BORN SOBER

BORN SOBER

PROHIBITION
IN OKLAHOMA, 1907-1959

BY JIMMIE LEWIS FRANKLIN

WITH A FOREWORD
BY J. HOWARD EDMONDSON

NORMAN
UNIVERSITY OF OKLAHOMA PRESS

International Standard Book Number: 0–8061–0964–5

Library of Congress Catalog Card Number: 70–160492

Copyright 1971 by the University of Oklahoma Press, Publishing Division of
the University. Composed and printed at Norman, Oklahoma, U.S.A., by the
University of Oklahoma Press. First edition.

To My Mother

FOREWORD

LIKE IT OR NOT, the political realist cannot ignore the fact that there have been few, if any, public issues with the impact of prohibition and repeal in Oklahoma. In this heart of the so-called "Bible Belt," where outspoken dry convictions inevitably provoked an equally violent backlash, the neutral constituency was extremely small. Almost every voter had strong convictions one way or the other on whether Oklahoma should have legalized alcoholic beverages and, if so, how. That is why this scholarly, but colorfully written, book is indeed an important and interesting social commentary on Oklahoma.

The liquor question in Oklahoma has always been—and still is—emotionally volatile. Although our administration fought hard for many other reforms—such as the merit system, central purchasing, tax equalization and more—that would be considered more significant than repeal to the political science scholar, I had feared that I might be remembered only as "the Governor who brought legal liquor to Oklahoma." I am pleased this has not been the case at this point a decade later.

Jimmie Franklin has accurately portrayed in this book the part our administration played on this issue. I would like to re-emphasize it. I came into office with the legal background and experience of strict law enforcement, particularly with a conviction against corruption of public officials. While our campaign position on the repeal issue—to submit it to a vote within ninety days—was politically popular, it also was our firm and sincere conviction. The problem of unequal law enforcement, or selective justice, that was later to promulgate the serious generation gap of the late sixties, was a frustrating problem to me. Prohibition clearly was not being enforced in Oklahoma—and couldn't be—because too many adults wanted it otherwise. This made every enforcement officer in the state work under a cloud of suspicion. While prohibition was not being enforced, on the one hand, we were, on the other hand and at the same time, telling our young to abide by the law of the land. If the people of Oklahoma wanted it that way, I reasoned, this is still a Republic. But I was committed to do all within my power to give them a chance to express their voice one more time in the new era. And that was my only commitment on this issue: to let the people vote.

Some of our campaign supporters were involved in the battle to legalize liquor after it came to a vote. But the author accurately reports the activities of my full-time office staff and myself. Inside my office, my assistants, Leland Gourley, Sam Crossland, and John Criswell, all helped formulate the plan finally approved by the legislature for referendum. But they, and I, scrupulously avoided becoming personally involved in the campaign after that point.

Since some of our campaign supporters were involved in that election campaign and the build-up to it, we agreed to keep the franchise system out of the plan. It could have been politically embarrassing and could have had an adverse effect on our whole reform program if some of my supporters had wound up with lucrative liquor distributorships. Another key feature, little publicized, that we felt was important was not placing a ceiling on the number of licensees. This could have led to a temptation for licenses to be "for sale" from future authorities. I was also happy to see county option defeated at the polls. Otherwise, enforcement again would have been complicated.

Basically, faced with the same political options, if I had it to do over, there would be few changes in the decisions we made in 1959.

As a result of the careful research of Jimmie Franklin, we now have the full story of one of the most interesting and controversial chapters in our state's history—the story of prohibition in Oklahoma.

J. HOWARD EDMONDSON
Governor of Oklahoma, 1959–1963

May 14, 1971

PREFACE

DURING the latter part of the nineteenth century and the early years of the twentieth, few questions of national social significance generated more interest and heated debate than that of prohibition. With the founding of the powerful Anti-Saloon League in 1893, prohibitionists won determined adherents to their cause and realized important legislative victories. The Progressive Movement, which roughly encompassed the first two decades of the twentieth century, gave the antiliquor forces added incentive, since a number of its reformers regarded intoxicants as a major source of many of the country's social ills. Increasingly, state after state, especially in the rural and fundamentalist South and West, adopted restrictive statutory liquor provisions.

Oklahoma entered the prohibition column in 1907, thus joining the crusade then sweeping the nation with inexorable force. With the approval of prohibition, people of the Sooner State established a social policy which endured for more than half a century. Although the struggle for restrictive laws in Oklahoma and the effort to maintain them greatly resembled the fight in other states, especially in the South and West, there were very important differences. The first and most significant observation is that Oklahoma had the marked distinction of being the only state to enter the Union with prohibition written into its constitution. The state's unique claim to this position represented the relentless endeavors of the Anti-Saloon League and the Woman's Christian Temperance Union, which militantly espoused the virtues of prohibition and the evils of drink for more than a decade prior to statehood. Loosely organized though they were, these two groups made their power and influence felt through the Protestant churches, which fervently articulated their program and which rendered them financial support. Collectively, they represented the church in action.

The constitutional prohibition of liquor in 1907 forecast the bitter dry-wet struggle in the years following Oklahoma statehood, for to repeal the restrictive provision of the state's organic law would require much political maneuvering and abundant finances. Moreover, to repeal an ordinary statute usually required only a majority vote of the legislators, but to repeal a section of the constitution required a majority of the voters who went to the polls, except at a special election. It is understandable, then, why the repeal election assumes such importance throughout this study, especially after 1933. It is here that one can measure the strength of the prohibition crusade and can examine the structure and function of special-interest groups. The political aspects, however, are only part of our concern, for in the final analysis prohibition was essentially a social movement, the product of a political process which represented the collective values of society.

During Oklahoma's fifty-two years of dryness, the prohibition movement remained narrow in its objective. Never did drys flirt with other reform issues which could dissipate their strength, tax their finances, or divide their ranks. Likewise, they rejected third-party movements. Significantly, the

Prohibition party in Oklahoma hardly got off the ground and never registered any real impact. To achieve its goal, the established prohibition leadership sought support from both Democrats and Republicans. But since Oklahoma remained a strong Democratic bastion throughout the period, that party became the political vehicle for the drys, although Republicans shouted the praises of prohibition as loudly as their adversaries.

The last notable observation about Oklahoma prohibition is that the presence of the Indian greatly influenced the movement in its early years. If in the South ardent spirits had to be kept from blacks, in Oklahoma they had to be kept from the red man, for his protection and that of society. For drys appealing to fundamentalist-inclined Anglo-Saxons who had not completely brushed the frontier experience into historical oblivion, it was a powerful argument.

The rock upon which constitutional prohibition in Oklahoma faltered was enforcement. Vigilant drys convinced a majority of the populace of the value of dry laws, but they never succeeded in fostering an assertive public sentiment which engendered strict enforcement. At the termination of the first state administration, Governor Charles N. Haskell bemoaned the disrespect for law; forty-seven years later, J. Howard Edmondson, then the state's chief executive, echoed the very same sentiment, complaining that Sooners simply did not want to obey the law. It was this chronic enforcement failure and the profit-conscious ambitions of business men which spawned intermittent efforts to abolish the state's hypocritical policy.

Not until 1933 did the prohibition section of the Oklahoma constitution undergo slight alteration. Encouraged by congressional approval of the Twenty-first Amendment and the passage of an act permitting the sale of 3.2 per cent beer, wets in Oklahoma inaugurated an intense campaign to force the

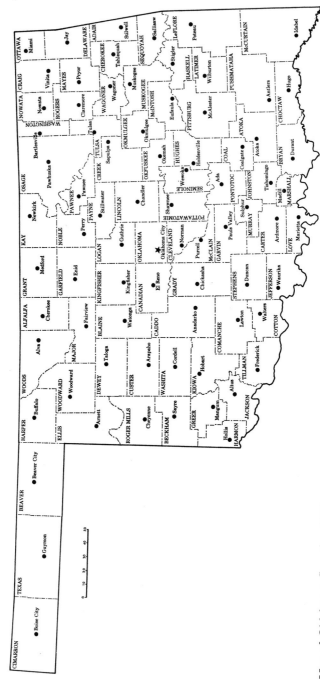

Map of Oklahoma Counties, 1960

acceptance of the beverage, although it had been declared illegal under the 1907 constitution. With the state staggering from the blows of the country's worst depression, those favorable to beer employed the identical revenue argument advanced by Franklin D. Roosevelt when he sought favorable liquor legislation from Congress. Strong legislative leadership, the need for revenue, and political bargaining finally gave Oklahoma wets their first modified victory. For twenty-four years after its adoption, the beer bill remained on the books undisturbed by drys, but in 1957 they launched a determined, although unsuccessful, campaign to bring about local option, the first step toward total exclusion of beer from within the state's borders.

The assault upon beer in 1957 signaled the beginning of the end for Oklahoma's long-standing prohibition experiment. The immediate effect of the drys' failure was the projection of repeal into the governor's race the following year. Prohibitionists, organized under the United Dry Association, were divided over a suitable candidate, which, as a result, contributed to the political triumph of J. Howard Edmondson, a young reform-minded Democrat. Edmondson responded decisively, and his methods yielded results wets long desired. Aided by a vigorous enforcement program, the Governor pushed a historic liquor referendum through the legislature; and he then continued to use his office to deny Oklahomans illegal liquor. Ominous signs reflected disaster for Sooner drys. When Oklahomans trooped to the polls in April, 1959, and approved the Twenty-seventh Amendment to their constitution, the forces of traditionalism, Bible-belt fundamentalism, and agrarianism, which had sustained prohibition, gave way to a new era.

While this book is ambitious in scope, its pretensions are modest. The author shares the view of Professor Norman Clark who, in his excellent study of the prohibition movement in Washington State, asserted that the history of American liquor control can be better understood through regional studies. Wherever possible, every effort has been made to integrate the Oklahoma story with that of the broad national experience, as arduous as that task sometimes proved to be. The work has been designed for both the general reader and the specialist in American social history. It is hoped that it will reflect the often expressed philosophy of one of the author's professors at the University of Oklahoma who never tired of saying, "History is written to be read."

To a few of the many persons who made this study possible, I wish to express my appreciation. Mrs. Dorothy Williams, Mrs. O. C. Cooke, and Mrs. Manon Atkins of the Oklahoma Historical Society Library were especially helpful in locating materials. The staff of the Manuscripts Division and the Phillips Collection of the University of Oklahoma rendered invaluable service. Without the assistance of Dr. W. Neil Franklin, Chief, Diplomatic, Legal, and Fiscal Branch of the National Archives, and his staff, the chapters on the twenties could not have been written. To Professors John S. Ezell, Donald Berthrong, and Gilbert C. Fite, of the History Department in the University of Oklahoma, I owe a special debt. The person to whom I am most indebted, however, is Professor Arrell M. Gibson, truly one of the most unselfish men I have ever known. For nearly eight years he watched the unfolding of this work, rendered generous criticism, and offered timely words of encouragement. Finally, to my wife, who should stagger at the mention of the word *prohibition*, I pay my deepest and warmest appreciation. That she endured and soberly paid deference to what liberally passed for scholarship is a moving tribute to woman's humanity to man.

JIMMIE L. FRANKLIN

CONTENTS

BORN SOBER

I

TOWARD SOBRIETY: THE FIGHT FOR TEMPERANCE IN OKLAHOMA TERRITORY

ALL OF WHAT is now present-day Oklahoma, with the exception of a strip of land north of the Panhandle of Texas and a section claimed by Texas, once comprised Indian Territory. For many years Congress made a determined effort, at least through statutory provisions, to prevent the introduction and sale of liquor in this domain.[1] Enforcement, however, proved difficult and any resourceful person could acquire strong drink from clever peddlers who plied their trade in violation of federal regulations. In the area which is now commonly known as the Oklahoma Panhandle, but once referred to as "No Man's Land" before its incorporation into Oklahoma Territory in 1890, there was virtually no law at all, and the sale of ardent spirits constituted a thriving business. The section claimed by Texas, later known as Greer County (and attached to Oklahoma Territory in 1896), had licensed saloons under the laws of Texas.

For more than a dozen years prior to 1889, Congress was subjected to great pressure to open for settlement the so-

[1] For commentary, see Grant Foreman, *Five Civilized Tribes*, 171, 391, 268, and his *History of Oklahoma*, 32.

called Unassigned Lands, located in the very center of the Indian Territory. By special proclamation President Benjamin Harrison opened these lands, totaling more than 2,000,000 acres, to settlement as of April, 1889. The dramatic details of the historic "run" to acquire portions of the Unassigned Lands are too familiar to warrant repetition. In the haste to throw open the area for homesteading, Congress made no provision for territorial government, thus leaving to the settlers themselves the arduous yet necessary task of law enforcement. As was the case in many western frontier communities, a relative degree of lawlessness characterized the initial stages of settlement, but gradually, in typical frontier tradition, concerned elements arose and through co-operative efforts secured protection of life and property. Technically, congressional statutes forbade liquor in the region opened by the President's proclamation and federal officers had instructions to enforce them. Despite legal restrictions, enforcement was as difficult as it had been in previous years.

Congress provided for the creation of Oklahoma government with the passage of the 1890 Organic Act. Among other things the act established the territory's seven original counties: Canadian, Cleveland, Kingfisher, Logan, Oklahoma, Payne, and Beaver, the last of which was subsequently subdivided into two others—Cimarron and Texas. Importantly, Congress specified that all lands in the western portion of Indian Territory when opened to settlement automatically became part of Oklahoma Territory. By the summer of 1890, the people had selected a legislature, and the new lawmakers began the business of erecting a legal structure for the new province.[2]

The Oklahoma legislature accorded liquor a favorable position. Very early the lawmakers passed an act which regulated the sale of and traffic in intoxicants. It required the

[2] A. M. Gibson, *Oklahoma: A History of Five Centuries*, 293–97, 308–309.

Board of County Commissioners to grant licenses for the sale of malt, spirituous, and vinous liquors upon application by petition of thirty of the resident taxpayers of the town, if the county came under the township plan. Where this form of organization did not exist, commissioners granted a license when they received a petition from thirty citizens of the precinct where the sale of intoxicants was to take place. Applicants were required to be of "good" character and of "respectable" standing in the community.[3]

The board acted upon applications only when requests for permits were published in the two largest newspapers in the county. In the absence of such journals, notices were posted in five public places, and if residents of the town registered no objections in writing, the board issued a retail license upon the payment of a two hundred-dollar fee.[4] Wholesalers, unlike retailers, paid an annual tax of one hundred dollars in all counties where they established business. To discourage violations, the territory established severe penalties. The statute of 1890 decreed that persons who sold intoxicating drinks without having first complied with the provisions of the act were to be fined no less than one hundred dollars or imprisoned up to one month.[5]

According to those who opposed the sale of alcoholic beverages, the sale of liquor encouraged disorder in the new territory.[6] The licensed saloon, they contended, was simply

3 W. F. Wilson, comp., *Wilson's Revised and Annotated Statutes of Oklahoma*, 1903, I, 481.

4 *Ibid.* It was not unusual for an applicant to have his character challenged through the filing of a remonstrance by one of his fellow citizens. As a general rule, the commissioners gave objections great consideration. On occasions cases were even appealed to the supreme court of the territory. For cases in point, see *Watkins* vs. *Grieser*, 66 Pac. 332, and *Swan* vs. *Wilderson*, 62 Pac. 422.

5 *Statutes of Oklahoma*, 1890, art. 1, chap. 48, 655.

6 Ernest H. Cherrington, ed., *Standard Encyclopedia of the Alcohol Problem*, V, 2056 (hereafter cited as Cherrington, *Encyclopedia*).

"licensed crime," and the government which sanctioned it was morally responsible for the evil it wrought.[7] That the bar was a "dark shadow" which rested upon every community where it was found was the considered opinion of one of Oklahoma's "dry" journals.[8] One devout prohibitionist in the territory wrote that Oklahoma City, the hub of the whisky traffic, was given over to "revelry, debauchery, throat cutting, robbery, and all the usual industries accompanying and being part of the saloon system."[9] There is some question, however, whether liquor and the "denizens of the saloons" could claim all credit for the city's moral ills.

Supporters of the law, on the other hand, maintained that a direct correlation existed between saloons and prosperity. If by chance they did foster crime and violence, it was all incidental to progress; the problem resided in the individual, not the bars. It was this group which fought so vigorously but vainly to maintain the saloons in 1907, and when the constitution outlawed them, their advocates worked long and hard for their restoration. Had it not been for the militant and determined activity of the Woman's Christian Temperance Union (WCTU) and the Anti-Saloon League's success in mobilizing sentiment against the whisky traffic, the liquor forces might have realized their objective.

The WCTU was the pioneer temperance organization in Oklahoma and Indian territories. A branch of the union was founded at Muskogee in 1888, roughly two years before Congress passed the Oklahoma Organic Act. Organized by Frances Willard and Anna Gordon, president and secretary respectively of the national association, the group soon affiliated with the central body formed at Cleveland fourteen years

[7] Watonga *Republican*, January 24, 1894.
[8] *Ibid.*
[9] William E. Johnson, *Ten Years of Prohibition in Oklahoma*, 7. For a very brief comment, see also Gibson, *Oklahoma*, 308.

earlier.[10] Upon the creation of Oklahoma Territory, a unit of the temperance society was established at the First Methodist Church in Oklahoma City. After statehood the two branches united, thus forming the Oklahoma WCTU. By the end of 1907, chapters existed in all the larger cities and towns of the new state,[11] and the organization had become a powerful social and political force.[12]

The WCTU attacked the liquor interests with revivalistic fervor. With its watchwords, "Agitate, Educate, Organize," and its methods, described as "Preventive, Educational, Evangelistic, Social, and Legal," the WCTU religiously pushed its campaign for sobriety throughout the territory.[13] During the 1890's the women undertook an intense campaign to repeal the law permitting the sale of liquor, but to no avail.[14] Far-reaching accomplishments in building sentiment against the saloon had to await the arrival of the Anti-Saloon League, an organization which in less than a decade did more than any other in bringing Oklahoma into the Union as a dry state.

The passage of the territorial liquor statute in 1890 prompted a stern reaction from the prohibitionists. An eventual result of that reaction was the summoning of a temperance meeting at the insistence of several Oklahoma City ministers, to "secure legislation tending to better the conditions

---

[10] Abbie B. Hillerman, *History of the Woman's Christian Temperance Union of the Indian Territory, Oklahoma Territory, and the State of Oklahoma*, 35. Frances Willard led an extremely interesting and exciting life. Two notable accounts of it deserve mention: Anna Gordon, *Frances Willard*; and Mary Earhart, *Frances Willard: From Prayers to Politics*.

[11] *The Oklahoma Almanac and Industrial Record, 1908*, 89.

[12] Unfortunately, few records exist covering the early years of the WCTU. Most of what is known is contained in Miss Hillerman's work, cited above, and in newspaper accounts.

[13] Oklahoma Woman's Christian Temperance Union, *Minutes* (1907), 7 (hereafter cited as WCTU, *Minutes*).

[14] Cherrington, *Encyclopedia*, V, 2057.

then existing." James L. Brown, a member of the first territorial legislature and a devout prohibitionist, was its most in-
strumental leader. He believed that the only way to realize the
group's objective was "to form and bring into existence,
slowly and in a quiet way, the most powerful organization that
could be obtained, composed entirely of men who were opposed to the liquor traffic on principle."[15] Familiar with the
success of the eminent Howard H. Russell, general superintendent of the National Anti-Saloon League, in organizing
local and state leagues across the country, Brown extended
him an invitation to visit Oklahoma City. Early in 1898 a
group of Oklahomans met the renowned reformer at the First
Baptist Church, and from this assembly came the Oklahoma
Anti-Saloon League.[16]

The league clearly stated its policy—"The Saloon Must
Go."[17] It pledged to organize the territory relentlessly and
agitate the liquor question "so that . . . Oklahoma might come
into the Union with a stainless banner and with constitutional
prohibition."[18] To further its goal, the league endeavored to
expose the lawlessness of the saloons and to show that they
opened on Sundays, that some conducted gambling rooms,
and that others operated houses of prostitution in conjunc-

[15] *American Issue* (Oklahoma ed.), October, 1912. All citations hereafter
refer to this edition.

[16] *Ibid.*

[17] The league enjoyed remarkable growth. By the turn of the century, the
Oklahoma Anti-Saloon League claimed a membership of 15,000. Its real
strength, however, was perhaps much greater since many prohibitionists gave
the organization their support but were not formally associated with it. See
El Reno *News*, November 1, 1900, and Cleveland County *Leader*, November
1, 1900. Some idea of the founding and growth of local leagues may be
followed through the papers. See, for example, Cleveland County *Leader*,
December 16, 1899; Frederick *Enterprise*, May 31, 1906; Chickasha *Daily
Express*, September 17, 1900; Eufaula *Indian Journal*, August 2, 1901; El
Reno *News*, December 21, 1899; Stillwater *Gazette*, January 31, 1901; *Daily
Oklahoman*, January 21 and February 7, 1900; and Kingfisher *Free Press*,
January 4, 1900.

tion with what already constituted a "morally depraved" business. The men also strove to focus attention on what they described as the dominance of the saloon element not only in politics, but also in law enforcement.[19]

When the league commenced its activities in Oklahoma, the liquor reform movement in the United States had already gained much ground. The Anti-Saloon League's object, as one writer has pointed out, was not so much to form new opinion as to mobilize an already existing attitude for political action. Since the days of Dr. Benjamin Rush's publication on the baneful effects of alcohol upon the human mind and body in the 1790's, temperance had been preached; and for three-quarters of a century, the moral aspect of the liquor question had been proclaimed. But the Anti-Saloon League was not content to rest its case upon the moral issue alone; it appreciated the value of political action, and it demonstrated its power by influencing voters.[20] Although its methods were political, the league was not partisan. As one of its exponents once remarked, "It is not playing the elephant or the donkey as a favorite but it is in politics to help elect good men to office and to keep bad men out."[21]

If the prohibitionists had resolved that the tavern and the liquor system must go, a strong commercial interest had determined that they must stay. Shortly after the announcement that the Anti-Saloon League had been organized, those concerned with the future of the whisky business called a

18 *American Issue*, October, 1912.

19 For material on the alleged alliance between the liquor element and politicians in one Oklahoma city, see Albert McRill, *And Satan Came Also: An Inside Story of a City's Social and Political History*, 59 (hereafter cited as McRill, *And Satan Came*).

20 H. G. Furbay, "The Anti-Saloon League," *North American Review*, Vol. CLXXVII (September, 1903), 434.

21 Peter H. Odegard, *Pressure Politics: The Story of the Anti-Saloon League*, 35.

meeting in Oklahoma City for the purpose of counteracting the expected temperance crusade. Henry Overholser, a future mayor of the city, expressed the sentiment of most of the businessmen when he suggested that drys were out to ruin them:

> I believe that the best interests of Oklahoma City are threatened, and thought it well for the businessmen and taxpayers to get together and consider what has to be done to uphold Oklahoma City in her march of progress. The people who are pushing this Anti-Saloon League have imported a man to manage their campaign, a man who neither knows nor cares anything about the conditions . . . here. He pays no taxes here, and when he has done the business interests what damage he can, will draw his salary and seek greener pastures. The small towns have succumbed to the on-slaught of these people . . . . There is a brilliant future before us and I . . . do not propose to see it marred and ruined by a set of people who would be much better minding their own business.[22]

Whatever merits Overholser's statement may have contained, he was correct in one respect—the league was enjoying an increasing amount of success. In the year prior to statehood, for example, one of the territory's papers estimated that there were as many as forty completely dry towns;[23] another counted one hundred.[24] In Woods County only five towns had saloons in 1906—Alva, Ingersoll, Carmen, Aline, and Helena. Washita County compiled an impressive record; the last saloon at Cordell, the county seat, was refused renewal of its license in April of that year, and the lone whisky establishment which remained in the entire county was at Bessie. At Hennessey, home of the Anti-Saloon League's first president, Tipton Cox, where there had been four saloons in

22 McRill, *And Satan Came*, 57.
23 *Daily Oklahoman*, May 4, 1906.
24 Sayre *Headlight*, November 8, 1906.

1905, the town "had the lid on tight."[25] Beaver and Comanche counties, with the exception of Lawton in the latter, had fallen in line with the growing sentiment against the liquor traffic.[26] At Weatherford, which had fourteen saloons in 1900, all had been closed by statehood.[27]

Decisions of the courts greatly aided the prohibitionists in their endeavor to dry up Oklahoma. Many judges required applications for licenses to comply strictly to the letter of the law. In some localities the bench ruled that newspapers had no obligation to publish requests for permits.[28] The territorial statute, it will be recalled, required that notices of application appear in the two papers of largest circulation in the county.

Temperance had been promoted to such a degree that by 1906, the year before Oklahoma's admission to the Union, prohibition throughout the territory seemed possible. The *Daily Oklahoman*,[29] which fought to the bitter end to maintain the saloons, ventured the opinion that if a vote had been held in 1906, a majority of the people would have declared against liquor. While the wets may have carried Guthrie,

[25] *Ibid.*

[26] *Ibid.*

[27] Personal interview with Mrs. Nellie Holmes, Tulsa, March 16, 1963. Mrs. Holmes and her family came to Weatherford in 1900. For years she has been an active member of the WCTU and has won national recognition for her untiring work. Weatherford, she recalled, had a population of 2,500 people and 14 saloons in 1900, but "one by one, they went out." Mrs. Holmes's husband was also active in temperance work, and for several years he served as president of the Weatherford Temperance Society. For brief sketches of Mrs. Holmes's work, see the Oklahoma *Messenger*, November, 1962; Union *Signal*, Vol. LXXXVIII (December, 1962), 11; and Tulsa *Tribune*, January 12, 1963.

[28] Sayre *Headlight*, November 8, 1906; and also Dora A. Stewart, *The Government and Development of Oklahoma Territory*, 316.

[29] The *Daily Oklahoman* was founded in 1894 by the Reverend Samuel Small, a roving evangelist and a former editor of the Atlanta *Constitution*. Small's paper had two major objectives—single statehood and prohibition. After miserable failure he sold the paper, left Oklahoma City, and never returned. Under new management the paper fought for single statehood, but opposed prohibition.

Oklahoma City, Shawnee, and a few other large towns, the rural vote would have easily carried prohibition. And indeed if there was any real friend of prohibition, it was the farmer. At statehood Oklahoma was predominately rural and over-whelmingly Protestant. There were only five towns in 1907 with a population of 10,000 or more: Oklahoma City, Guthrie, Enid, Muskogee, and Shawnee. There were only six with a population of between 5,000 and 6,000: Ardmore, McAlester, Chickasha, Tulsa, El Reno, and Lawton. Of the church groups, Methodists and Baptists had the most numerous memberships, with 68,611 and 67,541 respectively. Those of the Roman Catholic faith totaled 31,123, followed by the Disciples with 23,575 and the Presbyterians with 14,352.[30]

The drive for Oklahoma statehood and the presence of the Indian heightened the controversy between wets and drys. If Oklahoma and Indian territories should come into the Union as a single state, prohibitionists were determined to have Congress restrict the liquor traffic in the new state's constitution. Since the national government had a moral responsibility for the Indians, and inasmuch as various treaties had guaranteed the tribes protection from alcohol, prohibitionists believed it would be just and legal to continue this policy after statehood.[31] Regulation should not, and legally

[30] Bureau of the Census, *Thirteenth Census of the United States*, 1910. *Abstract, with Supplement for Oklahoma*, 590–91; Bureau of the Census, *Special Reports: Religious Bodies, 1906*, Part I, 252. There were 239,837 church members in Oklahoma in 1907.

[31] Long before the Five Civilized Tribes left the Southeast, they had enacted prohibition laws. Indeed, the Choctaws claimed that Neal Dow, the Maine apostle of temperance, was still a boy when they kindled the first council fire against whisky. Upon removal to their new home in the West, the Choctaws and other tribes included restrictive liquor provisions in their statutes. But despite the efforts of the tribes, the federal government, and the moral preachments of the missionaries, the traffic continued to defy suppression. A useful study on the subject is Gwen W. Zwick, "Prohibition in the Cherokee Nation, 1820–1907"; Grant Foreman, "A Century of Prohibition," *Chronicles of Oklahoma*, Vol. XII (June, 1934), 133–41, is also valuable.

could not, they held, be left to the police power of the state; and if Congress did not have the opportunity to outlaw the manufacture and sale of liquor in all parts of the new state, it did have the power to restrict it on the eastern side and on Indian reservations within old Oklahoma Territory. Ideally, drys contended, the ban should include the entire state, for if the territorial side voted for liquor, its very proximity to the Indian country would pose a threat to temperance among the Indians.

Consequently, opponents of the whisky traffic directed their attention to Congress. The national Anti-Saloon League favored the continuation of the federal prohibitory policy whether Congress granted single or double statehood. "While we remain absolutely neutral on the question of the kind of statehood *per se*," one dry resolution directed to the congressional Committee on Territories stated, "we nevertheless record a firm conviction that the people of Oklahoma . . . are not warranted in asking statehood with Indian Territory at a disregard of their solemn treaty contracts with the Indians."[32] The Inter-Church Federation, the Lake Mohonk Conference, and other special-interest groups across the country representing millions of members also sent resolutions urging the Congress to act favorably on prohibition.[33] Congress could hardly remain immune to such persistent pressure.

While Congress debated the liquor question, prohibitionists

Peter J. Hudson, "Temperance Meetings Among the Choctaws," *ibid.*, 130–32, is brief but colorful and informative.

[32] House of Representatives, *Hearings on Prohibition in the Proposed State of Oklahoma Before the Committee on Territories*, 59th Cong., 1st sess., 10. Prior to Oklahoma's admission to the Union as a single state, there had been much debate over whether two separate states should be created from Oklahoma and Indian territories.

[33] *Ibid.* In the South the drys and the churches had stressed the danger of making legalized liquor available to the Negro. It is significant to note that in Oklahoma, probably because of its small Negro population, prohibitionists seldom played upon the race issue.

in Oklahoma and Indian territories took steps to ensure sustained temperance sentiment. A special organization within the Anti-Saloon League known as the Indian Territory Church Federation, founded at McAlester in 1904, with A. S. McKennon as president,[34] pledged itself to a local promotional program which would help render the new state bonedry. Baptists and Methodists became increasingly vocal. The liquor traffic, the Methodist Temperance Committee reported in 1905, was an enemy of the church and one of Satan's "most successful agencies for destroying souls." The exclusion of liquor from the state was absolutely necessary to protect the church.[35] Both the Anti-Saloon League and the WCTU intensified their campaign as the possibility of statehood improved.

In 1905, Oklahoma drys received the aid of an unexpected but valuable ally—Carry Nation. Widely known for her hatchet destruction of saloon stock, this apostle of prohibition came to Guthrie, capital of Oklahoma Territory, and hurriedly established headquarters. Fortunately for saloon men Carry left her hatchet behind. Most of her time was directed toward making speeches and founding branches of her Prohibition Federation which sought to advance a number of things: destroy the liquor business, obtain constitutional prohibition in Oklahoma, foster legislation against swearing, and elect a prohibitionist president of the United States. Finally, Carry and the federation encouraged woman suffrage, an issue intricately related to the national prohibition controversy.[36]

The Prohibition Federation possessed great appeal, especially to the women of Oklahoma, mainly because Carry had

[34] E. M. Sweet, "C. N. Haskell and Oklahoma Prohibition" (Charles N. Haskell Collection, University of Oklahoma Library), 3.

[35] Oklahoma Methodist Episcopal Church (South), *Minutes*, 1905, 77 (hereafter cited as Methodist *Minutes*).

[36] Herbert Asbury, *Carry Nation: The Woman with the Hatchet*, 288.

organized it. The organization worked closely with the Anti-Saloon League, the WCTU, and local temperance groups in the territories. To disseminate her propaganda, the "woman with the hatchet" purchased property in Guthrie and installed a press on which she printed the *Smasher's Mail* and the *Hatchet*.[37] The federation quickly became an important agency in generating positive sentiment in favor of constitutional prohibition.

Wets did not stand idly by while temperance groups pressed their unrelenting fight. The organization of prohibition forces aroused saloon men to such a degree that in 1904 they formed the Liquor Men's Association to raise funds to turn back their aggressive enemies.[38] The German American Association, founded in the same year, also vowed to protect the right of its members to determine what they should or should not drink.[39] To the Citizens League the prohibitionist fanatics were nothing less than a totally "destructive element."[40]

By 1906 it was readily apparent to wets that the fight for saloons would apply only to Oklahoma Territory. In the Oklahoma Enabling Act, Congress declared for single statehood and required continuation of prohibition in the Indian Territory, which before 1907 roughly comprised the eastern half of present Oklahoma. The dry clause, imposed as a condition for statehood, provided that:

> The manufacture, sale, barter, giving away, or otherwise furnishing . . . of intoxicating liquors within those parts of said state [Oklahoma] now known as the Indian Territory and the Osage Reservation and within any other parts of said State which existed as Indian Reservations on the first day of January, Nineteen hundred and six, [shall be] prohibited for a

[37] *Ibid.*, 289.
[38] Cherrington, *Encyclopedia*, V, 2059.
[39] *Daily Oklahoman*, April 4, 1907.
[40] *Ibid.*, May 17, 1907.

period of twenty-one years from the date of the admission of
said State into the Union, and thereafter until the people of
said State shall otherwise provide by amendment of said constitution and proper state legislation.[41]

The new state, however, was permitted to establish an
agency, or dispensary, to supervise the sale of liquors for
medical and other prescribed purposes. The act outlined penalties for violation of the prohibitory clause. Significantly,
except for the former Osage Nation, it placed no restriction
upon old Oklahoma Territory, which was free to continue its
policy. Clearly, the action of the Congress toward the prohibition issue represented a partial victory for the antiliquor
organizations, but could they convince Oklahoma's founding
fathers to write prohibition into the state's constitution; and
if they did, would the people accept it?

[41] *Statutes at Large*, XXIV, 269–70.

II

BORN SOBER

WHEN THE Oklahoma Constitutional Convention assembled at Guthrie, both wets and drys energetically sought to advance their interests.[1] Prohibitionists sought in the constitution a restrictive liquor clause covering the entire state, while wets were equally determined to fight any limitation on the sale of intoxicants within old Oklahoma Territory.[2] The WCTU, headed by Miss Abbie Hillerman, organized a postal campaign and later established headquarters at Guthrie so that the women could maintain close contact with convention delegates. Miss Hillerman, with enviable enthusiasm, carried petitions containing 5,000 names to the convention and placed them on delegates' desks.[3] The Anti-Saloon League, anxious to sustain the success it enjoyed throughout

[1] See the firsthand comments of a participant in the convention in Paul Nesbitt, ed., "Governor Haskell Tells of Two Conventions," *Chronicles of Oklahoma*, Vol. XIV (June, 1936), 212 (hereafter cited as Nesbitt, "Haskell Tells of Two Conventions"). It is virtually impossible to determine the actual delegate strength of the two factions at the convention. The prohibitionists, however, were able to win to their side the convention leadership.

[2] James R. Scales, "Political History of Oklahoma, 1907–1944," 47.

[3] WCTU, *Minutes*, 331.

the country, imported its top lobbyist from Washington, the Reverend E. C. Dinwiddie, to conduct its fight. On the other side were the liquor interests, led principally by the Citizens League, headed by I. B. Levy of Guthrie and J. P. Goulding of Enid, which stressed temperance without prohibition.

The antiliquor forces achieved what appeared to be an impressive victory before the stormy debate on the issue began. After the convention had been in session several days, members of the Anti-Saloon League requested the support of Charles N. Haskell of Muskogee, convention majority floor leader, in securing a friendly Committee on Liquor Traffic. He advised them to make a list of men upon whom they could rely and indicated his willingness to present it to William H. Murray, president of the convention. Finally the league named fifteen men whom they considered "safe," and then Murray, at the suggestion of Haskell, appointed the entire committee as recommended by the league.[4] Eight of the members came from the Oklahoma side and seven from Indian Territory.[5] After hearing both dry and wet points of view, the committee filed its report, recommending *prohibition for Indian Territory and local option for Oklahoma Territory.*

The Anti-Saloon League, which through the leadership of the Reverend Mr. Dinwiddie became the dominant voice of the dry forces, was stunned. In a surprising about-face the league "swallowed its ambitions" and accepted the compromise report. When Dinwiddie and members of his organization approached the influential Haskell and urged his support of the recommendation, the outspoken floor leader replied, "Now look here ... let's not waste any time. I won't support [the] report. I am here for statewide prohibition." He thought the league had conceded its original objective because

4 Nesbitt, "Haskell Tells of Two Conventions," 213–14.
5 *Proceedings of the Constitutional Convention of the Proposed State of Oklahoma,* 72.

of Robert L. Owen who acted as an adviser to the group. Haskell wrote some years later that the liquor interests had "bluffed" Owen into believing that they were an all-powerful force in the convention, and that, in turn, he had persuaded the drys to go along with the compromise report. The ardently dry Haskell emphatically pointed out to the temperance reformers that the enabling act had already guaranteed prohibition for Indian Territory. Thus the committee's report was no "compromise" at all; it was defeat. The constitution, exclaimed Haskell, must be uniform; and he was "opposed to any calico constitution that makes a thing a law in one part of the state and not in the other."[6] The prohibitionists left Haskell once more pledged to their original goal of statewide prohibition. Indeed, they were not oblivious of the future governor's political powers and his many friendships.

Upon hearing petitions, amendments, substitutes, and amendments to substitutes, the convention delegates decided to adopt prohibition for the entire state. Very cleverly, however, they chose to submit the question separately for approval in the forthcoming election,[7] lest the uncertainty of public sentiment jeopardize the ratification of the constitution. The prohibition section as finally drawn was written by W. A. Ledbetter, and the suggestion to submit it separately came from Robert L. Williams, himself an imbiber.[8]

As election day, September 17, 1907, neared, both wet and dry factions intensified their campaign. The German American Association saw prohibition as a threat to personal freedom and liberal institutions, and declared against it. Nonpartisan, it clearly advanced its position in a public statement prior to the referendum on the proposed constitution and the prohibition provision:

---

[6] Nesbitt, "Haskell Tells of Two Conventions," 215.
[7] *Proceedings of the Constitutional Convention*, 415.
[8] Scales, "Political History of Oklahoma," 48.

when a political issue is raised which is antagonistic to our views of life, threatens [our] liberal institutions . . . and infringes upon the personal privileges and rights of men, then we band together for the preservation of right and freedom. Such an issue is at hand just now. The German vote will be cast solidly against prohibition . . . and we will support such candidates for state offices . . . who are known to uphold the liberal institutions of the country.[9]

The Citizens League continued its campaign to convince the public that prohibition aided neither temperance nor business. The league warned that it would lead only to hypocrisy and that "the habitual disregard of the prohibition law [would engender] disrespect for all law." Moreover, the organization maintained that prohibition "benumbed the moral sense and leads to evasion and subterfuge . . . resulting not infrequently in perjury."[10] Beyond this, however, were the economic consequences of a restrictive liquor ordinance. It would cut off a valuable source of revenue; it would stifle business, discourage investment, depreciate the value of real estate, and encourage illegal sales; prohibition was totalitarian in nature, for "force is not a proper or successful instrument of moral reform."[11] The league also raised the question, had not history shown that in other states prohibition could not dam the flow of ardent spirits?

The liquor interests agitated the question with such intensity and bitterness that many observers believed they were jeopardizing their own cause. In a meeting with wets, William H. Murray warned that by their methods they were "digging their own graves." If they persisted, he cautioned, many people would vote for the constitutional restriction of liquor. "Why not let up a little bit and let the public mind relax? You

9 *Daily Oklahoman*, April 4, 1907.
10 *Ibid.*, May 17, 1907.
11 *Ibid.*

might win if the people are not too deeply aroused."[12] While Murray admonished wets to relax, he consummated a bargain with drys which helped to ensure both statehood and statewide prohibition.

Shortly after his talk Murray held a conference with H. T. Laughbaum, E. C. Dinwiddie, and E. M. Sweet of the Anti-Saloon League. During this meeting he promised that if the league backed statehood, he would support prohibition. President Theodore Roosevelt, he reminded them, had expressed opposition to the Oklahoma Constitution and had threatened to refuse the state admission to the Union unless a Republican, Frank Frantz, was elected governor. Roosevelt would need some encouragement, and Murray set forth the league's chore:

> If you will merely put your best workers to work and you devote [your efforts to] . . . writing letters to every Temperance Organization, every church, and every person of prominence in the United States, covering every section of the country [urging them to write Roosevelt], you will guarantee statehood; and if you will guarantee statehood, I will guarantee prohibition will be adopted. Leave that to me and I will leave to you the guarantee of statehood.[13]

With the Murray bargain sealed, drys felt profoundly confident of victory. The Tulsa *World* predicted that prohibition would carry, especially in the Indian Territory which, under the provision of the enabling act, had to remain dry.[14] A sizable segment of the population in that territory believed that there should be no sectional discrimination of any kind within the new state and had decided to vote for prohibition, if for no other reason than to "play a joke on [the] Okla-

[12] Gordon Hines, *Alfalfa Bill: An Intimate Biography*, 212.
[13] William H. Murray, *Memoirs of Governor Murray and True History of Oklahoma*, I, 333–34.
[14] April 13, 1907.

homa [side] by making that end dry."[15] On the eve of the
election the *Daily Oklahoman,* although it hated to admit it,
thought the drys would win.[16] The Anti-Saloon League and
its followers, however, did not relax their efforts, and on the
day before the election, they staged a large demonstration in
Convention Hall in Guthrie to unify the various groups for
prohibition.[17] As the roar of drums slipped into silence and
the drys made their way home, uncertainty still existed about
the effectiveness of the campaign which had been pushed forward with full force since the 1890's.

On September 17, 1907, the people of Indian and Oklahoma territories accepted the constitution by a vote of 180,333
to 73,089. The prohibition clause carried 130,361 to 112,258.
Contrary to previous speculation, however, Indian Territory
did not play a joke on the Oklahoma side; it was just the other
way around, for fifteen of the counties which opposed the dry
proposition were in the eastern part of the state: Carter, Coal,
Craig, Creek, Johnston, Latimer, McIntosh, Nowata, Osage,
Pittsburg, Rogers, Sequoyah, Wagoner, Washington, and
Pushmataha.[18]

In that same election the Democratic candidate, Charles
N. Haskell, defeated Republican Frank Frantz for the governorship. Haskell, of course, was no stranger to the prohibitionists. At the constitutional convention he had nourished
a close friendship with Dinwiddie and other drys, had urged
Murray to appoint the men suggested by the league to the
Liquor Traffic Committee (although they did prove a disappointment), and had always voted favorably on prohibition.
During the gubernatorial campaign he reinforced his position.

[15] *Ibid.*
[16] September 16, 1907.
[17] *Ibid.*
[18] Seth Gordon and W. B. Richards, comps., *Oklahoma Redbook, 1912,* I, 295.

Both party platforms had judiciously avoided the liquor question, but the two candidates had been pressured to state their views. When pushed to declare his position, Frantz replied that "every man has a right to vote his individual opinion," and "my own views are binding to no one." He stated further that it should matter little to the public how he cast his vote since it would "in no way influence my course as Governor."[19] Frantz's evasiveness did not satisfy the drys.

At Norman, Haskell was questioned about his attitude. His answer demonstrated much more political prudence than his adversary's. "If I were not a candidate for public office," he informed his listeners, "I would have the privilege of telling you that this was none of your business," but "I . . . would not vote for a man who tried to conceal his personal or political intentions."[20] The criticism of Frantz's stand showed through Haskell's subtlety. "The man who hides," he continued, "is a coward and this is no time to have a coward in charge of the new government. I intend to vote for statewide prohibition."[21] As if that were not enough to damn his opponent, Haskell charged Frantz with intemperance.[22] Doubtless, Haskell's stand at Norman and his record at the constitutional convention, plus Frantz's failure to refute successfully the allegation that he occasionally imbibed, endeared Haskell to many a dry heart.

Oklahoma's first governor wasted little time in setting forth his policy. In his inaugural address he promised to enforce the law:

> By a majority of more than eighteen thousand voters, the people of Oklahoma have declared in favor of statewide pro-

[19] Oscar Fowler, *The Haskell Regime: The Intimate Life of Charles Nathaniel Haskell*, 120.
[20] *Ibid.*
[21] *Ibid.*
[22] Shawnee *Daily Herald*, September 3, 1907.

hibition. That is now the law in this state; not placed in our constitution as a political requirement nor for mere sentimental purposes, but because a majority of the people believe that humanity will be better by having such a law and by having it enforced. I stand here today as one of your officers to assure you that law will be enforced, and I hope that when tomorrow morning's [November 17] sun rises and forever thereafter as long as this law shall be the will of the people, that there will be no one within our borders disposed to violate [it], because that violation is bound to meet with the punishment presented in the law.[23]

While prohibitionists joyously congratulated each other, and as Haskell steadfastly pledged to stand by the constitution, wets prepared for an age of legal sobriety. In Oklahoma City it was reported that all saloons were doing a rushing business.[24] One whisky establishment, the Wetzenhoffer and Turk Company, began to dismantle early, and it printed a three-column spread in one of the local papers advertising "Alfalfa Bill Bourbon" for one dollar a quart and pints of "Old Crow" for fifty to sixty cents. The owner of the company wrote, "It would be useless . . . to go into details with you as you all understand our *reason* for giving these extremely low prices."[25] A Ponca City saloonkeeper posted above his shop this consoling statement, "Hush little saloon, don't you cry; you'll be a drug store, by and by."[26] A dispatch from Lawton noted that "much liquor is being stored away" for dry times.[27] The New State Brewery Company at Oklahoma City, owned by Anheuser-Busch, also closed its doors

---

[23] *Inaugural Address of Governor C. N. Haskell, November 16, 1907*, 9.

[24] Oklahoma *News*, November 16, 1907.

[25] *Daily Oklahoman*, October 13, 1907.

[26] Mary Goddard, "Well Went Dry Just 50 Years Ago," *Daily Oklahoman*, November 13, 1957 (Magazine section).

[27] *Ibid.*

and some 27,000 gallons of beer went into the sewers.[28] Prohibition spelled disaster to 550 retail saloons, 30 wholesale houses, and 2 breweries.[29]

As Saturday, November 16, 1907, drew to a close, citizens gathered at the bar to sip farewell to the past and to toast the new order destined to take place the next day. In Oklahoma City "good fellows, soaks and all" assembled to pay their respects to the parting of the ways. By eleven o'clock one writer has noted with a bit of colorful exaggeration, "hades had taken a recess and was using Broadway and Main for a playground."[30] By midnight there was nothing but a drunken mob.[31] Pandemonium finally staggered to an end, and it appeared there would be peace in the new state.

In December, Governor Haskell asked the First Legislature for enforcement legislation vitalizing the constitution. Vigorously maintaining that "prohibition will prohibit," he thought successful and uniform enforcement could only reach realization by giving the governor unhampered authority.[32] County attorneys had already informed the executive that conditions were serious in their jurisdictions; thus Haskell asked for a firm statute so that law officers would not have to remain "silent witnesses" to evasion of the constitutional mandate.[33]

Responsive to the Governor's request, the legislature considered an enforcement measure. A bill in accord with Haskell's thinking was introduced in the senate by Richard A. Billups, an attorney from Cordell and chairman of the Senate

28 *American Issue,* July, 1912.

29 Eufaula *Indian Journal,* February 7, 1908.

30 McRill, *And Satan Came,* 118.

31 *Ibid.*

32 *Seventh Special Message of the Governor to the First Legislature, December 12, 1907,* 18.

33 *Ibid.,* 18–19.

Prohibition Committee. The Billups Prohibition Bill passed the upper chamber by a vote of 36 to 7 on December 18, but not without vigorous objection from a very vocal minority.[34]

In light of future developments, some of these objections are significant enough to note very briefly.[35] Senator G. O. Johnson, although favoring prohibition "if it can be enforced," emphatically exclaimed that the proposed measure struck down the "strong arm of personal rights to gratify fanaticism." He also opposed the law because it would impose upon the people an "unjust" expense. Senator P. J. Yeager advanced two of the arguments propounded by the Citizens League and the German American Association during the election. He claimed the proposed enforcement legislation would make good citizens violate the law and thereby make criminals of honest men. "It abridges the great domestic principle that we shall each enjoy ourselves as conscience dictates so long as we do not interfere with the rights of others or the public good." The law, said Yeager, was undemocratic and unjust, and besides adding undue expense upon the citizenry, it would bolster the Republican party by 25,000 votes. Senator J. P. Goulding added that the law was "inquisitorial," and could subject the people to a "star chamber investigation." And to Senator H. E. P. Standford the spirit of the bill was "akin to that which, in the days of our Puritan Fathers, led to the burning of witches at the stake."

Objections aside, the senate sent the bill to the house. At the insistence of William H. Murray, speaker of the house, the lower chamber added a dispensary feature which provided for a state agency in accordance with the enabling act and the constitution, *and* in those towns with a population of one

---

[34] Oklahoma Senate *Journal*, 1907–1908, 65.

[35] Those voting against the bill were Senators P. S. Curd, H. S. Cunningham, G. O. Johnson, Frank Mathews, H. E. P. Standford, P. J. Yeager, and J. P. Goulding. *Ibid.*

thousand or more. Irritated by this change, the senate rejected the amendment by unanimous vote (32–0). In February, 1908, Senator J. Elmer Thomas suggested that the legislature postpone consideration of the bill until a committee of senators and representatives, along with Governor Haskell, drafted a measure in compliance with the prohibition section of the constitution.

The committee considered the Billups bill until March, 1908. Senator Billups then presented the committee's version of his bill to the senate and recommended acceptance of the dispensary (state agency) provision added by the house. The senate was divided over the measure, but finally decided to pass it provided that the dispensary provision of the constitution became effective at once, and that agencies to be established in towns of one thousand for the sale of liquors for medicinal and scientific purposes not be created until approved by a vote of the people.[36] Under the leadership of Speaker Murray, the house passed the measure by a slim margin,[37] and on March 24, 1908, Governor Haskell signed the "Billups Booze Bill," as opponents of the measure derisively dubbed it.

Oklahoma's first statutory liquor law, like its constitution, was very detailed. It consisted of three articles: the first two dealt with the dispensary, and the other contained provisions designed to prevent the sale of liquor except through the agencies established by the state. The law provided for a state agency system (dispensary) operated by a superintendent appointed by the governor. In each incorporated town of two thousand or more a local agency could be created; but counties with towns of less population were entitled to one dispensary at a place designated by the superintendent. The

---

[36] For the comments of senators and the vote in the senate, see *ibid.*, 65–66, 179–80.

[37] Oklahoma House of Representatives. *Journal*, 1907–1908, 160.

Billups bill stipulated, however, that agencies could be established in towns of one thousand people *if* Oklahomans approved such a provision in the November, 1908, referendum. Unquestionably this legislative concession violated the section of the enabling act which provided for *one* dispensary in towns of two thousand; where towns of no such size existed, Congress had specifically granted that a county "shall be entitled to have only one such agency."

Persons could purchase liquor only upon prescription from licensed doctors. A "patient" who wished to secure "medicine" from the dispensary had to make a sworn statement including his name and the purpose for which the liquor was bought. Physicians who recommended intoxicants except for a disease which required such treatment were liable to a fine of from $200 to $1,000, or imprisonment from thirty days to one year, or both. Other notable provisions of the law provided penalties for drinking in public, bootlegging, advertising of liquors, and delivery of intoxicants by common carriers to fictitious names.[38]

Between April, 1908, and the November election, the dispensary feature of the Billups bill was debated pro and con. One of the most vocal spokesmen for the system was Governor Haskell. Although he originally opposed the sale of whisky for medicinal purposes, Haskell reversed his stand because of "pressure from the public."[39] In ardent defense of the agency, he pointed out that it did not represent a "beverage" dispensary—it was not a "barrel of whiskey with the head knocked in and a tin cup hanging conveniently near." The operation of the system, he assured Oklahomans, would be well guarded. Scolding the opponents of the dispen-

[38] See the full text of Billups bill in *Session Laws of Oklahoma*, 1907–1908, 594–614.

[39] *Address of Governor C. N. Haskell ... Before the Oklahoma Prohibitionists, April 15, 1908*, 10 (hereafter cited as *Haskell's Address to Prohibitionists*).

sary, the chief executive stressed its importance to "practical" enforcement of the liquor laws:

> The complaint that the state is degrading itself and degrading its women and children by putting these medicinal sales of liquor under its control and direction, is a sudden awakening of pretended morality when it comes from a class of . . . individuals, who, in the [last] election were so unmindful of the morals of the state that they bitterly fought prohibition. I warn you that they are utterly unfit to advise [those] who are engaged in fighting for practical enforcement of prohibitions and the elevation of moral conditions.[40]

Haskell, nevertheless, confessed a doubtful attitude about the economic value of the agency system to the state, but he supported it because of its "moral" worth. It total sales, he said, amounted to $50,000 a year, the state would lose very little money. But in a speech to the Prohibition party,[41] the Governor admitted that the agency could represent an annual loss of $25,000.[42] The truth, however, seems to be that the Governor, as well as many legislators, actually anticipated a *profit* from the agency, not a loss.

The Anti-Saloon League also supported the dispensaries. Leaders of the organization claimed that opponents misrepresented the Billups law by using the term *dispensary*, notwithstanding the fact it appeared nowhere in the constitution or the enabling act. The liquor interests wanted to prompt

[40] *Daily Oklahoman*, March 25, 1908. For an interesting comment on the Billups bill, see "Billups Booze Bill," *Outlook*, Vol. LXXXIX (June, 1908), 311 (hereafter cited as "Billups Booze Bill").

[41] The Prohibition party held its first convention in Oklahoma in 1902. As was generally true of the organization throughout the nation, it never became a powerful political entity; nor was it an effective agent in molding temperance sentiment. For a sketch of the party's history, see D. L. Colvin, *Prohibition in the United States: A History of the Prohibition Party, and of the Prohibition Movement*. For a brief summary of its principles, see "The Prohibition Party," *Independent*, Vol. LXVII (April, 1909), 929–30.

[42] *Haskell's Address to Prohibitionists*, 12.

the people to repeal prohibition by making it impossible to get badly needed "medicine." The difference between the Oklahoma agency and the South Carolina dispensary, wrote the editor of the *American Issue,* official organ of the Anti-Saloon League, "is the difference between alcohol for purposes of debauchery" and "medicine when the doctor prescribes it." It was not "booze when any boozer wants it."[43]

Taking a cue from the Anti-Saloon League, the Protestant churches swiftly swung into line. The Baptists urged adoption of the Billups bill in its entirety at the polls.[44] To defeat the agency, Presbyterians conjectured, was a clever attempt by the wets to bring back the saloon with all its attendant evils. Their convention in 1908 condemned the "combined host of liquordom." It deplored the efforts of "brewer, distiller, joint keeper, bootlegger, sons of darkness who disgrace . . . the father of our country by calling themselves 'Sons of Washington,' the lower class German American[s] . . . the Citizen's League, gamblers," and disgruntled politicians "of the baser sort and all the lawless anarchist class to overthrow our law." The liquor interests would like nothing more than to defeat the church and all good Christians by making the

[43] *American Issue,* September, 1908. The father of the dispensary in the United States was "Pitchfork" Ben Tillman of South Carolina. As governor of the state, he succeeded in having a provision incorporated as a part of the 1895 constitution that provided for government ownership of the saloon business and attempted to eliminate the worst features of the liquor traffic. See John Eubanks, *Ben Tillman's Baby: The Dispensary in South Carolina, 1892–1915* and Ernest Cherrington, ed., *The Anti-Saloon League Yearbook, 1909,* 177–78 (hereafter cited as Cherrington, *ASL Yearbook*). For the operation of the system in another state, see Daniel J. Whitener, "The Dispensary Movement in North Carolina," *South Carolina Quarterly,* Vol. XXVI (January, 1937), 33–48.

[44] Oklahoma Baptist General Convention, *Minutes,* 1908, 18 (hereafter cited as Baptist *Minutes*). The year before, however, the Baptists had opposed the establishment of dispensaries, declaring that they were "subversive of morals and good government and tended to destroy the value of the . . . victory won . . . for prohibition." *Ibid.,* 1907, 86.

law inoperative, "bring it into disfavor [and] secure its [re]peal by re-submission."[45] The Methodists, meeting at Shawnee a month before the election, urged members to vote for the only "proper way of handling the sale of . . . liquor under the constitution."[46]

Opponents of the agency system were equally as vocal as its advocates. Strangely enough, opposition came not only from antiprohibitionists, but from many devoted drys who thought the dispensaries practically nullified the constitution.[47] The Kay County Civic League, for example, an organization pledged to complete prohibition, adopted a resolution committing the group against the referendum.[48] While the Anti-Saloon League held that the WCTU was supporting the agency, the women claimed they were not.[49] J. E. Wolfe, a prohibitionist from Vinita, ridiculed the system in the following humorous, but meaningful, language:

> Strange what a panacea for physical ills is wrapt up in a jug full of Sunnybrook [the agency's brand] liquid kill-devil, or a schooner of Budweiser rotgut . . . . For let it be known that the patient who loves this liquid hell-fire and damnation, has a disease that is chronic and established in its nature, and therefore required a continual application of the "curative agent" . . . .
>
> What a run on this lovely, beautiful . . . institution called the State Dispensary there will be! Day in and day out these poor thirsty and sick mortals will be seen wending their way to the open door of this humane and sanctified state saloon

[45] Synod of the Oklahoma Presbyterian Church (USA), *Minutes*, 1908, 95 (hereafter cited as Presbyterian *Minutes*).

[46] Methodist *Minutes*, 1908, 70.

[47] "Billups Booze Bill," 311.

[48] Lexington *Leader*, October 2, 1908.

[49] Mrs. Nellie Holmes, a long-time member of the organization, related to the writer that the union considered the agency a "slip through." Personal interview with Mrs. Nellie Holmes, Tulsa, March 16, 1963; see also Tulsa *Times*, March 27, 1908.

.... Parsons ... deacons, and dead-beats, and all sorts of thirsty citizens [will crowd] around to obtain the precious sip. Who could have conceived a more ingenious scheme to people hell than this State Dispensary Institution?

Come Out From Among Them And Be Ye Separate, Saith The Lord, And Touch Not The Unclean Thing.[50]

Others opposed the agency for a variety of reasons. The Sons of Washington,[51] organized to remove Oklahoma from the ranks of the dry states and to protect the personal rights of its members, called the state's policy hypocritical. There were also those who believed that local agents would seek to maximize their profits by illegal sales. That a public agency could possibly develop into a powerful and corrupt political machine as had been the case in some other states was a genuine fear shared by many. Republicans contended the system would be too expensive to operate.[52]

Although the state medical association agreed to endorse the dispensaries after extended debate, favorable opinion was far from uniform. Many doctors shared the view of the Canadian County Medical Association which resolved that "we condemn such system as being derogatory to our vocation and agree not to lend support toward the dispensary by refusing to write prescriptions ... in any cases whatsoever."[53]

While the public argued the merits of the agency, local dispensers and dispensaries already in operation experienced financial difficulties. There was a total of seventy-nine towns

[50] Prohibition files, Frederick S. Barde Collection, Oklahoma Historical Society (hereafter cited as Prohibition files, Barde Collection).

[51] Care should be taken not to confuse the Oklahoma Sons of Washington with the Sons of Temperance, which was an outgrowth of the Washington movement of the 1840's. The Oklahoma group was incorporated in 1908 as the Grand Lodge of the Sons of Washington. See the Lexington *Leader*, July, 1908.

[52] *Daily Oklahoman*, March 25, 1908.

[53] Prohibition files, Barde Collection.

in Oklahoma entitled to a dispensary.[54] When the Billups bill passed the legislature, great glee had prevailed over the economic possibilities of the system. It was not long, however, before the cold truth became evident—the "medical" dispensaries were "sick." At Guthrie citizens seemed remarkably free of ills; the local agent there for one five-week period sold only $3.20 worth of liquor. In Oklahoma City, with some 50,000 population, total sales between May and August of 1908 amounted to only $8.00. Purchases at other representative cities up to August included: Hugo, $15.57; Lawton, $6.00; Blackwell, $3.20; Shawnee, $9.85; Ardmore, $28.27; Durant, $22.50; Alva, $34.00; Arapaho, $1.60; and Mangum, $15.85.[55] In the sixty-five day period following the establishment of the agency system, the report of Superintendent Robert Lozier showed that the state spent $8,437.96 in selling $3,811.88 worth of whisky and $1,000 worth of alcohol. Total expenditures came to $25,051.95.[56] Such figures did not readily commend the agency to the taxpayers in November.

The issue in the election became very confusing. As indicated, both the constitution and the enabling act permitted the establishment of dispensaries in towns of two thousand or more, and if an Oklahoma county had no town of that size, one dispensary could be created at some place determined by the state. The proposed amendment would have altered the constitution by granting the legislature power to establish agencies in communities of one thousand population *and at other localities*. The proposition appeared simple, but the ballot title made it an extremely perplexing issue. It read in part:

State Question No. 1 is a proposed constitutional amend-

[54] *Haskell's Address to Prohibitionists*, 11.

[55] Prohibition files, Barde Collection; see also New York *Times*, August 1, 1908.

[56] Prohibition files, Barde Collection.

ment and related to the law now in force, establishing a State
Agency and local agencies for the sale of intoxicating liquors
for medical and scientific purposes only; each sale to be registered; no sale to be made except upon prescription signed
by a registered practicing physician; if adopted will amend
the Constitution so as to authorize the Agency Superintendent,
with the approval of the governor, to establish one such agency
in each town of one thousand population, or wherever else a
public necessity exists therefor.[57]

In the November election the amendment met with defeat,
105,392 to 121,573. Governor Haskell, therefore, closed *all*
the dispensaries. Immediately friends of the agency proclaimed that the vote had not been on the dispensaries then
in operation, but on whether or not the people wanted to
amend the constitution permitting them in towns with 1,000
or less population. The ballot title, they said, was contra-
dictory and void, as it prevented a voter from recording his
wishes, since he might have been for one proposal and against
the other, but could only vote yes or no.

The courts finally resolved the issue. In *Robert Lozier* vs.
Alexander Drug Company, Judge A. H. Huston of Logan
County ruled that a voter may have been opposed to amend-
ing the constitution so as to authorize the agency superintendent to establish an agency in towns of one thousand population and still have been in favor of the dispensary system,
which was in accord with the constitution. But in such case,
said Judge Huston, "he had no opportunity to express his will
at all, and it cannot be presumed from information on the ballot that he could have known that a vote against the proposed
amendment to the constitution should have operated as a vote
in favor of the repeal of the dispensary law." Therefore, the
Judge declared that the state agency as originally enacted was

[57] *Biennial Report of Benjamin F. Harrison, Secretary of State of . . .
Oklahoma . . . 1912*, 20.

still law, except the unconstitutional part providing for agencies in towns of one thousand population.[58] Governor Haskell objected to the decision of the court, and he urged the legislature to take favorable action on the dispensary system.[59]

It was not difficult to comprehend Haskell's ignorance of the agency, especially its financial status. Robert Lozier, its first superintendent, was perhaps honest but, nevertheless, an incompetent administrator. The state examiner sent the Governor and the Democratic party into a roar when he reported that "during the period . . . Robert Lozier was superintendent, the accounts and records made of the transaction in the State Agency was very incomplete, erroneous . . . indefinite and were improperly kept." He also found cases "where acid had been used to make erasures on the books, checks, etc."[60] Haskell condemned Lozier's poor methods, but upheld his honesty.

When the Oklahoma Supreme Court sustained the decision rendered by Judge Huston, Haskell had no choice but to reopen the dispensaries. In a special proclamation he reactivated the agency system.[61] By the end of 1909, however, only nineteen agencies had been established under a new superintendent, S. W. Stone, who replaced the inefficient Lozier.[62] Before the repeal of the agency law in 1911, never were there more than twenty dispensaries in existence.

[58] On appeal Judge Huston's decision was upheld by the Oklahoma Supreme Court. See *Robert Lozier* vs. *Alexander Drug Company*, 23 Okla. 1.

[59] *First Message of the Governor to the Second State Legislature, January 5, 1909*, 10–11.

[60] "Report of the Special Committee on the State Agency," Special Collection on Prohibition, Oklahoma Historical Society.

[61] See Governor Haskell's proclamation in the Beaver County *Herald*, June 10, 1909.

[62] Vinita *Weekly Chieftain*, June 11, 1909.

III

HASKELL EXPERIENCES ENFORCEMENT WOES

THE BILLUPS bill made provision for state control of the liquor traffic by establishing an enforcement office under the governor. Primarily, however, the execution of the law depended upon local officials, often aided indirectly by such groups as the WCTU and the Anti-Saloon League.[1] Although granted that most county and city officers were honest, conscientious public servants, they had neither the time nor the resources to cope effectively with small bootleggers, to say nothing of powerful ones. Thus, long before the days of national prohibition, Oklahoma had experienced the frustrations attendant to enforcement of the noble experiment.

The public attitude toward the question of enforcement varied during the Haskell period. Some citizens applauded the liquor law as an unqualified success, while others, even drys on occasion, denounced its enforcement as outright failure. Unquestionably, prohibition was not as effective as

[1] About the time Oklahoma entered the Union, the Anti-Saloon League was becoming increasingly significant as a social and political force throughout the nation. Politicians feared its influence, and the liquor interests respected its power. See Herbert Asbury, *The Great Illusion: An Informal History of Prohibition*, 94–104, and Odegard, *Pressure Politics*, 22–23.

the friends of the movement desired. Indeed, before the end of 1908 (the year the liquor enforcement statute passed the legislature), Fred S. Caldwell, Haskell's prohibition-enforcement attorney, reluctantly admitted that he had not "been able to do all I hoped to, because local sentiment largely controls the enforcement of the law in the community," and that in some places progress had been slow in getting "citizens of influence to uphold the officers."[2] Caldwell's appraisal of the law, incidentally, coincided with what wets had preached during the 1907 campaign. In a prohibition state, they had maintained, wet and dry zones were as inevitable as winter and summer.

Governor Haskell, nevertheless, was determined to see the law uniformly enforced. The state realized some success in the prosecution of bootleggers, to be sure, but it was at best only temporary, and violators, eager for profits at the expense of chance, returned to ply their trade in defiance of the Billups bill. The state's enforcement officers raided sporadically throughout Oklahoma, but the liquor traffic confounded their best efforts. In Creek County, for example, in 1909 officers brought indictments against nearly two hundred bootleggers,[3] but the very next year wets and drys complained concertedly (although for different reasons) that bootleggers presented a greater problem than at any other time.

In an effort to compel obedience to the law, the state proceeded occasionally against county officials who failed to enforce the liquor measure. In 1908, Governor Haskell sent state Attorney General Charles West to Pottawatomie County to investigate an alleged unlawful combination between officials and bootleggers. West succeeded in forcing the resignation or removal of a county attorney, a judge, and a county commissioner, all of whom had received money from the

2 *Daily Oklahoman*, December 5, 1908.
3 *Ibid.*

whisky interests for protection.[4] Later in the year West went to Tulsa County, where he ousted other officers for neglect of duty. The prohibition-enforcement attorney, Fred S. Caldwell, forced the resignation in Creek County (which he personally considered the "rottenest" county in the state from the standpoint of law enforcement), of the county attorney on the grounds that he had violated his oath of office by failure to enforce the prohibition law.[5] In 1910 the county attorney and the sheriff of Beckham County lost their jobs.[6] By the end of the Haskell administration, no less than twenty county and city officers had been removed for failure to enforce the liquor statute.

The state expended roughly $35,000 for enforcement during the first four years of statehood.[7] While state efforts may have been conscientious, they were not sufficient to enforce the law; in short, the administrative task was too great. Had there been bountiful resources of men and money, it is doubtful whether enforcement could have been anywhere near absolute in areas where public sentiment did not support prohibition.

Unfortunately, criminal statistics in Oklahoma, especially of prohibition violations, were not systematically kept. Examination of the available data, however, revealed the immense difficulties involved in enforcing the law. Although the records of arrests for drunkenness do not indicate the exact degree to which the law was enforced, figures for certain representative cities showed that violations usually increased with the passage of time. In Oklahoma City, for example, liquor cases rose from 274 in December of 1907 to an average of 311 a month in 1908. Where there had been 37 arrests for drunk-

[4] *Harlow's Weekly*, June 5, 1914.
[5] *Daily Oklahoman*, August 8, 1908.
[6] *American Issue*, March, 1910.
[7] Cherrington, *ASL Yearbook*, 1911, 140.

enness in January of 1908, there were 75 for the next month. By 1910 the city's condition had improved very little.[8] The same was true for other cities across the state, especially the larger ones. Lawton, for example, which registered 114 arrests for drunkenness in 1908, had 204 in 1910; Tulsa jumped from 769 to 1,366 in the same period; Shawnee spiraled from 517 to 867; at Sapulpa arrests were up to 727 in 1910 compared to 598 in 1908; El Reno, which had 72 arrests in 1908, increased to 282 two years later.[9] In six of the smaller towns of the state—Watonga, Geary, Blackwell, Newkirk, Kingfisher, and Perry—the number of arrests tripled between 1908 and 1910.[10] Generally, enforcement in the larger cities and towns presented greater trouble than in the less populated areas. Whatever these statistics may or may not suggest, they clearly indicate the presence of a considerable traffic in liquor.

The economics of enforcement complicated the suppression of the liquor traffic in many parts of Oklahoma. In fifteen counties—Grady, Comanche, Caddo, Kiowa, Murray, Carter, Johnston, Canadian, Seminole, Muskogee, Tulsa, Creek, Oklahoma, Pottawatomie, and Nowata—more than 9,000 cases arose out of the illicit sale of liquor between 1908 and 1910, at a total cost to these counties of $231,000. In Pottawatomie, less than a year after statehood, County Attorney Virgil Biggers lamented that the continuation of liquor-law enforcement at the present rate would break the county. By June of 1908 he had prosecuted 326 cases, two-thirds of which resulted in no convictions. These, the attorney estimated, cost an average of $20.00 each, or a total of $6,520.[11] Fines collected amounted to only $2,000. Condi-

8 Figures for 1908 may be found in the *American Issue*, September, 1908, and the *Daily Oklahoman*, July, 1908. See statistics for 1910 in the *Daily Oklahoman*, November 2, 1910.

9 *Daily Oklahoman*, November 2, 1910.

10 Cherrington, *ASL Yearbook*, 1910, 168.

11 Shawnee *Daily Herald,* June 8, 1908.

tions improved little the following two years. Of 1,150 cases filed in county court in 1910, 1,100 were alleged liquor violations, prosecuted at a total cost to the county of nearly $32,000.[12] State officials, however, claimed that counties came out even in the enforcement of the law, on the whole, although some definitely incurred a financial deficit.

Governor Haskell held tenaciously to the belief that vigorous enforcement would yield enough income to cover all expenses. He contended that where officers saw that the convicted violators worked out their sentences when unable to pay, the county came out ahead, but where prisoners remained idly in jail, expenses increased, and thus helped to discredit the law. Most counties, however, were not as fortunate as Canadian, Custer, Comanche, or Adair, all of which reported a profit resulting from enforcement.[13] In Canadian County, for example, there had been 222 actions under the prohibition law between November of 1907 and July of 1908. The cost of operation of the county seat, which included salaries of the judges, clerks, and jury fees, totaled $5,300, while the collection of fines came to $9,500; the value of all liquor seized amounted to approximately $5,000.[14]

Despite the cost of enforcement and the record of prohibition in the new state, Governor Haskell's attitude remained unalterable. It was principally the liquor interests from outside Oklahoma, he said, that discouraged respect for the law. The Governor once noted that "strenuous effort and organization [have] been made from the beginning of statehood . . . [by] persons and corporations [from] outside our own state, who would profit by a traffic now prohibited in our state." These lawless elements, said Haskell, had neglected no opportunity to discredit enforcement of the liquor statute and "to

12 Prohibition files, Barde Collection.
13 *American Issue*, March, 1910.
14 *Ibid.*

throw in the way of enforcement every possible barrier, and to discredit the public officers whose duty it is to enforce the law, and to which every honest effort is being made." He scolded drys who had not given active support to law enforcement, and who by their indifference enabled wets to "create false impressions" among honest and law-abiding citizens.[15]

Haskell also blamed policies of the federal government for much of the state's troubles. The use of the mails by out-of-state whisky companies to advertise in Oklahoma, the protection of interstate shipments of liquor under the commerce clause of the federal constitution, and the national government's policy of selling liquor stamps to persons in prohibition territory only undermined the efforts of the dry states.[16] The executive's analysis of the role of the government was partly correct. In 1908, for example, 2,135 persons in Oklahoma bought federal liquor stamps,[17] and in no year during the Haskell period did the federal government sell less than 1,000 to Sooners. Surely an element of truth showed through in the statement of wets that if further evidence were needed to demonstrate how statewide prohibition broke down, "it is at hand in the number of persons who pay a special tax to sell liquor where all sale is forbidden."[18]

Those who held permits could, and did, obtain shipments of liquor from outside the state through interstate commerce. At Elk City in Beckham County, to illustrate, the records of the Rock Island Railroad revealed that between January and December of 1909 more than 1,033 barrels of beer and 482

[15] *Daily Oklahoman*, August 28, 1909.

[16] *Ibid.*, February 16, 1910.

[17] In that year the names of all persons holding federal liquor stamps in Oklahoma were compiled by Governor Haskell's special enforcement attorney and distributed to law officials across the state. This list may be found in the Oklahoma Historical Society's Special Collection on Prohibition.

[18] *The Yearbook of the United States Brewers' Association*, 1909, 195.

cases of whisky were received.[19] At Purcell in McClain County the railroad agent reported that between July and September of 1909 a total of 2,502 gallons of whisky came into that small rural town.[20] Most liquor sold in Oklahoma throughout the prohibition period arrived in the state through interstate commerce.

It was not difficult, then, to comprehend Haskell's fight to subject such shipments to the police powers of the state. In November of 1909 the Governor wrote President William Howard Taft requesting his assistance in securing national legislation which would place the transportation of intoxicants under state regulation.[21] The Governor's letter was forwarded to Taft's attorney general, George Wickersham. In a letter to the President, a copy of which subsequently came to Haskell, Wickersham pointed out that efforts had been made to enact legislation designed to limit the introduction of intoxicating beverages into those states which forbade or restricted their manufacture or sale. Congress, he said, had recently passed a statute which permitted the sale of liquor only to bona fide consignees and which required intoxicants sent under interstate commerce to be plainly marked as to content and quantity.[22] The Attorney General noted that since the subject had been recently investigated, the administration had no intention of recommending any legislation to Congress.

In his correspondence to Taft, the Governor also complained of the acceptance of the federal revenue tax from dealers in intoxicants in dry territory and of the "improper" use of the mail service by out-of-state liquor firms in advertising their products. On the latter point Wickersham replied

[19] See "Prohibition Hypocrisy," a leaflet distributed by the Local Option Committee, Special Collection on Prohibition, Oklahoma Historical Society.

[20] Cherrington, *ASL Yearbook*, 1911, 149.

[21] Haskell's letter cited in Attorney General to President William H. Taft, November 15, 1909, Haskell Collection, University of Oklahoma Library.

[22] See the legislation in *Statutes at Large*, **XXXV**, 1136.

that in the absence of legislation, he could do nothing. As to the complaint about the federal tax, he pointed out:

> I may say that, in view of the well-settled rule that the payment of taxes imposed by statute for national purposes does not give those who pay them authority to engage in the manufacture or sale of the articles upon which they are collected in any state which lawfully forbids such manufacture or sale and it seems clear to me that the Executive branch of the Government may not, under such circumstances and in the absence of legislation to that end, refuse to receive payment of such taxes. . . . Certainly, the Government could not properly refuse to accept such payment and then prosecute those who would thus become violators of the Federal revenue law.[23]

Haskell was correct when he asserted that Oklahoma would continue to experience interference with prohibition enforcement as long as the federal government maintained such policies.[24] And he could have added that it would prove difficult, if not impossible, as long as the people of his state furnished a market.

One could hardly leave the question of enforcement during the early period of Oklahoma statehood without mentioning the activities of William Creekmore,[25] acknowledged "king" of the bootleggers. Soon after statehood, state Attorney General West estimated that there were one thousand bootleggers in Oklahoma City, most of whom belonged to the Creekmore organization. When Oklahoma entered the Union in 1907, the "king" was already in the illicit liquor business at Sapulpa, Indian Territory. Under an agreement made with a Joplin,

---

[23] Attorney General to President William H. Taft, November 15, 1909, Haskell Collection, University of Oklahoma Library.

[24] See *Haskell's Address to Prohibitionists*, 14.

[25] The activities of Creekmore have been traced in McRill, *And Satan Came*, 175–81; also see *Daily Oklahoman*, May 30, 1917. Helpful information was also obtained from personal interview with J. F. Shallenberger, Tulsa, May 27, 1966.

Missouri, wholesale dealer, he received one dollar a case for all the liquor sold. Soon Creekmore's operations included the entire state, and it became what many have alleged to be one of the greatest contraband liquor organizations in American history. Along with his expanding business, bootlegger Creekmore developed a powerful political machine. Whatever the protection cost, that was what Creekmore paid.

In Oklahoma City seldom did officers arrest a Creekmore man, but if independent or small-scale bootleggers attempted to gain a foothold in the business, they met with little success.[26] When law officers conducted raids, they usually fell on helpless and unfortunate souls outside the Creekmore organization. Although the "king" worked out of Joplin, he spent much of his time in Oklahoma City, the hub of the operation, or traveling over the state mapping strategy or keeping in touch with the local situation. Until convicted in 1915 for violating federal liquor laws, Creekmore prospered. Finally, a jury gave him three years and three months in the federal penitentiary at Leavenworth. Following his release, he returned to Oklahoma, gave up the whisky business, and decided to raise hogs for a living.

The existing method of enforcement which permitted men like Creekmore to ply their trade strengthened the efforts of the wets who sought in 1910 to have the prohibition law repealed. To many, prohibition appeared as one huge joke. *Gulick's Review* denounced the state's hypocrisy in the following cryptic language:

> Prohibition in Oklahoma is the rankest farce that ever cursed a state and the most stupendous piece of legislative folly that ever found its way inside the covers of the statute books of a commonwealth. Prohibition! When there are thousands of bootleggers traveling up and down the country; prohibition, when the streets of every town smell of whiskey;

[26] See McRill, *And Satan Came*, 176.

prohibition, when the cost of enforcement is [impoverishing] the counties and the state; prohibition, when drunkards reel from door to door . . . . And this is what the Billups Law amounts to in this state, a sumptuary law, mixed with the most questionable politics; a police regulation that is the laughing stock of the state; a mixture of demagogic dogmatic and pious puerilities, a combination of political piracy and religious [fanaticism]; a mixture of all that is doubtful in sumptuary restraint . . . . It is Belial smirking at virtue and virtue flirting with the devil. Prohibition in Oklahoma? Ye Gods, what a farce.[27]

If prohibition were indeed a farce, as the *Review* asserted, the second Oklahoma legislature did nothing to stop the comical show. The Billups bill went unaltered. The lawmakers did, however, pass an act which made it a felony, punishable by from one to five years in the penitentiary, to barter, give away, or sell intoxicants to habitual drunkards, persons of unsound mind, and minors.[28] Legislators gave a concession to those who drank apple cider by exempting it from the provisions of the whisky statute.[29] An outstanding feature of the session developed when Senators Clarence Davis of Bristow and J. P. Goulding of Enid introduced unsuccessfully a local-option measure.[30]

With the failure of the Davis-Goulding resolution, wets for the first time in Oklahoma history employed a new technique in an effort to realize repeal, the initiative process. Soon after the adjournment of the legislature, the Sons of Washington announced its intention of circulating a petition requesting a special election on local option. By February, 1910, the liquor forces had secured a sufficient number of signatures, but when they submitted their petition to the secretary

---

[27] Quoted in the Vinita *Weekly Chieftain*, April 8, 1910.
[28] *Session Laws*, 1909, 64–65.
[29] *Ibid.*, 387.
[30] Senate *Journal*, 1909, 307–308.

of state, William Cross, he refused to honor it, claiming that the measure was unconstitutional.

Governor Haskell supported Cross in his action. He declared that the initiative process was not intended for the introduction of unconstitutional measures. Moreover, he maintained that the prohibition question had been settled for twenty-one years by the enabling act and by the constitution. Temporarily occupying the role of judge, the executive declared that a vote on the issue would be null and void. "Where the possibility exists," said Haskell, "that a law may be deemed void by the courts, the taxpayers of the state should not be burdened by the cost of an election." He would not place upon the state the cost of a vote certain to be invalidated.[31]

The wets went to court to compel acceptance of their petition by Haskell and his secretary. They argued before the Oklahoma Supreme Court that the enabling act merely required the constitution to contain the twenty-one-year provision for Indian Territory, but it could not force the retention of that provision since the authority of Congress ceased after statehood. The court refused to take jurisdiction on the constitutionality of the legal questions involved until the amendment had been presented to the people, but it did order Cross to file the petition. Haskell accepted the judgment of the court, and he reassured wets that he had not intended to "deprive any element of our citizenship of any right . . . they [sic] may have under the Constitution or laws of this state."[32] Accordingly the Governor set the vote on the amendment for the general election in November.

The prohibition election, like the one at statehood, generated a great deal of enthusiasm and activity from both wets

[31] Governor Charles N. Haskell to the Secretary of State, February 15, 1910, Office of the Secretary of State, Oklahoma City.

[32] See the decision and comments on the case and those of Haskell in the Beaver County *Democrat*, September 22, 1910.

and drys. The prohibitionists, again led by the Anti-Saloon League, opened their campaign in Oklahoma City with a speech by Governor Haskell. He admitted that the prohibition law had its violators and often proved expensive, but he urged that the combined efforts to destroy laws that encouraged morality and domestic happiness should not serve as an excuse for a backward step. Haskell opposed the amendment on both moral and economic grounds. Intemperance, he said, destroyed a man's intelligence and his physical ability to support and educate his family, and to discharge his duties as a citizen. Therefore, he reasoned, the liquor traffic went counter to the public welfare. And, moreover, bars did not increase the earning capacity of the people.

The major church groups, which had been on guard for the "resurrection of the unscrupulous foe" (the liquor interests), put their members on the alert. Bishop William A. Quayle, of the Methodist Episcopal Church Conference, called upon all good Methodists to "do what the Anti-Saloon League asks," and "do business for God . . . country and state." The church faced a "new war for independence."[33] Presbyterians declared that the battle between the forces of right and wrong "can never be terminated by a peace protocol," and that it would be no "holiday task to defeat this cunning, deceptive . . . anarchistic enemy."[34] The Baptists thought the campaign one of "Law, Order, and Righteousness on one side, and Lawlessness and Sin on the other."[35]

The WCTU organized its statewide campaign with enviable skill. The group, headed by Mrs. Cora Hammet, sent out 25,000 copies of the local-option amendment and pointed out its defects; more than 30,000 copies of the song "Keep Oklahoma Dry" were also distributed.[36] With the able as-

[33] See the Bishop's comments in *American Issue*, August, 1910; but see also Methodist *Minutes*, 1910, 267–68.

[34] Presbyterian *Minutes*, 1910, 167.

[35] Baptist *Minutes*, 1910, 69–70.   [36] Cherrington, *Encyclopedia*, V, 2058.

sistance of Ernest H. Cherrington, noted temperance writer and editor of the *American Issue,* speakers of the WCTU and the Anti-Saloon League toured the state warning of the dangers of the liquor traffic to home, church, and civilization.

The wets' program was supported principally by the Sons of Washington and the Oklahoma Business Men's Protective League. The latter organization was led by Henry Overholser and claimed a membership of 2,000 in Oklahoma City, headquarters for both sides in the prohibition fight. By October, 1910, the league had established branches in all the larger towns of the state, and before the election it claimed a membership of 30,000 with representation from all the counties.[37]

The repealers hammered upon two major points. First, they said that prohibition had been given a fair trial, yet it had not significantly diminished the sale of liquor or drunkenness; secondly, wets emphasized the revenue which would accrue to the state from the legalized sale of liquor.[38]

Under the proposed plans counties would receive about $3,000,000 from approximately 1,500 whisky establishments. Much of this money would go to the road and bridge fund for the development of better highways in the state.[39] Besides this, repeal would release the taxpayers from the burdensome cost of enforcing the present law.[40] Overholser of the Business League pictured what he considered an alliance between the church people and bootleggers which he said actually robbed the taxpayers and worked to the disadvantage of a progressive state. In return, drys accused wets of trying to buy the election.[41]

[37] *Daily Oklahoman*, October 9, 1910.

[38] Local Option and High License Committee to Dr. George Conger, superintendent of the Oklahoma Anti-Saloon League, September 8, 1910, Prohibition files, Barde Collection.

[39] *Daily Oklahoman*, October 28, 1910.

[40] *Ibid.*, November 6, 1910.

[41] *Ibid.*, October 24, 1910.

In November, 1910, the people defeated the second of six repeal amendments in Oklahoma history. Of a total vote of 254,730, the local-option measure picked up 105,041 votes.[42] Twelve counties gave the amendment a constitutional majority, while nine others voted yes but lacked a constitutional majority. Compared to the 1907 election, drys increased their strength by some 3,000 votes.

In the gubernatorial race, held the same year, Democratic nominee Lee Cruce defeated the Republican candidate J. W. McNeil. Both parties seemed anxious to avoid entanglement in the prohibition issue. The Democratic platform, without specific mention of the liquor law, declared for "vigorous enforcement of all laws" and pledged its representatives to a continuation of that policy. The Republicans condemned the Democratic administration for nonenforcement and pledged the party to uphold the law as long as it remained on the books.[43] Both Cruce and McNeil were endorsed by the Anti-Saloon League, but a small number of prohibitionists seemed skeptical of the Democratic candidate because of his willingness to accept any petition presented to him resubmitting the liquor provision of the constitution. Cruce's personal abstinence and his belief in prohibition as a desirable social experiment no doubt outweighed the disadvantages incurred by his attitude on resubmission.[44] Prohibition seemed in good hands.

[42] Gordon and Richards, *Oklahoma Redbook*, II, 307. To carry, the amendment had to receive a majority of *all* the votes cast at the election.

[43] *Ibid.*, 368, 377.

[44] The Prohibition party entered candidates in the election for governor, lieutenant governor, secretary of state, and state treasurer. All were unsuccessful. Seldom did the party receive more than fifty votes in any county. Throughout Oklahoma history (when it did appear on the ballot), it made almost no impact upon the political scene or the prohibition movement. In fact, it was almost a nonentity.

IV

CRUCE AND WILLIAMS INHERIT A MOVEMENT

THE DEFEAT of local option in 1910 clearly indicated Oklahoma's satisfaction with the status quo, despite cries of hypocrisy from a very vocal minority. After three years of the noble experiment, there was little doubt in the minds of the drys that the "theory" of prohibition was well established, although enforcement, complicated by a number of problems, was impractical in most areas of the state. In fact, the Anti-Saloon League, previously devoted mostly to the creation of public sentiment, influencing legislation, and fighting the proposed constitutional amendment permitting the sale of liquor, shifted its policy to include greater emphasis upon enforcement, on the assumption that the prohibition "spirit" had thoroughly penetrated the hearts and souls of a majority of Oklahomans. The league was correct; the prohibition spirit abided, and so did the ardent ones. That Governors Lee Cruce and Robert L. Williams, pushed by the prohibitionists, demanded more stringent legislation during their administrations not only indicated insufficient laws, but also implied John Barleycorn's continued presence.

Before Governor Haskell left office, he made a final appeal

to the legislature to truly vitalize the constitution by granting the governor more power in the enforcement of prohibition. If succeeding governors were to be a strong factor in law enforcement, as most people of the state expected, sufficient legal authority must be granted. Addressing himself to the dispensaries established shortly after statehood for the sale of liquors for medicinal and scientific purposes—which had proved a total disappointment to the drys, a hypocritical joke to the wets, and a minor irritation to the bootleggers—the Governor spoke in vague terms, suggesting that their continuance was a matter of "judgment." Haskell also asked the legislature to request that Congress forbid the sale of liquor stamps in prohibition states and restrict intoxicants from interstate commerce.[1]

Once Cruce had received the dry heritage from Haskell, he followed unerringly the beaten path laid out by his predecessor. Seconding the legislative recommendations advanced by Haskell, he made plain his position on prohibition. Cruce promised that he would use the full force of his office to give the state honest and effective enforcement.[2] He would grant no pardons to bootleggers; and if they wanted to avoid confinement in jail, he admonished them to defeat the case in court or prepare to remain behind bars. Cruce asked the legislature for greater power to remedy the problem of enforcement, and he called for the abolition of the dispensary system. The people had declared against the dispensaries by popular vote; and moreover, he moralized, if it was wrong for the individual to sell liquor, the same held true for the state.[3]

The Governor's reasoning regarding the dispensaries, however admirable, served only to camouflage real issues. The

---

[1] See Haskell's message to the third legislature in House *Journal*, 1911, 61–62.

[2] *American Issue*, February, 1911.

[3] See Cruce's message to the third legislature in Senate *Journal*, 1911, 117–18.

sober truth was that the dispensaries had incurred general disfavor among the citizenry, while failing to live up to the financial expectations of once hopeful politicians. The Anti-Saloon League, which had once staunchly advocated the dispensaries and had claimed that wets misrepresented the idea in 1908, had now become a bitter opponent of the agencies. In commenting on the issue early in 1911, Dr. George Conger, the league's superintendent, denounced the system as "distasteful to us as to everyone else." In an attempt to vindicate the organization's past action, Conger remarked that the dispensary system "was put in as a temporary measure in the first place [and] was not altogether satisfactory . . . but seemed to be about the best we could do at the time."[4]

From the time of their re-establishment by Governor Haskell, the dispensaries had been confined largely to the reception and sale of confiscated liquors to out-of-state firms. Since the small state liquor-enforcement office provided for by the Billups bill came under the agency system, its superintendent also directed the activities of this branch.[5] With a profit of only about $4,000 for the year ending March 21, 1911, the frugal Cruce believed that the system did not warrant continuation.[6]

The idea of abolishing the enforcement activities of the agency system occasioned bitter utterances from two of its top officials. In his 1911 annual report, Caldwell said in substance that the expensive work carried out by the enforcement department had generally been without any appreciable results, and he urged its destruction by the forthcoming legislature. The work that had been done by the state enforcement officers

[4] *Daily Oklahoman*, January 5, 1911.

[5] The Anti-Saloon League also believed that the state enforcement office had not lived up to expectations. See, for example, the statement by C. F. Stealy, president of the Oklahoma league, *ibid.*, February 26, 1911.

[6] *Ibid.*, May 16, 1911.

as a special department of the state agency under the direction of F. F. Cain, said Caldwell, "has done the cause of bona fide law enforcement . . . injury."[7] He pointed out, for example, that Cain and his men had operated almost continually in Oklahoma City for several months, yet very few places had closed as a direct result of their action. As if that was not enough to damn the department, he charged that officers were too frequently presented with exceedingly strong temptations to accept money from law violators in consideration of small privileges; and Caldwell subtly intimated that some had taken advantage of a few of these lucrative offers.[8]

Cain countered Caldwell's attack with the charge that he had drawn a "nice fat salary," hired "sleuths," criticized more Democratic officials, advanced more theories, and gotten less done than any other one man. "I believe the majority of the officers connected with the department will agree," said Cain, "that under his plan of management, it would have been much better for the state if it had abolished it ten minutes after his appointment." Alluding to accomplishments under his leadership, he noted that not less than $30,000 worth of goods had been turned over to the state for sale in nonprohibition territory. Contrary to the faulty accusations leveled at him by the misinformed Caldwell, operations in Oklahoma City had reaped success. He had "swamped" the jails, arresting "dozens" of violators with only a small force of ten men. What Cain carefully, and perhaps judiciously, avoided men-

[7] *Ibid.*

[8] *Ibid.*, January 15, 1911. For alleged instances of bribery, see G. A. Reinmiller, "West vs Reardon," *Sturms*, Vol. IX (February, 1910), 35–36. In commenting on enforcement, Caldwell pointed up a significant problem voiced by more than one officer. On many occasions when bootleggers were convicted, especially in city courts, they appealed their cases to county court, thus placing financial responsibility upon the county. Confronted by such a number of these cases, many prosecuting attorneys of the counties often dismissed them in the face of more important matters.

tioning was that little of lasting value had been done to curtail the liquor traffic in the city.[9]

The politicians, too, recognized the failure of the agency system, and thus sought to redeem themselves of the error committed nearly three years earlier. In January, 1911, the legislature considered a bill designed to abolish the dispensaries and to provide for the suspension of derelict officials.[10] As finally drawn, the legislation significantly altered the Billups bill. The provision granting the governor authority to remove officers who did not perform their duties was deleted, but the state agency (including the state enforcement department as well as the dispensaries), a constant headache since its inception, faded into history. The lawmakers, however, gave the governor the right to appoint one roving enforcement officer.[11]

The legislature also addressed Congress regarding the interstate commerce problem and the federal tax paid by liquor dealers.[12] As a result of national pressure from various dry groups and legislatures such as Oklahoma, Congress in 1913 passed the Webb-Kenyon Act designed to subject interstate shipments of liquor to closer supervision.[13]

Despite the passage of more stringent legislation, successful control of the liquor traffic in Oklahoma proved difficult. After grappling with the prohibition puzzle for two years, Governor

[9] *Daily Oklahoman*, January 8, 1911.

[10] For comments on the proposed legislation, see *American Issue*, January, 1911, and Vinita *Weekly Chieftain*, January 6, 1911. Views of various senators may be found in the *Daily Oklahoman*, February 11, 1911.

[11] The law has been outlined above in extremely abbreviated form. For the statute in its entirety, see *Session Laws*, 1910–11, 154–66.

[12] See Senate *Journal*, 1911, 142–43.

[13] *Statutes at Large*, XXXVII, 699–700. The best discussion of the relationship of progressivism to the Webb-Kenyon law is found in James H. Timberlake's excellent book, *Prohibition and the Progressive Movement, 1900–1920*, 162–65. For Oklahoma's response to the law, see *Harlow's Weekly*, March 15, 1913, and *Daily Oklahoman*, March 1, 5, 7, 1913.

Cruce lamented that enforcement in many instances "has been weak, lax, and absolutely ineffective . . . "; he was convinced, nevertheless, that the state could force respect for the liquor law.[14] The passage of the Webb act and the existing state of enforcement gave the Governor additional justification for demanding a law which would grant him authority to remove derelict officials. One special enforcement officer, he said, was not sufficient to solve the problem: "When the mayor of a city with dozens of policemen . . . will publicly acknowledge that he can't enforce the prohibition law in a single city, it would seem that enforcement not only in such a city," but in any other city "by a single individual is a physical impossibility."[15]

Mindful that public sentiment played a highly significant role in the execution of the law, and that in some areas of the state bootleggers were active in politics, Cruce saw his "ouster" plan as a solution to the state's enforcement trouble. The proper respect for the law could only develop through uniform enforcement:

> To permit one sort of enforcement in Oklahoma County, another in Muskogee County, and still another sort in Carter County, amounts in the end to no enforcement. Laws statewide in their application should be statewide in their enforcement, and what is prohibited by state laws in Muskogee County should be prohibited in Oklahoma County and in every other county.
>
> In order that the Governor's authority may be defined and that his requests may be observed by local officials, [the] Legislature should give him the power to remove summarily from office any local official whose duty it is to enforce the

14 *Regular Biennial Message of Governor Lee Cruce to the Legislature of 1913*, 15 (hereafter cited as *Message of Governor Cruce*).

15 *Message of Governor Cruce*, 20; also Edward E. Dale and Jesse L. Rader, *Readings in Oklahoma History*, 734–35 (hereafter cited as Dale and Rader, *Readings*); for related statements, see Vinita *Weekly Chieftain*, September 29, 1911, and *Daily Oklahoman*, June 27, 1911.

. . . laws of Oklahoma . . . . Clothed with this authority the
question of local sentiment would play very little part. It would
[also] result in another thing which would immediately be
helpful to better government; it would remove the bootlegger[s] . . . from local politics . . . . They are sufficiently numerous in many localities to hold the balance of power.[16]

Although cognizant of the enforcement problem, Oklahoma's Democratic Fourth Legislature defeated the Cruce
proposal. The politicians feared that the power the Governor
demanded could be used as a political weapon in the hands of
a chief executive anxious to strike at his enemies; they were
not afraid of the proper use of power, but of its possible mis-
use. From subsequent events it appeared that the legislature
was not only determined to keep Cruce from acquiring the
power he craved, but was also equally as determined to place
enforcement absolutely under the jurisdiction of local officers.

With the Governor's proposal rejected, the most heated
debate during the session developed from the attempt to
abolish the office of special enforcement officer. Later, in
March, 1913, the legislature passed a bill to eliminate the
position. Governor Cruce, whose relationship with the law-
making body was far from amiable, especially when it came to
curtailing his power, vetoed the bill. He believed that better
enforcement could be carried out by retaining and strengthen-
ing the present office. And he criticized the statute which permitted the appointment of only one officer as "a lame attempt
to give a majority of the citizens . . . the prohibition they voted
for." W. J. Caudill, who then occupied the post, concurred in
his chief's opinion and argued for a much larger force.[17]

Cruce's veto did not resolve the matter, for at the special
session of the legislature held in 1913, supporters of the bill
revived it. The Governor, however, once again vetoed the

[16] Dale and Rader, *Readings*, 735.
[17] *Daily Oklahoman*, March 6, 1913.

measure, and he scolded the legislators for their "bad faith" in raising the issue a second time.[18] In the meantime, Caudill, on the assumption that many lawmakers had been inspired in their actions by animosity toward him rather than the office, resigned, hoping to check the attempt to push the bill through. He was wrong. In April the legislature passed the bill over the Governor's veto.[19] Although the destruction of the office could have been justified in the name of frugality, it is doubtful whether the usually economy-minded Cruce interpreted the move in any way other than as a direct blow to his appointive power.

Disenchantment with enforcement during the Cruce period showed among drys and wets alike. Early in 1911, before the abolition of the state agency, B. J. Baugh, one of the enforcement workers, noted that conditions in Oklahoma were "rotten."[20] The superintendent of the Anti-Saloon League echoed the same sentiments in remarking that "it will not be seriously claimed . . . by those well informed, that the prohibition law is not violated throughout the state . . . especially in the larger cities."[21] The league called upon the people to get rid of crooked officers "whether it be judge of the court, county attorney, sheriff, mayor, or chief of police."[22] Near the end of the Cruce administration, Oklahoma Baptists, while taking pride that their state was the first ever born sober, mourned that "it has not been sober ever since." They may have been right in declaring that "we are all to blame."[23]

18 Eufaula *Indian Journal*, March 6, 1913.

19 See *Session Laws*, 1913, 45–50.

20 *Daily Oklahoman*, February 3, 1911.

21 *American Issue*, June, 1911; see also the statement of W. J. Caudill in the Vinita *Weekly Chieftain*, September 29, 1911, for an appraisal of enforcement.

22 *American Issue*, October, 1912.

23 Baptist *Minutes*, 1914, 84. Perhaps the best sources on general conditions in Oklahoma for the Cruce period are *Harlow's Weekly* and the *American Issue*. The latter, however, should be used with much caution.

In response to this apparent lack of sobriety, the Anti-
Saloon League urged the formation of law and order groups
or other similar organizations in areas where widespread violations persisted. Thus many cities during the Cruce period
experienced clean-up campaigns, a movement of potential
magnitude, but which ended stifled by general apathy, unholy politics, or lack of perseverance on the part of the reformers. Oklahoma City afforded a typical example of the
clean-up campaign action. Little effort had ever been made
by local officials to curtail the activities of bootleggers, and
in any given year no less than one thousand conducted their
business without undue difficulty. Indeed, few genuinely
honest people denied that the town stood "wide-open." The
Anti-Saloon League decried the alliance between the law-
breakers and top city officials, asserting that "the practice of
collecting monthly fines from bootleggers was in force."[24]
Early in 1913 the Central Hundred, a committee of church
people, decided to organize to work for public decency and
morals.

Supported by the WCTU and the league, the Central Hundred had as one of its specific objectives the ouster of Mayor
Whit Grant who allegedly conceded free reign to the bootleggers. Led by John Embry, a local attorney, and Fred Caldwell, former counsel to Governor Haskell, the organization
began a recall movement. When requested to publicly state
his views, Grant replied, to the obvious consternation of the
drys, that he doubted whether it would ever be possible to
eliminate the hip-pocket bootlegger and small jointkeeper in
the city.[25] The Mayor went further to outline the problems
connected with enforcement (which by no means were pe-
culiar to his city). Although it may not have been an adequate defense for his alleged inability to "put the lid on the

24 *Ibid.*, September, 1911.
25 *Daily Oklahoman*, February 4, 1911.

town," one particular statement by the Mayor contained a great deal of truth, and it cut to the very heart of the issues involved in the execution of the law:

Perhaps the most serious drawback of all is that when the most strenuous crusades are being made to enforce [the] . . . liquor ordinance, arrests are being made day after day and convictions imposed in municipal court; the offenders uniformly avail themselves of the right to appeal to the county court, where each one has the right of trial by jury and where the docket is so crowded that only a very few days can be allowed per term for the trial of city appeals; the result being that these appeals are delayed for months and months, until the arresting officers cannot remember very clearly the facts of a particular case, or the other witnesses, if such there be, cannot be found, and conviction can then only be had in a very small per cent of the cases . . . and during all this delay the police continue to make arrests of persons charged with such violations, and they continue to perfect appeals.[26]

The Central Hundred dismissed Grant's rambling explanation as weak and evasive, but it could never muster enough strength to unseat the Mayor. As was generally true of the clean-up campaign throughout the state, any success realized was transitory.

If the drys encountered monumental enforcement troubles during the Cruce period, the wets faced overwhelming difficulty in creating favorable sentiment for local option. Fitful attempts to initiate petitions continued to appear, but all faltered from public lethargy. Misled into believing that a majority of the people did not sympathize with prohibition, the Oklahoma Local Option Association launched a program in June, 1911, to give the state a "clean" liquor bill.[27] Like the Sons of Washington, the Business Men's Protective League,

26 *Ibid.*, February 5, 1914.
27 *Ibid.*, June 11, 1911.

and all their predecessors, the association condemned prohibition hypocrisy and argued the economics of a liquor traffic.[28] Some wets, however, not yet recuperated from the trouncing a year earlier, discouraged another vote on the issue. The Tulsa *World*, a "whisky" paper by Anti-Saloon League standards, complained that "this thing of holding elections every time the moon changes is not only expensive, but keeps the state in a turmoil." The editor of the *World* cautioned that the constant appeal to the initiative and referendum would bring both political instruments into disrepute; Oklahoma needed a rest.[29]

Others, however, considered political and social tranquility impossible until the dry dynasty was displaced. Following the unsuccessful efforts of the Local Option Association, the Business Men's Protective League endeavored to generate interest in a liquor bill in 1912 and again in 1913, but it lacked a favorable response.[30] Never conceding defeat, wets organized the next year under the United Civic Association. It blasted prohibition as a product of "cheap politicians" and "fake reformers."[31] The repealers proposed through their amendment to place two whisky establishments in towns of less than one thousand population, three in towns of one thousand but less than two thousand, and one additional liquor store for each one thousand population in towns of more than two thousand.[32] The *Oklahoman*, vigorous advocate of option since statehood, looked upon the move with pessimism and

[28] See the leaflet distributed by the Local Option Association in the Oklahoma Historical Society's Special Collection on Prohibition.

[29] Tulsa *World* quoted in the *American Issue*, July, 1911. The Anti-Saloon League's reaction to the petition may be found in the *Daily Oklahoman*, June 13, 1911.

[30] See Cherrington, *ASL Yearbook*, 1912, 185; *American Issue*, February, 1912, and October, 1913; and *Harlow's Weekly*, September 12, 1914.

[31] *Daily Oklahoman*, March 6, 1914.

[32] *American Issue*, July, 1914.

predicted defeat.[33] The paper reconciled itself to the grim fact that sentiment had developed in favor of the liquor law.[34] Time proved the truth of the statement; indeed it appeared that Oklahomans had perfected the curious ability to live in two worlds—one where the law was esteemed as beneficial to the public welfare, the other where it was trampled under the feet of men who defied an assertive public sentiment to make its voice heard.

With applause from the drys, Governor Cruce's administration came to an end. In the gubernatorial campaign of 1914, the Democratic nominee, Robert L. Williams, triumphed over John Fields, the Republican. Although a personal wet, Williams was a political dry; thus, he stood firmly by the party's pledge to uphold the law. Fields competed with Williams in his verbal support of the law. At that same election the people also approved a constitutional amendment which made drunkenness by state officials grounds for impeachment.[35]

Although the Williams era became noted for the passage of legislation designed to prohibit *completely* the traffic in liquor in *any* form whatsoever in the state and to ensure adequate enforcement by granting the Governor more power, very little was achieved during the Governor's first few years in office. Neither the executive's inaugural address nor his first message to the legislature contained any reference to prohibition. While several radical enforcement proposals did come before the Fifth Legislature, however, all met with overwhelming defeat. Misgauging the spirit of the times, Senator Lewis Hunter of Comanche and Cotton counties introduced a local-option bill, which he said was based on the "Jeffersonian doc-

[33] *Daily Oklahoman*, June 8, 1914.

[34] See *ibid.*, August 5, 15, and 19, 1914.

[35] For comments on the amendment, see *Harlow's Weekly*, July 4, 1914, and the *Daily Oklahoman*, July 17 and October 13, 16, 1914.

trine of local self government and home rule and the abolition forever of the Hamiltonian theory of centralization."[36] The resolution got nowhere.

Long obscured by the Anti-Saloon League, the WCTU re-entered the temperance limelight by urging upon the Governor and the legislature a scientific prohibition-instruction measure. The president, Abbie Hillerman, who had worked untiringly at the Oklahoma Constitutional Convention, presented the bill to the House Prohibition Committee. The measure passed both houses with only one dissenting vote, and was subsequently signed by Governor Williams. The new law provided that the nature of alcoholic drinks and their effects upon the human system should be taught in "the common schools of this state and in all institutions supported wholly or in part by money from the state." The measure required no additional textbooks since temperance was taught as a part of physiology and hygiene.[37]

The fact that the legislature failed to pass more stringent enforcement statutes did not imply that the prohibition movement had lost its thrust. Following the defeat of one of the local-option amendments in the legislature, one prominent state editor remarked with a great deal of truth that "prohibition has ceased to be an issue and is now and in all probability . . . will be a fixed institution in Oklahoma." That point, he said, was definitely settled in the lower house of the legislature in 1915 when the lawmakers turned down the local-option measure. "No matter what the sentiment of those voting," the journalist commented, it was apparent that most politicians "regarded further attempts to consider the [issue] . . . as absolutely futile—that the overwhelming majority of the people are firm adherents to prohibition."[38]

36 *Daily Oklahoman*, March 20, 1915.
37 *Session Laws*, 1915, 8.
38 *Harlow's Weekly*, March 27, 1915.

CRUCE AND WILLIAMS INHERIT A MOVEMENT

In response to continuing enforcement failures, however, the Anti-Saloon League had to agitate for additional legislation designed to subject local officials to the "will of the constitution." Although Governor Williams did not have an official prohibition-enforcement staff, since the legislature had abolished it, he had, nevertheless, directed the attorney general to conduct investigations of liquor-law violations. Williams held that enforcement could be greatly strengthened if the legislature gave the supreme court concurrent jurisdiction with the lower courts in cases involving derelict officials.[39] The Governor, therefore, urged upon the Sixth Legislature the immediate passage of such a bill. Essentially, Williams' request embodied the same idea contained in the removal proposal presented under Cruce, the only difference being that the judiciary rather than the chief executive had ultimate power in ouster proceedings.

The legislature displayed a favorable mood for the passage of extreme statutes. One journal remarked before the beginning of the session that "if legislation will make the state dry[,] it will be . . . after the adjournment of this assemblage."[40] Such speculation came close to the truth. A very positive opposition to Williams' proposal, however, came from Senators W. K. Snyder and T. H. Davidson of Oklahoma and Tulsa counties respectively, who argued that the supreme court was already too busy to deal with such cases and that the bill could easily build a political machine for the attorney general who would prosecute derelict officers. Senator Clarence Davis thought the act useless and that outside intervention by a state official in local affairs could not possibly advance the cause of prohibition. "Jesus Christ," he said, "couldn't have been sheriff of the Kingdom of Creek

[39] *Message of Governor Robert L. Williams to the Sixth Legislature . . . January 4, 1917*, 35–36.
[40] *Harlow's Weekly*, January 24, 1917.

–63–

[County] and closed the joints," because of inexperience. Another senator prophesied that if the bill passed "there'll be more hell a-popping in this state than there is popping under the present condition."[41]

The favorable voices in support of the measure, however, held sway. While many legislators agreed that the bill was drastic medicine for enforcement ailments, they acknowledged that the disease was terrible and the remedy must be severe. Perhaps the most articulate spokesman for the measure was not a member of the legislature, but the actual father of the ouster plan, Attorney General S. P. Freeling. H. T. Laughbaum of the Anti-Saloon League also argued forcefully for the bill, and he made himself conspicuous to legislators by subtle reminders of the good voters back home.[42]

Despite every articulate dissent, the "attorney general's bill," as some labeled it, passed both houses with little trouble. In the house the vote was 86 to 16, and in the senate 31 to 6.[43] As was generally true of all prohibition measures throughout the state's history, voting showed no division along party lines. In essence, the removal statute provided that the attorney general when directed by the governor should investigate complaints of negligence and institute proceedings before the supreme court to oust any official who failed to perform his duty.[44]

About the time the legislature was debating the attorney general's bill, a significant event of national importance occurred beyond Oklahoma's borders. That was the validation of the Webb-Kenyon law by the United States Supreme Court in January of 1917. The objective of this bill, as already seen, had been to protect dry states in the exercise of their

[41] See comments by various senators in *Daily Oklahoman*, January 26, 1917.
[42] *Ibid.*, January 17, 1917.
[43] Senate *Journal*, 1917, 602–603; House *Journal*, 1917, 688–89.
[44] *Session Laws*, 1917, 379.

sovereignty over their own affairs in the matter of interstate shipments of liquor. Contrary to widespread belief at the time, it did not entirely prevent the transportation of intoxicants into prohibition states; it merely forbade shipments which were in violation of state laws. President Taft, who held office at the time the bill was being considered, vetoed the measure on the ground that it was unconstitutional, but Congress had passed it over his objection.[45] Yet four years elapsed before the liquor interests were able to carry an appeal all the way to the United States Supreme Court. Once the court sustained the act, drys heralded it as another step toward national prohibition. Laughbaum of the Oklahoma Anti-Saloon League lauded the decision as a "brilliant victory that gives impetus to the national fight. It is the criterion of Congress' stand on the liquor question," and it could, he said, "presage the beginning of the end of the prohibition fight —that is, the end of the liquor interests."[46]

Inspired by the court ruling and the forward force of the national movement, prohibitionists proposed to render the state bone-dry. Early in the Sixth Legislature, Senator Walter Ferguson introduced a bill drawn by the Anti-Saloon League

[45] *Congressional Record*, 62d Cong., 3d sess., 1913, Vol. XLIX, pt. 5, 4291–92.

[46] *Daily Oklahoman*, January 10, 1917. Shortly after the court sustained the Webb law, the *Oklahoman* in highly poetic language bade farewell to the wets and liquor in dry territory with these amusing lines: "To Oscar Pepper, adios, the same to dear Old Crow; a fond goodby to all the rye that blossomed long ago. The Bourbon and the Scottish Kings of all their role are shorn; the requiem's sung, the knell is rung for John D. Barleycorn. The vintages that sparkled red . . . are *de trop*: its H_2O for you, dear Mirabel. The bubble that bedecked the brims where silver gleamed and flowers and repartee held lively sway—farewell to all such hours. Wrap up the wines of Burgundy in weeping blackest crape . . . they've stepped aside for the unfermented grape . . . . The drought upon the statutes writ spreads across the land; what once was acts are arid facts—the real thing understand. Beneath our smiling southern sun, beneath Maine's fearful sky, when Kansas chatters in its sleep—all this and more is dry." Quoted *ibid.*

which would have forbade the shipment of liquor into the
state for *any purpose*. Although this measure was unquestionably one of the most radical ever considered, all signs immediately forecast its quick passage. In fact, the bill displayed
such extreme tendencies that Governor Williams (no doubt
constantly battling to shield his firm belief in the principle
of local option)[47] threatened to veto the act if passed. In an
effort to stem this tide of legislative radicalism, the chief executive called in members of the legislature, together with
Laughbaum of the Anti-Saloon League, and proposed a substitute measure. The Williams proposal would have granted
an individual the right to ship into the state one quart of whisky or one case of beer each month of the year.[48] His suggestion fell on deaf ears.

With the Anti-Saloon League more militant than ever, urging citizens to pressure their representatives to support the
Ferguson bill,[49] the legislature proved past predictions of ex-
tremism correct. The bill passed the house by a vote of 89 to
7, and the senate 32 to 5.[50] Governor Williams compromised
his original position and allowed the act to become law without his signature. By the terms of the newly enacted bill, the
legislature made it illegal for a person to receive liquor from
a common carrier *regardless of the purpose* for which it was
to be used; and the statute made it unlawful for anyone to
possess intoxicants received directly or indirectly from such
carriers.[51]

---

[47] Governor Williams once remarked that he would rejoice "when the
National Prohibition Amendment will be effective." This did not reflect his
true sentiments. See Edward E. Dale and James D. Morrison, *Pioneer Judge:
The Life of Robert L. Williams*, 296.

[48] *Harlow's Weekly*, February 7, 1917.

[49] For commentary, see *Daily Oklahoman*, January 31, 1917.

[50] Senate *Journal*, 1917, 632; House *Journal*, 1917, 745.

[51] *Session Laws*, 1917, 350. The year 1917 saw a number of prohibition
victories in the United States Congress, including submission of the Eighteenth

The bone-dry law was destined for a bitter battle in the courts, which eventually left it virtually ineffective. Oddly enough, the first attack did not come from organized wets, but from an unexpected quarter—the Roman Catholic church. In August of 1917, a barrel of sacramental wine which had been shipped into the state prior to the Ferguson law was confiscated at Norman, Oklahoma. Father John Metter of Saint Joseph's Church directed a complaint to Attorney General Freeling and asked him to devise a method by which priests could legally acquire shipments of wine for religious services. Freeling replied that the Ferguson bill was universal in its application and that under absolutely no circumstances whatsoever could intoxicating beverages enter the state by common carriers. Determined to test the law, the Roman Catholic church, acting through Father Urbane deHasque of Oklahoma City, sought to ship from Oklahoma City to Guthrie by the Santa Fe Railroad "eight quarts of duly inspected and authorized, pure, unadulterated, fermented juice of the grape . . . to be used by priests within the state of Oklahoma for the purpose of the celebration of the mass."[52] The railroad, as expected, refused the consignment, and Father deHasque carried the case to court to compel delivery.

Opinions on the case in fundamentalist, Protestant-oriented Oklahoma drew mixed reactions. Laughbaum (actual author of the bill) said the law allowed for no exceptions, thus insinuating that the church would have to make the necessary adjustments. The Waukomis *Hornet*, setting itself up as a judge of ritual, did not believe that intoxicating wine was absolutely necessary in worship services, and the paper noted that "if Catholic communion wine is exempt from [the law's] provisions, all other denominations should be and that

Amendment. For a brief summary of the achievements during the year, see Edward B. Dunford, *The History of the Temperance Movement*, 24–27.

[52] *Daily Oklahoman*, October 12, 1917.

would make a pretty big leak. We don't think the good Lord would seriously object to the substitution of grape juice for wine."[53] Members of the First Baptist Church of Oklahoma City thought the measure should apply impartially to all citizens; and they went further to assert that the use of altar wine by Protestant churches in particular "is wholly unnecessary and . . . is deemed detrimental to the best interests of such churches."[54] The Ministerial Alliance of Oklahoma City accepted the bone-dry law as it stood, *but* left its interpretation to those in authority—meaning, of course, Freeling.

The Catholics and their supporters maintained that the statute as applied impinged upon religious freedom. Bishop Theophile Meerschaert described Freeling's stubborn refusal to permit shipment of the wine as "intolerable" and "outrageous."[55] Two of the most outspoken advocates of the Catholics' cause were the *Daily Oklahoman* and the Tulsa *Daily Democrat*. The latter saw the whole problem stemming from the dictatorial tendencies of the fanatical Laughbaum. "The state may regulate the traffic in liquors with perfect propriety and be within the law in doing so," said the *Democrat*, "but when it permits one man [Laughbaum] to set himself up as a dictator of the churches, the courts will decide that it is going too far."[56] To the *Oklahoman* the unbending statute did not "belong in the twentieth century."

> It is fair to assume that few, if any, members of the sixth legislature . . . imagined that [the] law could interfere with the age-long rites of certain Christian churches. It is fair to assume, too, that few, if any, of them would have voted for the bill, had they dreamed this would have been one of the results of the law. And further, it is fair to assume that comparatively few people in the state, however ardently they favor prohibi-

[53] Waukomis *Hornet* quoted in *Harlow's Weekly*, October 24, 1917.
[54] *Daily Oklahoman*, September 10, 1917.
[55] *Ibid.*, September 8, 1917.
[56] Tulsa *Daily Democrat*, October 13, 1917.

tion, approve of making prohibition an obnoxious religious tyranny. It would be regrettable indeed if any other assumption were possible. Yet that is one of the results of the bone dry law. If the law is literally to be enforced it is only a question of time when the Catholic and Episcopal churches will be unable to conduct their belief and custom. Such a Ukase is an anachronism.[57]

In the district court the Roman Catholic church contended that the Ferguson law, forbidding the delivery of intoxicants, was unconstitutional since it interfered with religious freedom. The state, which assumed the defense of the railroad, asserted that the act applied to sacramental wine. Moreover, the state argued that the framers of the bone-dry bill specifically and deliberately refused to exempt wine used by the church. The court sided with the state and the railroad, holding that the law was universal in its application.[58]

On appeal the Oklahoma Supreme Court reversed the decision of the lower tribunal. While the prohibition section of the constitution addressed itself to the evils of intemperance and to the use of liquor for the purpose of intoxication, wrote Justice Thomas Owen for the court, the use of wine in worship constituted no part of the evil the constitution tried to prevent. Consequently, the term "intoxicating liquors" did not include wine used for religious services. Even on the eastern side of the state, the court noted, where federal laws technically forbade the introduction of *any* sort of liquor, no one had attempted to prevent shipments of liquor for religious worship.[59]

[57] *Daily Oklahoman*, September 13, 1917. The Episcopal and Roman Catholic churches generally held aloof from the prohibition movement. Both maintained that alcoholic beverages were not of themselves an evil. The "right use" of intoxicants was the key to their approach, whether in personal use or in sacramental worship.

[58] *Harlow's Weekly*, December 26, 1917.

[59] *DeHasque* vs. *Atchison, Topeka, and Santa Fe Railroad Co.*, 68 Okla. 182.

The initial assault upon the Ferguson bill severely crippled the act; a second challenge practically destroyed it. Shortly after the wine battle, the court, in deciding a case from Harmon County, ruled that a person could introduce a small amount of liquor for his personal use, provided that he did not receive it by common carrier.[60] When asked about the court's decree regarding his bone-dry bill, Senator Ferguson moaned that "there's always an element of chance about any law—as to whether it will stand up or not. Pretty nearly all statutes have to go over the top against a withering fire from the lawyers." And then in a sad utterance, he lamented: "The zero hour came for my bone dry law. But it fell in the charge mortally wounded, and now lies punctured out in No Man's Land. It couldn't reach its objective. That's all." While the Senator regretted the casualty, he realized that the "fortunes of war ebb and flow."[61]

The removal statute also met with its problems. In the very first action brought before the supreme court to oust a local official, the effectiveness of the law was considerably diminished. Not long after the legislative session ended, the Committee of One Hundred of Tulsa, a law and order group, filed a complaint with Freeling alleging that the sheriff of the county, William McCullough, was guilty of negligence in the performance of his duty. Freeling enjoined the officer to enforce the prohibition law, but the request, according to the Attorney General, went unheeded. Thus he brought ouster charges against McCullough. In exercising his option concerning the court in which he would institute the proceedings, Freeling chose the supreme court in preference to the lower tribunal at Tulsa, believing that the facts in the case could be

[60] *Crossland et al* vs. *State*, 74 Okla. 58.

[61] See Senator Ferguson's lamentations in *Harlow's Weekly*, December 25, 1918.

more fully determined if the hearing were removed from the zone of local influence.

The supreme court, however, refused to hear the Attorney General's case. It declared that "where a court of last resort and inferior courts have concurrent jurisdiction to grant an original application of any kind, the same should be first made in the inferior court unless a good . . . showing is made . . . for invoking the jurisdiction of the court of last resort."[62] The tribunal did not decide upon the constitutionality of the law, but Freeling refused to pursue the case. The Tulsa *World* lauded the court's decision not to hear the case; and the paper expressed the hope that the action would reduce the weekly complaints from various persons requesting the Attorney General to remove a local official through the court.[63]

Perhaps the most encouraging development for the drys during the period was the conviction of William Creekmore. Since statehood "King" Creekmore had plied the state with his contraband, had bribed local officials and jurors, and, in the process, had accumulated one million dollars. When Creekmore's apparent invincibility was pierced by the keen edge of justice in 1915, many thought it spelled the death knell for organized resistance against prohibition. But on the ashes of the infamous bootlegger's fallen dynasty came other equally cunning and notorious personalities adept at dispensing their product.[64] From all available accounts, enforcement could not command a favorable comment at the end of the Williams years. Occasionally clean-up campaigns appeared, to be sure, but they soon dissipated and went the way of those of the past. The state held a few investigations and

[62] *Ibid.*, October 17, 1917.
[63] Tulsa *World*, October 9, 1917.
[64] McRill, *And Satan Came*, 179.

indicted a local official here and there, but such cases were an infrequent development.[65]

While the Ferguson law, the attorney general's bill, and enforcement encountered their hurdles in Oklahoma, the prohibition movement on the national level neared its apex. On December 18, 1917, Congress submitted to the legislatures of the states a resolution proposing the Eighteenth Amendment to the Constitution of the United States. By January 2, 1919, seventeen states had ratified the amendment. It came before the Oklahoma legislature on January 7, 1919, six days before Governor Williams was scheduled to give way to J. B. A. Robertson, a Democrat, who had triumphed over the Republican, Horace McKeever, in the 1918 campaign. Robertson had supported prohibition and had pledged himself to urge immediate ratification of the national amendment.[66]

Smashing all records for rapid action, the Oklahoma legislature ratified the prohibition amendment on January 7, 1919. In the lower chamber the tally was 96 to 8, and support was unanimous in the senate.[67] Most of the representatives who objected to the proposal admitted their prohibitionist leanings, but opposed it on constitutional grounds or for other reasons.[68] Thus Oklahoma became the eighteenth state to adopt the Eighteenth Amendment. Before the end of January enough states had ratified the proposal to make it a part of the Constitution; it became operative in 1920. For the Anti-Saloon League and drys everywhere, it was a magnificent victory; for the wets it spelled temporary despair; for Oklahomans, it only meant the continuation of a movement that had embraced the state since it entered the Union.

[65] For cases in point, see *ibid.*, September 4, 1915, November 27, 1915, January 8, 1916, March 25, 1916, and August 19, 1916; also *Daily Oklahoman*, December 2, 1918.

[66] *Harlow's Weekly*, April 3, 1918.

[67] Senate *Journal*, 1919, 22–23; House *Journal*, 1919, 34–35.

[68] *Daily Oklahoman*, January 8, 1919.

V

TO CATCH A BOOTLEGGER: EARLY YEARS UNDER THE EIGHTEENTH AMENDMENT

NATIONAL prohibition had not suddenly crept upon the nation like a thief in the night. If Oklahoma had seemingly accepted prohibition as a beneficial social experiment, it was not an isolated occurrence among the states. The state was a part of, and a contributor to, a movement that had become increasingly more potent since the founding of the National Anti-Saloon League. The aggressive tactics of this militant and politically conscious organization, ably augmented by the crusading WCTU and countless other temperance groups, caused the saloon interests steadily to lose ground until by the advent of national prohibition, more than one-half the United States was dry. In 1908 there were only five completely dry states, but eight years later twenty-three had adopted prohibition; three more joined the ranks at the beginning of 1917, and by the time the Eighteenth Amendment went into effect, there were more than thirty.

Prohibition gathered its adherents chiefly from the rural and fundamentalist-oriented states of the South and West.[1]

[1] For the development of the movement in these sections of the country, see Frank Foxcroft, "Prohibition in the South," *Atlantic Monthly*, Vol. CI

Its gains in the North and East were relatively unimportant. Of the twenty-six dry states in 1917 fourteen were west of the Mississippi, eight were in the South, and only four were above the Mason-Dixon line.[2] One of the least noticed, but most interesting, facts of the temperance movement was that, as one observer of the prohibition movement has pointed out, the consumption of intoxicating beverages increased despite the enactment of prohibition laws. While it would be fallacious to regard these statutes as the cause for this rise in bibulousness, it is certain, as pointed out in the special case of Oklahoma, that they failed to arrest it.[3]

In 1913, the year that the Anti-Saloon League commenced its campaign for national prohibition, per capita consumption of intoxicants in the United States had multiplied five times what it had been sixty years earlier. Since the league had alleged in 1913 that two-thirds of the country was dry, this claim meant that the other one-third of the nation consumed five times the amount of liquor imbibed in the 1850's, or it suggested that alcohol from wet states flowed into the dry states and counties from over their borders.[4]

(May, 1908), 627; R. W. Simpson, "Near Prohibition in the South," *Harper's Weekly*, Vol. LIII (July, 1909), 15; "The Saloon in the South," *Outlook*, Vol. LXXXVIII (March, 1908), 581–82; and "Prohibition Winning the West," *Literary Digest*, Vol. XLIX (November, 1914), 997–98. See also L. Ames Brown, "Nation-wide Prohibition," *Atlantic Monthly*, Vol. CXV (June, 1915), 735–47; "Number of Dry States Doubled," *Literary Digest*, Vol. L (March, 1915), 536.

[2] The maps in Cherrington's *ASL Yearbook*, 1918 (119–36) afford some visual indication of the progress of the prohibition movement.

[3] The above paragraph and the two which follow are based on the very fine study by Charles Mertz, *The Dry Decade*, 12–13.

[4] By 1913 the Anti-Saloon League had become convinced that prohibition could only succeed in a completely dry nation. As long as one state remained wet with the right to transport its goods into other areas, temperance stood in danger. Therefore, drys reasoned, the solution was national prohibition. In reality this had been the league's goal since its inception, although it had

A number of rapid-fire developments brought to fruition the long-cherished dream of the dry forces. The Progressive Movement gave the antiliquor forces an added push since it focused upon liquor as a pressing social ill. The outbreak of World War I also helped to spell the downfall of John Barleycorn. European hostilities brought a demand for conservation of food resources in order to counteract German tyranny. Responsive to the country's needs, Congress passed measures restricting the manufacture of alcoholic beverages.[5] During the war a majority of congressmen undoubtedly agreed with Senator Henry L. Myers from dry Montana who, in commenting upon wartime prohibition, exclaimed that "there is nothing to understand except one thing, and that is . . . bread will help us win this war more than whiskey."[6] With this prevailing congressional sentiment, and because of constant pressure from ever diligent drys from all over the country, President Woodrow Wilson, after some vacillation, had signed measures guaranteeing prohibition during the war period. But wartime dryness, of course, did not constitute the ultimate ob-

stressed local option in its early years. In 1913 the stage seemed set for the final onslaught upon the liquor interests. In launching the campaign for national prohibition, the delegates to the fifteenth convention of the Anti-Saloon League were greeted as an army preparing for combat. Wayne Wheeler, at the time superintendent of the Ohio League, told the gathering with unrestrained eloquence: "We welcome you to the launching of the most beneficial and far-reaching movement since the civil war. As Moses said to the children of Israel that they should go forward, just so the time has come for the moral forces of this nation to march on against the last bulwarks of the enemy. A great national evil has been localized and quarantined. Over two-thirds of the saloons are now in ten states. They are localized more today than slavery was when the last stage of the conflict was reached. Like . . . a great storm you can hear the determined demand from every [side for] national prohibition. I do not know how you may feel about this, but I would die rather than run from such a conflict." See Anti-Saloon League, *Proceedings of the Fifteenth Convention*, 1913, 14.

[5] For further discussion, see Andrew Sinclair, *Era of Excess: A Social History of the Prohibition Movement*, 157–58.

[6] *Congressional Record*, 65th Cong., 1st sess., Vol. LV, pt. 3, 2171.

jective of the prohibitionists; the pinnacle of success for them was a constitutional amendment that would banish liquor throughout the nation for all time. In the end, perseverance, the war, political pressure, desire for reform, the selfish interests of brewers and distillers, and even misinformation regarding the deleterious effects of liquor upon the human mind and body, all helped to carry the nation to those lofty moral heights envisioned by the patriots of righteousness.

The language of the Eighteenth Amendment reflected the creative talents of the Anti-Saloon League, principally those of Wayne B. Wheeler, its chief lobbyist. Essentially the amendment provided that after one year from its ratification, "the manufacture, sale, or transportation of intoxicating liquors within, the importation thereof into, or the exportation thereof from the United States and all territory subject to the jurisdiction thereof for beverage purposes is hereby prohibited." Very significantly, it gave Congress and the various states concurrent enforcement powers. Professor Andrew Sinclair in his careful and penetrating study of prohibition has noted that the drys, however, did not insist upon *total* prohibition of the *use* of liquors at the time the amendment was framed, lest they push legislators too far too fast. They were more interested in installing the practice of prohibition in the Constitution than in achieving a stringent measure. Their objective was to secure approval and ratification of the amendment, and then press for strong enforcement legislation.[7]

The measure passed to enforce national prohibition was the Volstead Act. A detailed document, it was full of loopholes that only time and bootleggers would reveal. In summary, it provided for the manufacture of industrial alcohol under a permit system and for denaturing to make it unsuitable for human consumption. Only patients, doctors, makers of vine-

[7] Sinclair, *Era of Excess*, 165.

gar and cider, and communicants at religious services had the right to use beverage alcohol. The act gave the commissioner of internal revenue responsibility for administering the law, and his agency had authority to investigate violators and to report them to United States attorneys who were to prosecute in federal court. The measure also provided penalties for bootleggers; it prescribed provisions for padlocking places used in the sale of intoxicants and for disposal of confiscated property at public auction. Notably, however, the Volstead Act said nothing of prosecuting purchasers of liquor.[8]

Drys in Oklahoma and other states greeted national prohibition with renewed hope that Washington could do what their state and local governments had been unable to accomplish. Ever aware of the tenacious character of the "enemy," Oklahoma Baptists urged the passage of other "legitimate measure(s)" to strengthen the Volstead Act.[9] Their national body, meeting in annual session in Washington in 1920, proclaimed the sixteenth day of January the "most glorious in the history of the American people; it was the *Mont Blanc* of a snowcapped range."[10]

Baptists realized, however, that the passage of the Eighteenth Amendment had done little to dispel what they considered the "deep seated spirit of anarchy" and rebellion characteristic of the liquor interests. And prayer alone would not still their voices or their trade: "We must see to it that only honest friends of law and order are elected to office whether the office be legislative or executive." If every officer did his duty, then he could count on Baptist support.[11] Oklahoma Presbyterians echoed similar sentiments. If the liquor interests were not permanently subdued by the Eighteenth

[8] See the complete text of the Volstead Act in *Statutes at Large*, XLI, pt. 1, 305–22. For a critical analysis, see Sinclair, *Era of Excess*, 168–70.

[9] Baptist *Minutes*, 1920, 96–97.

[10] Southern Baptist Convention, *Annual*, 1920, 94.

[11] *Ibid.*, 96.

Amendment, it was necessary for the church to put forth a continuing effort to make it plainly manifest that the industry would never rise again. All parishioners were warned that should the forces of right demobilize, power-hungry political leaders would rush forward to consummate deals with "the old liquor gang in exchange for votes."[12] And that would mean complete nullification of prohibition. Church leaders not only knew theology—they also knew the inner workings of practical American politics.

Rhetoric and resolutions alone, as both drys and wets realized, never ensured the enforcement of any statute. It was paradoxical that, supposedly, public opinion in Oklahoma, and other parts of the nation, supported both national and state prohibition, but that an official report in 1930 generally characterized Oklahoma as a prosperous haven for bootleggers.[13] Yet many citizens very soberly, and with perfectly clear consciences, staggered to the polls and paid allegiance to politicians who, with equally clear consciences, swore to uphold the law. And here, as the record testifies, resided much of the problem—the law was upheld but not enforced.

A feeble effort by the state accounted for much of the undoing of the Eighteenth Amendment in Oklahoma. Shortly after its passage, a keen political observer lamented that there was a disposition on the part of some state authorities to rely solely upon the federal government for the suppression of intoxicants. The assertion contained much truth, but federal officials could hardly afford to police every hamlet throughout the nation. Enforcing the federal and state prohibition laws in Oklahoma alone, with its 70,000 square miles of varied terrain, would have constituted a task much too monumental for even a sizable staff. Moreover, the economics of enforcement frustrated the operation of both the national and state laws.

12 Presbyterian *Minutes*, 1921, 38–39.
13 The report is discussed in detail in the following chapter.

It was only with great reluctance that economy-minded Oklahoma legislators appropriated funds to carry out the concurrent feature of the Eighteenth Amendment.[14]

The attempts at enforcement during the early years of the noble experiment in Oklahoma foreshadowed the pattern which the state was to follow during the period of federal prohibition. The confiscation of whisky stills became such a persistent occurrence that some persons no longer regarded it as noteworthy. A common belief prevailed that, in spite of the Eighteenth Amendment, liquor was freely available to all who could afford it. Drys, in rebuttal to what seemed obvious, quickly took defense behind statistics. They pointed to the records of the federal authorities in pressing their claims that violators were experiencing the terrible wrath of the law. Eagerly and enthusiastically, the prohibitionists noted that in the first two years following enactment of the law more than 1,400 arrests had been made in Oklahoma, 200 stills seized, and more than 350 illicit distilleries destroyed. Moreover, they took comfort in noting that during this period nearly 30,000 gallons of illegal liquor and beer, which otherwise would have quenched the thirst of the state's citizens, had been taken off the market.[15] Wets, however, accepted these figures as documentary proof that alcohol was truly accessible. Unimpressed by the statistics which purportedly sustained the dry argument, Oklahoma dissenters organized an effort to amend the law, arguing that the Eighteenth Amendment had been placed in the Constitution by a minority of the people.[16] Their endeavor proved futile, and

[14] *Harlow's Weekly*, October 28, 1921.

[15] Cumulative figures for 1920 and 1921 were tabulated from Treasury Department, Bureau of Industrial Alcohol, *Statistics Concerning Intoxicating Liquors*, 174 and 181.

[16] For a brief note on this organization, the so-called Sanity League, see the *Daily Oklahoman*, March 29, 1922. From all indications the league had a very brief existence.

increasingly, local citizens followed the national trend toward disrespect for prohibition.

With never ending persistency, drys throughout the nation stressed the glorious results of the new order. Citizens had only to look around to witness the results of prohibition: jails that once overflowed now lacked prisoners, almshouses and bread lines were deserted, children previously naked and hungry now had food. Public opinion, contrary to prohibition opponents' assertions, supported the law which had been achieved through the established democratic process.[17] To contend that the Eighteenth Amendment was unwise, unjust, or unconstitutional, said drys, represented an "old trick" of Satan's "to incite men to violation and to excuse the violator." Those who denounced the law as an utter failure, and who exhorted that it created criminals, sought to thwart the will of the majority and to bring insult upon the nation.[18]

The history of prohibition testifies that local community attitudes and pressures sometimes exert a strong influence which affects the operation of a national law and its enforcers. For example, in 1922, W. F. Seaver, prosecuting attorney of Tulsa County, dismissed fifteen liquor cases, acidly remarking that "I am not going to force anything down their (Tulsa residents') throats that they don't want."[19] Federal Judge Robert L. Williams, much to the dismay of Oklahoma drys and some officials in Washington, often applied leniency in the handling of prohibition cases. Personally, the former

[17] Southern Baptist Convention, *Annual*, 1923, 103–104.

[18] *Ibid.*, 1924, 115–16.

[19] Undated clipping in Department of Justice, General Records, Record Group 60, 1910–45, National Archives. (The files are hereafter cited as Department of Justice, General Records, followed by the appropriate record group.) Charles Prince [Young] of Lakewood, Florida, wrote the Department of Justice about the case and inquired, "can't you manage to send this old reprobate to jail for about 999 years? And then hang him." See Young's letter of December 8, 1922, *ibid.*

Oklahoma Governor had always been opposed to national prohibition. He believed that statewide prohibition could have been achieved by vigorous enforcement of federal legislation which prevented the importation of intoxicants into dry areas, but that the prohibitionists had rushed in and insisted on a nationwide law, which Williams asserted had led to a proliferation in law violations.

Whether the blame placed upon the shoulders of the drys by Judge Williams was a justifiable criticism or not, there were those who believed that enforcement constituted a problem of much significance. Early in 1921, Governor J. B. A. Robertson, a political dry, lamented that more whisky was being consumed in his state than in former years.[20] The Muskogee *Daily Phoenix* thought the Volstead Act was full of loopholes and that they had led to the situation described by the Governor.[21] Cognizant of Oklahoma's duty under the concurrent clause of the Eighteenth Amendment, and no doubt conscious of the political strength of the state's aggressive prohibitionists, Robertson authorized his attorney general, George F. Short, to call a conference of federal and state law officials to discuss enforcement.[22] Although the officers left the meeting pledged to a statewide assault upon the lawless, little developed in subsequent months to disturb the

[20] *Harlow's Weekly*, October 28, 1921.

[21] February 10, 1922. The newspaper noted that any person who desired liquor could obtain it with very little effort, just as he could get any other kind of "poison." The writer suggested that every man who died of poisonous liquor converted, by his death, many thousands to the cause of temperance; just as one's sins found one out, bootleg liquor "will kill and maim you." Thus the doctrine of self-preservation would eventually ensure enforcement, for no person dared take a sip while remarking, "Well this may be my last one." The editor of the *Phoenix* was too optimistic; poisonous drink continued to kill—and people continued to drink.

[22] The idea of the conference had been advanced by the United States attorney general, Harry M. Daugherty. See Governor Robertson's special call for the meeting in Department of Justice, General Records, RG 60, NA.

peace of a vast number of Oklahomans who liberally imbibed and who never gave the slightest thought of branding as a criminal their fellow citizens who supplied their demands. Ironically, however, a majority of them remained willing to stand *by* the constitution.

That local and state governments did not honestly and fully co-operate with the central government became increasingly clear.[23] "We have the laws clearly written into our (national) Constitution and in our statutes," bemoaned the editor of *Harlow's Weekly*, "yet the state government [in Oklahoma] is doing [little] whatever to cause those statutes to be respected." And he scolded the members of the legislature for not providing funds to meet the challenge they had taken upon themselves in 1919. If the electorate, the editor implied, retired several of the lawmakers and officers who indulged in liquor themselves, the state and the nation would profit.[24] Enforcement of national prohibition, however, involved the entire framework of government to such an extent that the attitudes of many legislators and law officers were changed. An example of this complexity was noted in the comment of Judge Williams that county attorneys often prosecuted those with money to pay, but left the prosecution of the poor to federal authorities.[25] Others suggested that county officers used the federal law as a convenient means of avoiding mounting court cost and of escaping tax increases to liquidate this and other expenses. Citizens often complained, to be sure, but when the respectable element, the backbone of the community, held the law in contempt by patronizing those who plied their outlawed trade, local lawmen had to weigh care-

[23] For an informative comment, see William Brown, "State Cooperation in Enforcement," *Annals* of the American Academy of Political and Social Science, Vol. CLXIII (September, 1932), 30–38.

[24] *Harlow's Weekly*, November 10, 1921.

[25] *Ibid.*, October 28, 1921.

fully whether they respected their jobs or their principles more.

Complaints sent to officials in Washington by Oklahomans testified to the difficulty of enforcement. While it proved impossible to investigate every single charge, the very fact that the Justice Department and the Prohibition Bureau received so many letters was enough to create much concern. From the mid-twenties up to the time the government issued its report on Oklahoma in 1931, these protests revealed that the state had fallen into the general pattern of the rest of the nation. Occasionally local residents extended their services to counteract this trend and to aid the government in trying to dam the flow of ardent spirits. A sixteen-year-old Tribbey, Oklahoma, youth, dismayed with the hypocrisy of his elders and dissatisfied with social conditions in his small town, wrote very ungrammatically, but sincerely, that things were so bad "people can't have no kind of [gathering] without it ending up in a drunken brawl." Although the young man could not prove it, he strongly suspected that county officers had conspired with the bootleggers. He could change things; all the government had to do was grant him and a few others the authority and they would "swoop" violators off their feet and "bring them in so fast it would make a man's head swim."[26] His employment of the common vernacular by no means disguised his seriousness, and no one could read his letter without realizing his determination.

Few perhaps could match the verbal enthusiasm of the Tribbey lad, but their appeals afforded an indication of Oklahoma's contribution to the dry age. That golden voice of the Anti-Saloon League, Wayne B. Wheeler, urged Mrs. Mabel Walker Wilebrandt, assistant attorney general in the Justice Department, to inquire of conditions in Oklahoma, especially

[26] Erwin Webb, Tribbey, Okla., to H. M. Daugherty, U.S. attorney general, March 26, 1924, Department of Justice, General Records, RG 60, NA.

of the attitude of the Criminal Court of Appeals. Seemingly, Wheeler conjectured, the court was too sympathetic toward transgressors of the law.[27] A Ravia, Oklahoma, man who had opposed national prohibition before its inception was so "fed up" with the traffic in "rot gut" that he wrote for a special agent to rid the town of its eighteen bootleggers.[28] The logical deduction from this letter and scores of others was that local and federal officials had abrogated their authority. In fact, the residents of Durant voiced this view when they accused one of the federal officers of dishonesty and discrimination in law enforcement.[29] Some whisky peddlers, they said, were protected while others met with swift justice.

Some persons concluded before the first decade of the noble experiment had passed that even the power of the federal government could not arrest the successful operation of what finally became one of America's most profitable underworld trades. Prohibition had become in their eyes nothing less than high comedy with judges, sheriffs, and prosecuting attorneys sharing center stage. And many in Oklahoma did not appreciate the professional performance. W. F. Hughes and John A. Robinson of Ara and Panola respectively were both convinced that only a secretive approach could break the alliance between the "protectors" of the law and bootleggers. It would only be useless, wrote Robinson, to inform county authorities since they were allegedly "getting part of the income to let these wildcat [stills] run."[30] A few citizens had come to believe that it was absolutely impossible to enforce the law

[27] Wayne B. Wheeler to Mabel W. Wilebrandt, November 27, 1925; and Wilebrandt to Wheeler, December 19, 1925, ibid.

[28] Unsigned letter from Ravia, Okla., to Department of Justice, January 8, 1925, ibid.

[29] Letter from the citizens of Durant, Okla., to the U.S. attorney general, February 20, 1925, ibid. For details of the machinery of national prohibition enforcement before 1929, the reader should consult Laurence F. Schmeckebier, The Bureau of Prohibition.

completely. H. C. Miller of Vinita, Oklahoma, for example, expressed the belief of millions of his countrymen when he informed Mrs. Wilebrandt that she "couldn't clean up Oklahoma with 300 men."[31] People would not dare change the law for they had exactly what they wanted—alcohol. No good lawman, except a "fanatic and a fool" would enforce a law just because it appeared on the books.[32]

The condition of the American judiciary also played a part in creating the conditions described by those who registered their reactions to the government. From the beginning of the twentieth century, the number of court cases had steadily climbed. In 1910, for example, federal tribunals handled about 15,000 cases, but a decade later, the figure had increased to more than 34,000; and 5,000 of these were prohibition violations.[33] In 1928, the very same year that prohibition helped to sweep Al Smith into political oblivion, federal courts handled some 58,000 prohibition cases; and by 1932 judges across the land received more than 70,000.[34] Anyone who has carefully studied the reports of the United States attorney general for the prohibition years will readily conclude that the court system simply could not cope with the

[30] W. F. Hughes, Ara, Okla., to Department of Justice, July 29, 1927; and John A. Robinson, Panola, Okla., to the U.S. attorney general [July ?], 927, Department of Justice, General Records, RG 60, NA.

[31] H. C. Miller to Mabel W. Wilebrandt, August 5, 1928, *ibid.*; and also the letter of Judge George C. Crump of the 9th Judicial District of Oklahoma to the U.S. attorney general, August 5, 1928, *ibid.*, in which he complains of the insufficient number of government agents in Oklahoma. The number of prohibition officers employed in the enforcement of national prohibition was never large. In 1920 there were only 948; a decade later this figure had not yet doubled; and by 1932 the force stood at only 2,300 men. See Treasury Department, *Statistics Concerning Intoxicating Liquors*, 1932, 140.

[32] Miller to Wilebrandt, August 5, 1928, Department of Justice, General Records, RG 60, NA.

[33] Sinclair, *Era of Excess*, 211.

[34] Treasury Department, *Statistics Concerning Intoxicating Liquors*, 1932, 140.

monumental task. Professor Sinclair has pointed out that nine
out of every ten convictions under the prohibition laws in the
United States were obtained during so-called bargain days, a
period set aside in which a reduced sentence was offered for
pleas of guilty.[35] Moreover, he found that until 1930 only one
out of every three convictions in federal court resulted in any
form of jail sentence. Unfortunately, the judiciary and enforcement officers spent too much of their time with small
violations and too little time with large ones. Prevailing conditions in the state of Oklahoma support these basic findings.

In June of 1927, W. F. Rampendahl, assistant United
States attorney for the Eastern Judicial District of Oklahoma,
wrote Mrs. Wilebrandt that the situation in Oklahoma had
become acute. Between January and June of that year, Rampendahl filed 490 indictments covering liquor offenses and
had prepared to undertake an additional 200, many of which
he termed "trivial." He complained that local officers preferred to file their cases in federal court because they received
better results and "are glad to relieve the state [and the
county] of the burden."[36] In her reply to Rampendahl, Mrs.
Wilebrandt consoled the overworked attorney with "we appreciate the situation which confronts you." Something should
be done, she said, to prevent overcrowding of the docket, but
under the Volstead Act anyone could file a complaint.[37] Unfortunately, Rampendahl had become part of a national problem which even the drys had never foreseen, and which some
wets hoped would continue until prohibition met with complete failure.

The problem of the judiciary did not force the supporters
of the law to retreat from their morally fortified position.

[35] Sinclair, *Era of Excess*, 211.
[36] W. F. Rampendahl to Mabel W. Wilebrandt, June 22, 1927, Department
of Justice, General Records, RG 60, NA.
[37] Wilebrandt to Rampendahl, July 14, 1927, *ibid.*

Instead they continued to laud what they regarded as prohibition advances. They pointed to the economic well-being of the country during the prosperous twenties. Millions of working men, proclaimed the Baptists, had been able to move to better homes; and they gleefully exclaimed that the building record in the United States since prohibition "is the greatest in the history of the world." Industrial efficiency, too, constituted a by-product of the new order. Just three years before the catastrophic developments of 1929, they praised the 30 per cent increase in the output of goods over that of 1919, the last full year of legalized liquor;[38] the supreme task was to perpetuate these benefits. Prohibitionists, however, were not willing to share in the blame for the disaster which struck in October, 1929. But the drys as well as their opponents were clever propagandists, and surely they knew that the economic upswing of the twenties could not be assigned to a single social reform; nor could the downturn.

Many honest drys by 1928 recognized the precarious state of the noble experiment. They reluctantly, but rightly, admitted that their greatest achievement had brought their greatest problem, and that it was still necessary to render forever sterile that "prolific mother of a multitude of ills."[39] At worst, they said, the horrors of the present could not compare with those of the old saloon days. Opponents disagreed.[40] Nor could drys easily ignore the fact that there had been much relaxation in the execution of the law. That, they asserted, was due to the small number of enforcement officers and to the inadequate enforcement funds appropriated by Congress, the judiciary, and politics. The *Baptist Messenger*, taking temporary respite from its attacks on Al Smith, the pope, and the 1928 election, added another important reason. The drys had

---

[38] Southern Baptist Convention, *Annual*, 1926, 107.
[39] *Ibid.*, 1927, 115.
[40] See *Harlow's Weekly*, April 10, 1926.

grown lax; and the *Messenger* perceived that the big task now was to get an effective public sentiment.[41] There was no need to think of repeal; there had been violations of the liquor statutes just as there had been of the laws against murder—why not repeal the laws against murder?

In spite of the inflated claims of drys and wets, few could deny that prohibition enjoyed the approval of a vast number of Oklahomans despite feeble enforcement. State legislation during the period, to a great degree, mirrored this sentiment.[42] Many of these statutes could be classified as drastic, but their application was far from austere. While many citizens agreed with the principle of national prohibition, they found it difficult to reconcile their views with the belief in individual freedom which enforcement necessarily curtailed. And that constituted the great enigma which troubled many minds.

[41] June 14, 1928; and also Methodist *Minutes*, 1925, 53.

[42] The serious student should see the *Session Laws* passed during the period. A summary, however, of the statutes may be found in Cherrington, *ASL Yearbook*, 1931, 88–89. The only scholarly commentary on Oklahoma's prohibition laws is William Bandy, *Commentary on Intoxicating Liquor Laws in Oklahoma*.

VI

AN OFFICIAL INDICTMENT AND MURDER

THE REPORT of the Wickersham Commission in 1931 confirmed what many people already believed—that prohibition had not been totally successful. From the issuance of the report to repeal, prohibitionists fought an uphill battle, although the members of the Hoover-appointed commission to study prohibition and law enforcement did not as a whole urge repeal of the Eighteenth Amendment. In co-operation with the commission, the Bureau of Prohibition submitted the results of several individual state investigations. The agency appointed one of its lawyers, Phillip N. Davison, to carry out the Oklahoma survey.[1] Davison's highly critical study amounted to a severe indictment of the noble experiment, but it was not sufficient to shake the faith Sooners had reposed in prohibition since statehood in 1907.

The bureau survey found that the governor's office and state officials gave only half-hearted support to prohibition

[1] See the report of Phillip N. Davison, "Prohibition Survey of Oklahoma," in National Commission on Law Observance and Enforcement, *Enforcement of the Prohibition Laws. Official Records of the National Commission on Law Observance and Enforcement* . . . ; IV, 807 (subsequently cited as Davison, "Prohibition Survey," *Enforcement of the Prohibition Laws*).

enforcement. Completed in 1930, the report singled out the Oklahoma governor at that time, William J. Holloway, for specific criticism. He had been, it said, "loath to accept [his] responsibility . . . in matters of liquor enforcement." Citizens throughout the state had appealed to the chief executive for help and relief from deplorable conditions, but he merely transmitted these complaints to the federal government.[2] When queried about his lack of response to letters Oklahomans had written about conditions in their communities, the Governor replied that his investigation bureau usually handled such matters. A former sheriff, however, administered this agency and since he knew most of the sheriffs in Oklahoma's seventy-seven counties, Holloway thought he could obtain better results by summoning assistance from Washington. Plainly implicit in this reply was possible distrust of his appointee, or an exaggerated belief in the power of the central government. But an even more damaging criticism remained. The Governor had refused to take forceful action in remedying corruption in his state, yet the most casual observer could attest to unfavorable conditions in many localities.[3] Holloway, in the tradition of other politically dry governors before him, denied any evasion of responsibility, and he caustically denounced the statements about him as utterly untrue. He emphasized that he had given support to law officials at every level of government.[4] Federal authorities did not deny that they had gotten their share of assistance, but what distressed them was that it had been mostly negative.[5]

Not only did Governor Holloway's attitude frustrate the operation of the Eighteenth Amendment in Oklahoma, but so did the limitation of the federal prohibition-enforcement machinery. An analysis of the government's local staff in 1930

[2] For example of such cases, see *ibid.*, 826–29.

[3] Holloway's attitude is reflected *ibid.*, 812–13.

[4] Norman *Transcript*, February 22, 1931.

clearly pointed up this fact. At the beginning of that year, the state had eighteen prohibition agents on duty; nine of them operated in the Northern and Eastern Judicial districts with the herculean task of patrolling a total of forty-three counties. Before 1930 the average number of agents for this entire sprawling area was six, while the Western Judicial District had a total of nine, who were responsible for a total of thirty-three counties.[6] Severely handicapped not only by the attitude of local officers, but also by the lack of powerful automobiles and other resources, agents found it difficult to compete with speedy bootleggers who rigged their machines to make the quick get away so vital in an enterprise as risky as theirs.[7] It was not unlike a nineteenth-century stagecoach against a modern-day aircraft. Even the young Oklahoma lad who boasted of his ability to bring bootleggers in so fast it would make a man's head swim would probably have retired to a slower tempo upon tangling with men who knew their business as well as any other American entrepreneur.

Davison's account of prevailing conditions in various counties in each judicial district revealed the breakdown in law voiced by the average citizen. He directed his most cutting criticism at corrupt or inefficient county officers. In the west-

[5] The Governor's attitude differed little from that of a great many other officials across the country who assumed that since the federal government had now "stepped in" to ensure enforcement of the liquor laws, state governments could "step out." For a criticism of such an attitude, see the address of James M. Doran, "The Problem and Policy of Prohibition," delivered at Yale University, February 20, 1929, to the Department of Economics, Sociology, and Government, found in the National Commission on Law Observance and Enforcement Research Records, Record Group 10, National Archives (subsequently cited as NCLOE Records, RG, followed by the appropriate number).

[6] Davison, "Prohibition Survey," *Enforcement of the Prohibition Laws*, IV, 813.

[7] Lack of sufficient funds and a small enforcement staff proved a continuing problem in all states. For comment, see James J. Britt, "Views as to the Improvement of Prohibition Enforcement," NCLOE Records, RG 10, NA.

ern area he paid unqualified respect to the officers in only Noble, Cimarron, and Woods counties for their diligence; but even in some of these counties, sentiment supported the liquor element. In the remaining counties there was laxity in the sheriffs' office or at other high levels. At Tonkawa, in Kay County, for example, considerable evidence pointed to the conclusion that bootleggers had considerable control over the police. One officer in that town was summarily discharged shortly after he gave federal authorities information resulting in the capture of some of the state's most persistent violators. On another occasion a federal agent actually overheard a powerful bootlegger dictating orders to policemen, which they subsequently executed. Surprisingly, Oklahoma County gave the government "fair" co-operation, thanks in great part to an active prosecuting attorney. This county's neighbor to the southeast, Pottawatomie, epitomized the very worst in liquor enforcement. Between 1927 and 1930 a liquor conspiracy had existed, aided and abetted by corrupt county officials. A grand jury eventually indicted more than one hundred persons during the period, including the county attorney and a former sheriff of the county.[8]

If Oklahoma prohibitionists became alarmed over liquor lawlessness in the western part of the state, they had cause for added concern when they read of developments in other areas. Nearly two years before the Davison report, Judge Robert L. Williams had irritated many drys with his assertion that four-fifths of the people in many communities of the eastern district opposed vigorous enforcement of the prohibition laws. He noted specifically that in Choctaw, Pushmataha, LeFlore, and McCurtain counties "a candidate for sheriff could [not] possibly be elected if it were definitely known that he intended to enforce the prohibition law to the

[8] Davison, "Prohibition Survey," *Enforcement of the Prohibition Laws*, IV, 811–20.

letter." And he surmised that the same was true for other counties in his judicial district.[9] The Davison report buttressed the Judge's opinion with the general conclusion that things were bad. Large stills, it noted, provided an ample supply of liquor, and as soon as federal agents appeared to clean up one section, operations immediately began elsewhere.[10] It was not at all uncommon for prohibition officers to arrive at a particular place to raid a still only to find that the news of their crackdown had preceded them. Conditions in Carter, Nowata, Craig, Rogers, Mayes, Cherokee, Delaware, Adair, Sequoyah, and Ottawa counties were also notorious for disrespect for the Eighteenth Amendment.[11]

Two of the worst offenders of the law were the counties of Tulsa and Muskogee, which contained two of the three largest cities in the state.[12] In 1930, Tulsa had a population of 180,-000. Considered the "Oil Capitol of the World," this city on the Arkansas River prided itself for allegedly having more millionaires per capita than any other city in the United States. Liquor flowed as freely in Tulsa as the black gold which often yielded profits lucrative enough to invite the

[9] Tulsa *World*, October 9, 1928.

[10] Davison, "Prohibition Survey," *Enforcement of the Prohibition Laws*, IV, 823. In 1923 the Oklahoma legislature passed a very stringent law against the manufacture, sale, or possession of a still. The statute, however, did not fully achieve its intent (see *Session Laws*, 1923, 1–2). The statistics on seizures of stills proved interesting. In 1930 a total of 502 were seized, and in the next year 681. During the last complete year of prohibition, a total of 729 were confiscated in Oklahoma. Whether federal enforcement was more vigorous, or stills more plentiful, is difficult to determine. (Calculations for the period made from Treasury Department, *Statistics Concerning Intoxicating Liquors*, 1930–33.)

[11] Davison, "Prohibition Survey," *Enforcement of the Prohibition Laws*, IV, 820–23.

[12] *Ibid.*, 821. In all of old Indian Territory, in which both Tulsa and Muskogee counties were included, roughly the eastern part of present-day Oklahoma, federal statutes forbade the sale of intoxicants, but these laws had been violated with the frequency with which they were passed.

envy of those less fortunate. Since statehood Tulsa had been rightly termed by many as "wide open," and those with any perspective entertained no illusions that the Eighteenth Amendment would change the city's drinking and gambling habits, or significantly alter the personal entrepreneurial arrangements of the "ladies." Neither of these vices, in the eyes of some, constituted a social menace inimical to a happy and prosperous society.[13] The dichotomy which characterized the thinking of many Tulsans was clearly demonstrated by city officials who eagerly and diligently sought to curtail such crimes as larceny and rape but who took little initiative in the matter of liquor enforcement.[14]

Muskogee bore a striking similarity to Tulsa. The sheriff of the county simply was not earnest about his job; and the city manager and council, while honest and well meaning, apparently were not fully awake, or were woefully indifferent to the real situation in the city. "One has only to make a trip to the fifth floor of the Manhattan Building, where a view of the roofs of some of the buildings adjoining may be [seen], interview the janitors, and talk with occupants of this and other buildings to be convinced," Davison reported, "that there is considerable use of liquor amongst many of the so-called respectable class of citizens of the city."[15]

Federal Judge Franklin E. Kennamer of the Northern Judicial District summed up better than anyone else the state of national prohibition in Oklahoma:

13 In 1925 a considerable number of Tulsans reacted with shock when federal and city officers raided a hotel where the Veterans of Foreign Wars held its national meeting. The attitude of the mayor of Tulsa, Herman Newblock, typified that of many businessmen of the city. He pointed out that convention cities invariably welcomed their guests by extending them special privileges for a few days. See *Harlow's Weekly*, September 25, 1925, and October 17, 1925.

14 Davison, "Prohibition Survey," *Enforcement of the Prohibition Laws*, IV, 821.

15 *Ibid.*, 821–22.

... the main trouble throughout Oklahoma ... is the incompetency and corruption amongst a large percentage of enforcement officers. This includes sheriffs, deputy sheriffs, prosecuting attorneys [and] deputy marshals .... The principle reason for [this] incompetency, corruption, etc., existing amongst these enforcement officials is the inadequate salaries that forces them to steal and become involved in collusion in order to make a living. Another outstanding trouble, if not the primary one, is that corrupt politicians control the appointment of enforcement officers. Enforcement officers in many cities and towns are controlled by a corrupt political ring.[16]

The execution of the national prohibition law often brought death to both the innocent and the guilty. By 1923 a total of thirty prohibition officers had lost their lives to uphold the law.[17] Although shootings usually involved only violators of the law and lawmen, others often lost their lives. It is highly unlikely, however, that the number of people killed ever approached that claimed by the Association Against the Prohibition Amendment (AAPA).[18] But whatever the number, the populace became increasingly aroused at such killings, especially when the government chose to defend officers whom many thought guilty. That such a small number of these agents were convicted produced antagonisms which played a significant role in the demise of the noble experiment.

The most celebrated of all killings in Oklahoma during the period of national prohibition was that of the famous frontier marshal, Bill Tilghman. His death in 1924 at the hands of a federal prohibition agent, Wiley Lynn, triggered a reaction seldom experienced in the state. Tilghman, whose picture now hangs majestically in the Oklahoma Historical Society Building at Oklahoma City, was not only praised, but loved, for his

16 See Judge Kennamer's statement *ibid.*, 825.
17 Roy A. Haynes, *Prohibition Inside Out*, 44.
18 For further discussion, see Dayton E. Heckman, "Prohibition Passes: The Story of the Association Against the Prohibition Amendment," 141–44.

bravery. To many Oklahomans his "cold-blooded murder" only served to illuminate the life of a man already considered a legend in Western history. Nearly three years after the acquittal of Tilghman's killer, an Oklahoma governor, who believed the murderer had been freed "in all probability by perjured testimony," wrote his attorney general that "whenever an officer is killed and his assassin is known, . . . we [should] keep a constant policy of watchfulness, and vigorously prosecute for every infraction of the law the offender may subsequently commit."[19] The governor's letter clearly revealed the attitude indicative of public opinion immediately following, and long after, the case was closed.

The facts of the Tilghman murder are confused, and to this very day many things remain unexplained and as puzzling to the historian as they were to the contemporaries of the prohibition period. Many parts of the story, however, have been well told; others have been so filled with unrestrained emotionalism and personal sentiment to fit the legend Tilghman himself created, that even the more objective and detached are sometimes led astray.[20] Mrs. Tilghman vigorously contended in the biography of her husband and in her correspondence with government officials in Washington that a vicious dope ring master-minded his murder, and Wiley Lynn has been regarded as the "trigger-man" paid to protect the operation.[21]

Despite Lynn's acquittal Tilghman's friends remained

[19] Governor Henry S. Johnston to the Honorable Edwin Dabney, Oklahoma attorney general, May 27, 1927, in William and Zoe Agnes Tilghman Collection, University of Oklahoma Library.

[20] Zoe A. Tilghman, *Marshal of the Last Frontier: Life and Services of William Matthew (Bill) Tilghman, for 50 Years One of the Greatest Peace Officers of the West*, 349.

[21] Prohibition agents also enforced the narcotics laws. For a brief note on the traffic in Oklahoma, see Davison, "Prohibition Survey," *Enforcement of the Prohibition Laws*, IV, 824.

thoroughly convinced of his guilt. W. E. Sirmans, secretary of the Cromwell Chamber of Commerce, for example, wrote that "there is no question [that] he was murdered in cold blood."[22] One of the most puzzling features of this case, nevertheless, was Sirmans' failure to appear to testify as a witness for the state. In an affidavit sworn at Ware County, Georgia, nearly three years after Lynn's trial, Sirmans said that a number of people had warned that he "would be killed if he did not leave Cromwell, as the dope and whiskey ring were [sic] going to protect Lynn and see that he was not punished."[23] The governor of Oklahoma, he said, had sent a detective and had advised his leaving the town at once.[24] But surely Sirmans must have been aware of all the dangers involved when he urged Tilghman to abandon retirement in Oklahoma City to take on the task of cleaning up Cromwell.

In a letter to Mrs. Tilghman from Waycross, Georgia, Sirmans again endeavored to explain his unexpected disappearance. In May, 1925, he left Weatherford, Oklahoma, for Florida and was traveling around the state looking for a location. Ten days after the conclusion of Lynn's trial, Sirmans received a letter with a telegram enclosed from Prince Freeling, former attorney general of Oklahoma, who served as the state's prosecuting attorney in the case, informing him of the date of the trial. Had the message arrived in time, he continued, he would have appeared to give his testimony.[25] For a man who had "grown to love Capt. Tilghman," and who had caught the frontier marshal in his arms as Lynn's bullet ripped through his body,[26] it seems odd indeed that he took no initiative in determining the date of the trial. That he had

[22] Sirmans to Nix, November 2, 1924, Tilghman Collection, University of Oklahoma Library.
[23] See the affidavit of November 28, 1927, *ibid.*
[24] *Ibid.*
[25] Sirmans to Mrs. Tilghman, November 28, 1928, *ibid.*
[26] Sirmans to Nix, November 2, 1924, *ibid.*

given evidence at two preliminary hearings[27] still does not satisfy the curiosity of some students of history.

For several years after her husband's death, Mrs. Tilghman sought compensation from the federal government, but she never achieved positive results despite the efforts of Oklahoma congressmen. Officials in the Bureau of Prohibition opposed any such appropriation. In a memorandum to one of the assistant attorney generals in the Justice Department, A. W. W. Woodcock of the bureau stated frankly that "I do not think the circumstances are such to call for an appropriation."[28] In 1934, Mrs. Tilghman directed a desperate appeal to President Franklin D. Roosevelt and sought direct intervention in the matter.[29] Her efforts bore no fruit; and slowly her cause, like her husband's death, slipped into the dim recesses of the distant past. But Tilghman's death at Cromwell, Oklahoma, had revealed part of the hideous drama acted out on other stages and at other times during the period of the so-called noble experiment.

Oklahoma and the nation witnessed another death during the era which lacked much of the sentiment of the Tilghman case—the political "killing" of Alfred Emanuel Smith. Again, prohibition played a starring role, although careful post mortems have not determined precisely whether it was a party, a religion, or the favorable reaction to the "great reform" which defeated him; some suggest all three.[30] Certainly the last two were of vital, if not overriding, significance in traditionally Protestant and dry Oklahoma. Smith's greatest asset in the

27 Sirmans to Mrs. Tilghman, November 28, 1928, *ibid.*

28 A. W. W. Woodcock, director of the Bureau of Prohibition, to Assistant United States Attorney General Youngquist, March 8, 1932, Department of Justice, General Records, RG 60, NA.

29 Mrs. Tilghman to President Franklin D. Roosevelt, June 4, 1934, Department of Justice, General Records, RG 60, NA.

30 Consult the very fine study by Robert M. Miller, *American Protestantism and Social Issues*, 48–62.

Sooner State was his party affiliation, but in 1928 even this attachment was somewhat weakened by Republican-induced prosperity. Moreover, the Grand Old Party, which had occupied the White House since 1921, had espoused the dry creed to the obvious pleasure of the prohibitionists; but Smith labored under the assumption that the nation was ready for a change. He was wrong, especially if he thought the country wanted a Roman Catholic who was also wet.

Both Republican and Democratic conventions in 1928 stood by the Eighteenth Amendment. The Republican platform pledged strict enforcement of the dry law as then on the books, but it said nothing about the party's adherence to the *principle* of national prohibition. Its nominee, Herbert Hoover, candidly proclaimed in his acceptance speech, however, that "I do not favor the repeal of the Eighteenth Amendment." To be sure, he realized that flagrant abuses had occurred and that crime and disobedience could not be tolerated, but prohibition still remained for the Iowan "a great social and economic experiment, noble in motive and far-reaching in purpose."[31] Modification of the Volstead Act to permit that which the Constitution forbade amounted to nullification. As one student of the prohibition movement has carefully noted, Hoover never came forward with a categorical statement in support of it.[32]

Al Smith, the Democratic candidate from New York, approached prohibition much more forthrightly than his Republican opponent. In spite of his party's platform, Smith's direct language fostered much political antagonism among those who had nominated him in Houston, Texas. Indeed, his running mate, Senator Joseph Robinson, a confirmed political dry from Arkansas, found it difficult throughout the campaign to square

[31] See the prohibition section of Hoover's acceptance speech in *The Memoirs of Herbert Hoover*, II, 201–202.
[32] Sinclair, *Era of Excess*, 300.

Smith's attitude with that of his party.[33] In his telegram of
acceptance, the New Yorker had boldly declared, to the dismay of many party leaders, that "I personally believe that
there should be [a] change in the Eighteenth Amendment
and I shall advise the Congress in accordance with my constitutional duty of whatever changes I deem necessary or
expedient." Corruption and ineffectiveness of the prohibition
law did not justify its continued existence without alteration;
the country, he said, had not realized temperance. The remedy was the "fearless application of Jeffersonian principles"
of local control—there had to be a differentiation of local
laws to allow for variation in habits. Smith was convinced
that the people of the United States after eight years of trial
should be permitted to say whether present conditions should
be rectified. The conclusion at which he arrived followed from
the premises he established: The prohibition article needed
amendment "to give to each individual state . . . after approval by a referendum . . . the right wholly within its borders
to import, manufacture . . . and sell alcoholic beverages."[34]

Stern opposition to Smith's candidacy had mounted prior
to his nomination, and it continued with inexorable force until his eventual political demise. Not since pre-prohibition
days had there been such cause for concerted action by the
drys. Early in 1928, Oklahoma Baptists had warned that
the antiprohibition forces had conspired to nominate the wet
Smith, and they cautioned every good citizen to stay alert
and to support "only such men for office who will agree to
uphold the law."[35] After Smith received the nomination and
proceeded to depart, with seemingly little apprehension, from

[33] See Nevin E. Neal, "A Biography of Joseph T. Robinson," 251–53.

[34] Smith's position is adequately summed up in Democratic National Committee, *Campaign Addresses . . . of Governor Alfred E. Smith . . .*, 12–14 (hereafter cited as Smith, *Campaign Addresses*).

[35] *Baptist Messenger*, February 15, 1928; see also Southern Baptist Convention, *Annual*, 1928, 87.

his party's platform, prohibitionists found him even more
vulnerable, although his religion alone was enough for some
to oppose him. As one writer has rightly suggested, "The religious campaign against Smith is impossible to distinguish
from the dry campaign against him. They were part and
parcel of the same attitude."[36]

As the campaign progressed, drys claimed with noticeable
vigor that the major issue before the country was not political or religious, but moral. Every effort to divert attention
from the question of morality, said the Oklahoma *Messenger*,
which spoke for thousands of drys, "is a smokescreen."[37]
When Smith delivered an address in Oklahoma City without
mentioning the prohibition issue, drys proclaimed that he
had deliberately harped upon the question of religious prejudice only to camouflage the real issue.[38] That politics was less
important than moralism, they said, was vividly demonstrated
by Smith's choice of John J. Raskob, a former Republican
and a wet, as his campaign manager. Therefore, prohibitionists contended that continuance of the great reform should
also overshadow partisan political alignments.[39]

One of the drys' strongest spiritual allies during the election in Protestant Oklahoma was the rapidly declining order
of the Ku Klux Klan. No public figure, writes Professor
Charles Alexander in his fine study, ever took as much abuse
from the Klan as the governor of New York.[40] In 1927, Oklahoma Klansmen considered plans for controlling the state
Democratic convention and sending an anti-Smith delegation
to the Democratic convention in Houston. Klansmen, however, failed in their efforts and the Smith forces were able

[36] Sinclair, *Era of Excess*, 301.
[37] *Baptist Messenger*, August 9, 1928.
[38] For Smith's speech at Oklahoma City, see his *Campaign Addresses*, 43–
61; and for comment, *Baptist Messenger*, September 27, 1928.
[39] *Ibid.*; Tulsa *World*, October 26, 1928.
[40] Charles Alexander, *The Ku Klux Klan in the Southwest*, 235.

to win a plurality.[41] After the convention the KKK declared political war on the nominee. In Oklahoma and in the traditionally solidly Democratic South, there appeared little support to counter Klan opposition. Even Hoover, some Democrats concluded grimly, looked better to them than this Tammany Hall–supported, wet East Sider from New York, who seemingly spoke in an indistinguishable tongue, completely foreign to southern speech.

The leader of the Oklahoma Klan had threatened in Houston to bolt the Democratic party and support Hoover; and no doubt there were many who pledged good-by and good riddance.[42] During the subsequent campaign the national office of the Klan regarded Oklahoma as a battleground for an open assault upon "the menace of which Al Smith is spokesman."[43] The Klan as an organization, however, had very little influence in Oklahoma or any other southwestern state in the 1928 presidential election. "In most places," writes one authority, "the Klan was more important spiritually than physically." And, very significantly, he concludes that "religious prejudice and stern moralism, elements that had given rise to the Klan in the first place, were still factors in southwestern politics, and they benefited the Republicans and anti-Smith cause in the region."[44]

Despite the almost fanatical opposition to Smith from many Oklahomans, he was not without his firm supporters. Governor Henry S. Johnston avidly defended the party's candidate while lashing at the Republicans, accusing the GOP of

[41] *Ibid.*; and *Daily Oklahoman*, September 23, 1927, and October 11, 1927.

[42] Professor Alexander believes that the size of the Klan in Oklahoma has been exaggerated. While some suggest a figure as high as 7,000 in the late twenties, he thinks that a more reasonable number would be 2,000 for the year 1929, and 1,500 in 1930. Obviously, any estimate runs the risk of error since the Klan did not willingly give out such information. See Alexander, *The Ku Klux Klan in the Southwest*, 241.

[43] Tulsa *World*, October 29, 1928.

[44] Alexander, *The Ku Klux Klan in the Southwest*, 239–40.

pushing prohibition forward as its own smoke screen. Moreover, he argued that prohibition was really not an issue in the campaign, and that the nation could not be any wetter under either candidate than it had been under Calvin Coolidge.[45] Former Governor Lee Cruce, while boosting Smith, did not concede that enforcement was an impossibility. Much like Johnston, he lambasted the Republicans for not making an honest effort to enforce the law during the seven and one-half years of Republican ascendency. The trouble, said Cruce, was that for all those years prohibition had been regarded simply as an experiment with little attempt to perfect it. No true prohibitionist could be satisfied with the past, especially with the discrimination in enforcement which permitted bootleggers of considerable means to roam free while smaller ones were subjected to prosecution. Cruce, like Johnston, believed Smith would stand by the law as long as it remained on the books although he did not agree with it in principle.[46]

The Tulsa *World*, the largest pro-Smith paper in the state, decried the tactics employed against the Democratic nominee. It critically commented during the election that there had been not only a "whispering" campaign against Smith's religion, but also some loud "shouting."[47] The Republicans, the *World* editorialized, only thought of breaking into the solid South for the first time since the Civil War because of Smith's Catholicism. "Deny it as much as they may," charged the *World*, "this is the real issue with which Republicans expect to win the electoral votes of the southern states." That could make victory possible, but "what a price!"[48] The use of religion as a political factor the editor of the paper regarded as "one of the most serious blows that the institutions of

---

[45] Tulsa *World*, October 21, 1928.
[46] *Ibid.*, October 31, 1928.
[47] *Ibid.*, October 14, 1928.
[48] *Ibid.*, October 23, 1928.

this country have ever had to face." What the paper clearly suggested was that the sectarian question could not be made a political issue without leaving behind incalculable harm to the state of the nation, especially if the Protestant churches became actively involved in the campaign.[49]

A strong reaction manifested itself in Oklahoma against the effort to line up the churches and the pulpit for Hoover. Judge Robert L. Williams, a long-time Methodist, was furious when the annual conference unanimously approved a resolution declaring the election of 1928 a "referendum on prohibition." The jurist, who resented his denomination's becoming, as he put it, an arm of the Republican party, declared for separation of church and state.[50] The Women for Smith-Robinson Club in a paid political announcement directed its fire at the spiritual exhorters of the Word who had turned their pulpits into political platforms. The ladies were convinced that an organized movement existed to align Oklahoma ministers against Smith, no matter what their political faith.[51] One brave pastor, however, informed the local branch of the WCTU that since it had become a political organization, it could no longer use the Lord's house to advance the cause of politics.[52]

Al Smith could not successfully counter the combination of forces that was arrayed against him. Thus the Republican party for the second time since Oklahoma statehood carried a presidential election. The party displayed surprising gains although Oklahoma remained basically Democratic, at the state and local level. Hoover polled some 394,000 votes to Smith's 219,000. What the election really indicated, however, was not altogether clear. To one religious group Smith's

[49] *Ibid.*, November 6, 1928.
[50] *Ibid.*, November 2, 1928; and also *Harlow's Weekly*, August 4, 1928.
[51] Tulsa *World*, November 3, 1928.
[52] *Ibid.*, October 17, 1928. The National WCTU openly campaigned for Hoover, and so did some, but certainly not all, of the local Oklahoma chapters.

AN OFFICIAL INDICTMENT AND MURDER

defeat meant that "mighty moral issues have precedence over partisan issues," and that the voters had served notice on politicians that the federal government would not be surrendered to the supporters of liquor.[53] From the many articles on church and state and on the pope, which appeared in some contemporary publications in opposition to Smith's stand on prohibition, one could not doubt that this assertion was oversimplified, if not totally untrue. That the election signified Oklahoma's acceptance of the Eighteenth Amendment, whether it wanted the law vigorously enforced or not, also transcended debate.[54] The Tulsa *World*, taking a national view of the election, believed that prosperity constituted a key ingredient in Hoover's success.[55] But intolerance, concluded the *World*, surely contributed to the Republican triumph. Oklahoma had merely joined hands with the rest of the nation; and the drys had achieved one of their most significant victories since the inauguration of prohibition. But disaster loomed beyond the horizon.

[53] *Baptist Messenger*, November 15, 1928.
[54] *Harlow's Weekly*, November 10, 1928.
[55] Tulsa *World*, November 8, 1928.

VII

"SUDS," THAT'S ALL: REPEAL AND BEER

THE ALLIED influences of the Great Depression and the unfavorable conditions which accompanied the noble experiment created a public opinion inimical to the continuance of
national prohibition. Wet propagandists, led principally by
the Association Against the Prohibition Amendment,[1] took
every possible advantage to expose the hypocrisy of prohibition and to emphasize its deleterious effects on social, political, and economic institutions. Aided by an increasingly large
number of pro-repeal city newspapers and other journals, the
"antis" with remarkable success carried their case to rustics
of the countryside as well as to urbanites. Try as they might
to reduce wet arguments to mere exaggerations or prevarica-
tions, drys confronted mounting difficulties in trying to offset
the combination of forces arrayed against them. By the early
thirties frustrating signs projected a dismal picture of terrible
things to come.

A reflection of, and a contributor to, the change in citizens'
attitudes toward prohibition were the massive polls con-

[1] The history of the Association Against the Prohibition Amendment has
been told in great depth in Heckman, "Prohibition Passes."

ducted in the twenties and the thirties, especially those of such journals as the *Literary Digest*. While the *Digest*, then with its reputation unmarred, may have overstressed wet sentiment,[2] it did capture the general opinion of the people. Drys, of course, never accepted the results of the polls as an accurate barometer of what people really thought. As Professor Andrew Sinclair has pointed out, however, "even if the findings of the *Digest* were biased in favor of repeal, the fact that they were widely believed to be accurate was a telling blow to the drys."[3]

The final poll conducted by the *Digest* in 1932 showed that more than 73 per cent of the national population favored abolition of the Eighteenth Amendment. Of the forty-eight states, only Kansas and North Carolina returned dry majorities. Oklahoma had a wet percentage of 54.53 per cent which represented an increase of 3.59 per cent over 1930.[4] Confirmed Sooner prohibitionists pointed out that many of their number refused to vote since they considered the poll unrepresentative. It was harder for them to deny, however, that dissatisfaction existed among a sizable faction of the population. Yet, one must take care not to misread the polls or the statements from dejected drys, for clearly most Oklahomans were not disgruntled with state prohibition but with national enforcement. (Both Republicans and Democrats in the 1932 election reckoned with the growing significance of the wet movement.)

The GOP, unwilling to admit openly the failure of an experiment the party had assumed responsibility for perfecting, asked for resubmission of the Eighteenth Amendment. The Democrats, however, boldly declared for outright repeal. Drys, then, had no alternative but to choose "moderate wets"

---

[2] Sinclair, *Era of Excess*, 313.

[3] *Ibid.*, 415.

[4] See the results of the poll in *Literary Digest*, Vol. LXIII (April 30, 1932), 6–7.

or "extreme wets";[5] the prospect was not very inviting. During the campaign Republican Herbert Hoover tried to woo drys and moderates, but he avoided any suggestion of total repeal, while his opponent Franklin D. Roosevelt preyed upon the sentiments of a depression-ridden populace which recognized the need for revenue, even if from hard liquor and beer. To the advantage of the wets, however, prohibition as an issue in the 1932 presidential contest did not take on great significance as a moral question. By and large the electorate concerned itself with the economic benefits of repeal, and, consequently, the Democrats were able to successfully utilize the possibility of additional revenue to their political benefit.[6] With the depression one of his strongest allies, Roosevelt rolled to an easy victory over Hoover and thus brought nearer to an end an era of social experimentation which wets later recounted as days of dark despair.

The Congress elected in 1932 followed the lead of the popular new president on prohibition. In February, 1933, it approved a repeal amendment and sent it to the states for ratification. An innovation was introduced in its submission since it called for the use of the convention method of ratification. Until the Constitution could be changed, Roosevelt also asked Congress to legalize beer by altering the Volstead Act.[7] Sensitive to the possibility of new sources of income, a bill permitting the sale of 3.2 beer was passed and sent to the President, who signed it on March 23, 1933. The country had now taken its first step back to where it had been in January, 1920.[8]

[5] Sinclair, *Era of Excess*, 386.

[6] *Ibid.*

[7] See the President's brief message to the Congress in Samuel I. Rosenman, ed., *The Public Papers and Addresses of Franklin D. Roosevelt*, II, 66–67.

[8] After the passage of the beer bill, the Southern Baptist Convention declared that "ostensibly Congress enacted [it] not for the sake of making legal intoxicating liquors, but for the sake of revenue, as though a purely destruc-

When Congress submitted the Twenty-first Amendment to the states, the Oklahoma legislature was in session. Despite the many grave economic problems which faced the lawmakers, repeal and beer attracted considerable debate. Even prior to congressional action, wets in the state legislature had pushed in vain to amend the prohibition section of the state constitution. Interested groups like the Muskogee-based Oklahoma Modification and Repeal Association urged legislators to follow the lead of the other states by abolishing the dry ordinance in anticipation of national repeal.[9] The move to achieve this objective netted nothing except a firmer determination on the part of drys to smother any repeal attempt.[10] While legislators had shown an aversion to altering the state constitution, wets believed that the lawmakers' antagonism would not prevent a state vote to consider the Twenty-first Amendment.

Accordingly, wets, led by Representative William Coe, called a Democratic caucus to map a legislative campaign for the establishment of machinery for submission of the Twenty-first Amendment. Coe believed that the house contained about fifty resubmissionists, and that with diligent work he could get enough votes to push a plan through the lower chamber. The caucus finally adjourned without taking decisive action, only recommending that the legislature study the problem.[11] Drys, of course, looked with utter contempt upon any move to act on the amendment. Both the Anti-

tive force in the social order could bring material prosperity." See Southern Baptist Convention, *Annual*, 1933, 112.

[9] Paul Mertz, "Oklahoma and the Year of Repeal, 1933," 20 (hereafter cited as Mertz, "Year of Repeal, 1933"). The author has relied very heavily upon many of Mertz's findings. He is very grateful not only for this fine study which has saved him much work, but for the many conversations with Professor Mertz which kept him on the right path.

[10] See the *Baptist Messenger*, January 26 and February 2, 1933.

[11] *Daily Oklahoman*, February 22, 1933, and Norman *Transcript*, February 21, 1933.

Saloon League and the WCTU charged that a state ratification convention would be too costly, but the women did not fear a clash with the wets since they felt certain of the outcome. The Norman *Transcript* adopted the position of the drys when it stressed the need for a "drastic" cut in expenditure of every kind at a time when people were starving. Oklahoma, said the editor of the *Transcript*, had no right to help other states acquire liquor by ratifying the amendment;[12] so why waste badly needed money on an election?

Eager to put Oklahoma on record for or against the Twenty-first Amendment, Representative James Babb championed a ratification measure, House Joint Resolution 32.[13] The introduction of a beer bill in the legislature at the time the ratification measure was up for consideration greatly improved the chances of success for the Babb proposal.[14] Drys in and outside the legislature recognized that if the nation scrapped the prohibition amendment, Oklahoma would probably remain legally dry, but the possible introduction of beer posed a new and more serious threat. Consequently, there was a tendency, during the discussion of the two bills, for them to give more on ratification and to concentrate their efforts on beer. There still remained, however, wide differences of opinion on the kind of convention plan which should be adopted, if any at all. Representative George Copeland introduced an unsuccessful bill for the Prohibition Thousand, a statewide dry group, which would have given rural areas a greater voice in repeal by selecting delegates from legislative districts.[15] Babb's resolution, however, eventually received favorable action although it encountered strong opposition in the senate.[16]

[12] February 22, 1933.

[13] For the resolution in detail, see House *Journal*, 1933, II, 2594–2601.

[14] Mertz, "Year of Repeal, 1933," 41.

[15] For elaboration on the Copeland measure, see the Norman *Transcript*, March 27, 1933.

[16] House *Journal*, 1933, II, 2601, and Senate *Journal*, 1933, 2524.

Governor William "Alfalfa Bill" Murray promptly vetoed House Joint Resolution 32. Murray, one of the state's founding fathers and self-assured experts on Oklahoma's constitution, had never openly registered any noticeable hostility toward a vote on the Twenty-first Amendment. In fact, he once voiced the necessity for such action. But he vetoed HJR 32 because it would begin the repeal process within ninety days of adjournment and because it did not have an emergency clause. The legalistically inclined Murray doubtless stood on solid and unshakeable ground, but as one student has noted, "the constitutional ninety-day suspension of a bill's effectiveness was probably never intended to apply to the processes incidental to approval of a federal amendment."[17] "Alfalfa Bill's" veto, however, temporarily snuffed out the movement toward a repeal convention just as the regular session of the Fourteenth Legislature ended, but most expected a hurried resurrection of the repeal attempt once the lawmakers reconvened.

The legislature had adjourned only after the passage of several tax measures advanced by the administration. To Murray's dismay he had been unable to secure sufficient votes to attach emergency clauses to his revenue bills. Following the regular session, discontent developed among Sooners over these new tax bills, and citizens threatened to circulate petitions bringing the recently enacted measures to a public vote. Murray hurriedly decided upon a special session to demand the necessary emergency clauses. Determined that only matters suggested by the Governor receive attention, Murray took care to remind the legislators in his special message that

[17] Mertz, "Year of Repeal, 1933," 48, and *Harlow's Weekly*, May 6, 1933. An emergency clause attached to the bill would have made it effective immediately upon passage by the legislature and the signature of the governor. Without such a clause the provisions of the bill could not have become operative until a ninety-day period had elapsed—thus the basis for the Governor's constitutional argument.

"no other measures will be considered or submitted for consideration under any circumstance."[18] Since the special session could only act on proposals specifically itemized by the Governor, repealists and pro-beer advocates found themselves placed in a very difficult spot. The Governor, they concluded, must be persuaded to expand his message.

Repealists moved rapidly toward success following favorable action on the emergency clauses for the Murray tax bills. In June, 1933, house floor leader John Steele Batson announced that he would personally request the Governor to grant the legislature authority to consider the repeal question. Batson's statement coupled with that of Senator Al Nichols, who was close to the administration, that Murray wanted a vote on the Twenty-first Amendment before the 1934 elections, increased confidence that the executive would yield to the wishes of the ratificationists.[19] "Alfalfa Bill," his tax bills already passed and now content to see the legislature discuss whatever it desired, sent a special message to the legislature July 8 which paved the way for a consideration of repeal.[20] But he cautioned the lawmakers to avoid any discussion of state prohibition.

A new repeal plan advanced by Representative Leon Phillips and similar to the old Babb resolution drew warm support from those anxious for a vote on the fate of the Eighteenth Amendment or those tired of toying with the issue.[21]

18 See his message to the special session of the Fourteenth Legislature in Senate *Journal*, Extraordinary Session, 1933, 10–19.

19 Norman *Transcript*, June 12, 1933.

20 Both houses had adopted resolutions asking the Governor to extend the call. See Murray's message to the Fourteenth Legislature on the question of repeal of the Eighteenth Amendment in House *Journal*, 1933, II, 4614. The forthcoming message had been successfully predicted in the *Daily Oklahoman*, July 8, 1933.

21 One paper reported that as many as eleven resolutions had been drawn up and awaited introduction in the house as soon as the Governor opened the session to repeal. See Norman *Transcript*, July 9, 1933.

Phillips' bill contemplated an election in 1934 unless Governor Murray called for an earlier vote. It also provided that the repeal process become operative the first Tuesday following the one hundred fifth day after adjournment of the legislative session. At that time the state election board would certify to the governor the names of two electors in each county, one wet, the other dry. Twenty days later county conventions would then be called to select delegates at a ratio of one for every five hundred persons; each of these county conventions would nominate two delegates to a state convention. Subsequently, two slates of delegates representing repeal and anti-repeal would be listed on the ballot at the next statewide election. Following the certification of the results, the law required the governor to call a final convention composed of the successful slate to act on the amendment.[22]

The intricately involved Phillips plan encountered little opposition in the legislature. The house approved the bill by a margin of 37 votes, but apathy and absenteeism played havoc with the resolution in the senate.[23] Although the upper chamber, as a whole, favored a repeal convention, many senators had already made their way home by mid-July, and the wet leaders had trouble in assembling a quorum. One very candid senator suggested that the lack of attendance had resulted because his colleagues had gotten the urge to "put on their hats and go down to the hotel to drink a bottle of [newly legalized] beer." He had no use for such "cattle."[24] Finally, two Oklahoma lawmakers, Senators T. Woody Dixon and Charles Moon of Marietta and Muskogee respectively, flew

[22] House *Journal*, 1933, II, 4616.

[23] Mertz, "Year of Repeal, 1933," 156.

[24] *Daily Oklahoman*, July 15, 1933. The debate on beer and repeal took place at the same time. To avoid much confusion, the two issues have been discussed separately. Beer was legalized *before* the approval of the repeal convention.

to the capitol, thus permitting the senate to pass the bill.[25]

By the time Oklahoma actually commenced its ratification procedure, thirty-two states had approved the Twenty-first Amendment. Unless Governor Murray acted with dispatch, it seemed doubtful if Sooners would get the opportunity to render their opinion on the noble experiment. But the economy-minded "Alfalfa Bill" had no intention of calling a special election and he informed his critics that if they objected "they can go to hell."[26] He saw no need to expend extra money at a time when the state went begging for funds. In December, 1933, Utah, the thirty-sixth state to ratify the Twenty-first Amendment, brought to an end the prohibition experiment begun in 1920, thus making the continuation of the Oklahoma repeal drive a useless affair.

Repeal had demanded its share of attention during the very important Fourteenth Legislature, but the battle over beer generated more discussion and political maneuvering. The adoption of the national law legalizing 3.2 beer had greatly inspired some Oklahoma legislators and business-minded citizens interested in the industry. In March, 1933, Representatives Bob Graham and R. C. Garland offered a measure, House Bill 647, permitting the sale of 3.2 in the state.[27] The passage of this law, they and their supporters contended, would not violate the provisions of the Oklahoma Constitution, for Congress had already adjudged beer nonintoxicating.[28] The section of the Oklahoma Constitution to which they referred, however, specifically stated that persons who furnished "any intoxicating liquor . . . including beer, ale and wine" were subject to fine and imprisonment.

[25] For passage of the bill, see Senate *Journal*, Extraordinary Session, 1933, 480–81.

[26] *Daily Oklahoman*, July 27, 1933.

[27] Mertz, "Year of Repeal, 1933," 22.

[28] See *Statutes at Large*, XLVIII, pt. 1, 16–20.

The legality of the beer bill confronted the House Legal Advisory Committee with a difficult task. Its chairman, the highly respected Bower Broadus of Muskogee, consented to hear testimony from the drys, but he refused to entertain moral arguments against 3.2; the committee's preoccupation, he said, was with the legal aspects of the beverage.[29] The members of the committee had to search long and hard for a judicial precedent which would justify beer. Eventually it unearthed an old 1910 state supreme court case, which gave its members a basis for their ultimate decision. After much grappling with conscience, Broadus' group concluded that the legislature could by statute define 3.2 beer as nonintoxicating, and that the Graham-Garland bill was constitutional.[30] The report came as a shock wave to the drys, but produced justifiable optimism among the wets.

Wets chalked up another victory in getting their bill assigned to a special committee. Had it gone to the hostile House Prohibition Enforcement Committee, presided over by the indescribably dry B. W. Todd, it probably would have witnessed the fate of other liquor proposals.[31] Led by A. F. Duke, a Nazarene minister, the special committee consisted of an equal number of drys and wets and one member of undetermined allegiance. Duke and Tom Anglin, speaker of the house, decided to dispense with hearings on the bill, an opinion which displeased wets who anxiously awaited the opportunity to air their case. Their reasoning could easily be understood, for they recognized that the hearing could serve as an edu-

29 *Harlow's Weekly*, March 18, 1933.

30 House *Journal*, 1933, I, 2107. Mertz maintains that the committee took a very enlightened view given the precedents available to them. Broadus, he said, was on "solid ground in ruling that the statute making all beer intoxicating was changeable." Indeed, it is difficult to disagree with such a sound conclusion. See Mertz, "Year of Repeal," 28.

31 For discussion, see *Harlow's Weekly*, April 1, 1933, and Tulsa *World*, March 29, 1933.

cational platform; in short, it would assist them in carrying the beer message to the people. With Graham and Garland threatening to hold a rump committee meeting unless Duke and Anglin changed their minds on hearings, the chairman acquiesced and conceded to the wishes of the wets.[32]

The hearings yielded little of real significance except occasional laughter balanced with spirited and deeply felt oratory. Drys, as always, relied upon their morally persuasive arguments, but they did not dismiss the necessity of rebutting those projected by economically inclined wets. The Reverend Lemuel Penn of Prohibition Thousand endeavored to dispel the contention that "booze," including beer, had benefited the nation; and he proclaimed that "there are other forms of human depravity you could tax."[33] Mrs. Elizabeth House of the WCTU prophesied economic austerity if beer was legalized. Money spent for beer could not be used for food and clothing, said the women's president. The Reverend H. E. Swan, soldier of many a battle, movingly related the death of his mother, a victim of a beer-drunken driver. It would amount to a disgrace if the legislature legalized the destructive 3.2 "poison." Another dry saw the real issue as the preservation of the home.[34]

Wets harped upon beer as a revenue source, its temperate qualities, and the hypocrisy of prohibition. In a statement fashioned for the public as well as for his colleagues, Representative Graham told the committee of his stern opposition to hard liquor, but added that the state needed the money from nonintoxicating beer. And Garland taunted the ministers who had testified, when he subtly intimated that they knew young people of the state obtained beer and hard liquor without undue exertion. Ross Lillard, Oklahoma City attor-

[32] Mertz, "Year of Repeal, 1933," 33.
[33] *Ibid.*
[34] *Ibid.*, 36.

ney, exhorted that 3.2 would remove the brewery from the home, much to the benefit of that institution and the state.[35]

If the testimony of the wets had been more convincing than that of the drys, it did not sufficiently impress enough members of the committee. By a vote of 4 to 3, it recommended that the legislature kill the bill. Committee wets—Graham, Garland, and Henry Timmons—vigorously dissented and then prepared a minority report. To offset many of the objections leveled at the bill, pro-beer members revamped it so thoroughly that it "was likened to a renovated car with all parts replaced but the radiator cap."[36] Drys wailed in amazement when the house in March, 1933, accepted the minority report and when the committee of the whole gave its approval to the bill the following month.[37] The pro-beer faction had advanced one step closer to success, despite the betrayal by the special committee.

The beer bloc needed sixty votes to carry the bill in the house. A few days prior to the April 1 roll call, wets appeared short of this number by at least two votes. Graham pleaded for party unity in seeking converts to his cause. In an effort to expel legal doubts held by some legislators, he noted that he had "pretty fair fellowship in my stand for near beer[38] when the U.S. Congress, the President and neighboring states say 3.2 per cent beer is not intoxicating."[39] Despite this appeal to authority, many representatives, including the speaker of the house, persistently maintained that the measure contravened the prohibitory provision of the Oklahoma Con-

[35] *Ibid.*

[36] *Ibid.*

[37] House *Journal*, 1933, II, 2593.

[38] The bill drawn by the minority members of the special committee and approved by the house declared all beverages with a minimum alcoholic content of .5 per cent and a maximum of 3.2 per cent nonintoxicating "near beer." The statute passed by Congress had not made this distinction.

[39] Mertz, "Year of Repeal, 1933," 39.

stitution. On April 6, however, it passed the house with
exactly the required number of votes, 60 to 54.[40]

Supporters of beer in the senate promised a speedy vote.
The influence of such powerful senatorial figures as president
pro tempore Paul Stewart, Al Nichols, and Hardin Ballard
steered the bill away from the dry Prohibition Enforcement
Committee, and, as in the case of the house, it was sent to a
special committee. Annoyed at what had taken place in the
lower chamber, Senator W. T. Clark, chairman of the Enforcement Committee, had earlier forecast his determination
to kill any bill which had escaped hearing in the proper house
committee.[41] After some revision the special committee reported the bill favorably, and on April 11 the senate gave its
approval.[42]

Progressively, sentiment for a referendum on 3.2 developed
in the legislature. This method would provide a means not
only for the people to register their opinion, but also for legislators to shift responsibility to the public. An election which
would cost at least $60,000, however, constituted a financial
problem. Governor Murray had emphatically expressed his
disapproval of any appropriation for that purpose, although
he personally desired a popular vote if expenses came from
nongovernmental funds. The burden of the election, therefore, would have to rest upon the shoulders of the wets. In-
itially the bill's backers thought that the collection of money
would prove no serious obstacle, and that brewers and other
interested parties would generously contribute. With this assurance the senate passed House Bill 647 by a vote of 28
to 15, less than a two-thirds majority.[43]

The discussion of the beer bill in the legislature and its

[40] House *Journal*, 1933, II, 2638–39.
[41] Norman *Transcript*, April 7, 1933.
[42] Senate *Journal*, 1933, 1938.
[43] *Ibid.*, 2117.

eventual passage quickened the activities of long-established prohibition organizations and also fostered the creation of a united front to meet the new challenge. Backed by the Protestant churches, drys always had at their command a potentially powerful machine easily conditioned for combat. In March, 1933, prohibitionists had met at the First Baptist Church in Oklahoma City to map their attack and to synchronize the efforts of various dry groups. They agreed at this time to co-ordinate their program through a centralized body called the Prohibition Thousand, commanded by the Reverend A. M. Jayne of Oklahoma City.[44] Acutely aware of the snow-balling sentiment for beer in the state resulting from the backing of powerful interests, the Prohibition Thousand pledged itself to counteract the trend toward the adoption of an immoral and a patently unconstitutional measure.[45] Although the drys were unable to defeat the Graham-Garland bill in the legislature, they did win a major victory in having it referred to the people.

By May, 1933, the Prohibition Thousand and its constituent dry groups had finalized their plan of attack. A central headquarters had been established, and county and precinct chairmen appointed.[46] Dry leaders originally anticipated the circulation of 500,000 printed declarations of intent in an effort to secure 50,000 pledges against beer, but they could never raise the necessary money. Not the least of their many headaches was their failure to get the right kind of responsible businessmen "to join the preachers in leadership positions." Throughout its history the Prohibition Thousand remained an association of clergymen and members of dry

[44] *Harlow's Weekly*, April 1, 1933, and Norman *Transcript*, March 27, 1933.
[45] This view was best expressed by the *Daily Oklahoman*, which pictured the 3.2 bill as a "deliberate attempt at nullification." The constitution, said the *Oklahoman*, forbade beer of an intoxicating nature. See excerpts from that paper in *Harlow's Weekly*, April 1, 1933.
[46] *Ibid.*

–119–

pressure groups recruited essentially from the Baptist, Methodist, and Presbyterian churches.[47]

Beer advocates in 1933 perfected an organization unequaled in the annals of the Oklahoma prohibition movement. On the same day that drys had assembled to mount their forces, their opponents had met at the Huckins Hotel in Oklahoma City and formed the State Modification and Repeal Association. Most of its backers came from the Hotel Men's Association, the Crusaders (a local chapter of a national repeal group), and wet legislators.[48] Some individual businessmen interested in profits, whether from the sale of beer directly or from goods related to its sale, were also present. The association chose as its president widely known and much respected Judge C. E. McLees, leader of a Muskogee repeal group.

The actual passage of the beer bill with the stipulation that the wets raise the required money for the referendum dictated the establishment of a new organization which could not only serve as a propaganda instrument, but also collect money and win the election.[49] Thus, in April, partisans of beer formed a "patriotic and outstanding committee of businessmen and political leaders" called the Committee of One Hundred, led by J. Harvey Maxey of Tulsa.[50] Among the members at the time of its organization were many illustrious persons prominent in Oklahoma's social and political life. There were former Judge George Ramsey, Norris Henthorne of the Tulsa *World*, the retiring president of the State Fed-

[47] Mertz, "Year of Repeal, 1933," 71.

[48] *Harlow's Weekly*, April 1, 1933.

[49] The State Modification and Repeal Association had as its major objective the passage of the beer bill. At the time of its formation, few expected the Governor to demand that beer interests defray the cost of the election.

[50] The events leading up to the creation of the committee and the subsequent organization of the Beer for Oklahoma League have been well described in Mertz, "Year of Repeal, 1933," 52–65.

eration of Labor, Joe Campbell, and B. G. Patton, once national commander of the American Legion. Ultimately, membership came to include such names as that of the former national Democratic chairman, prominent Republican leaders, fraternal leaders, and a past president of the American Education Association. Former Governor J. B. A. Robertson, who looked upon beer as a fight "for the rebirth of freedom," aligned himself with the champions of the "liberal" cause.[51] With this widely diversified following, the committee anticipated appealing to a large portion of the electorate which would contribute money and vote for 3.2.

Dissension within the Committee of One Hundred over fund-raising plans led to its reorganization. Some members, especially Henthorne and Maxey, thought that only Oklahomans should contribute to the campaign, but others favored soliciting from brewers. Publicly, the committee adopted the policy espoused by Maxey and Henthorne. Bob Graham, however, independently exerted himself and sought funds from Anheuser-Busch and Company of St. Louis, but his efforts, according to most reports, reaped no rewards.[52] As the prospects of raising the necessary money faded, and as members became more disgruntled, the committee turned to R. C. Garland to handle its financial drive and the election campaign. The choice was a wise one, for the co-sponsor of the beer bill had a number of valuable political and personal associations and was not regarded as a "dripping wet." With Garland in virtual control, the committee now changed its name to the Beer for Oklahoma League.

A difference in name, however, did not alter wet fortunes; the league could not generate the thrust necessary to cata-

[51] For a note on Robertson's stand, see the Tulsa *World*, April 26, 1933, and the Muskogee *Daily Phoenix,* April 26, 1933.

[52] Consensus was that funds to finance the election did not come from brewers. See Mertz, "Year of Repeal, 1933," 61.

pult the organization closer to the badly needed $90,000.[53] A desperate cry went out for monies from within the state, but depression-weary Sooners failed to respond. By establishing quotas for each of the counties, wets had hoped to realize their objective, but as of June 8, 1933, only about $20,000 had been collected or pledged.[54] Unable to reach their goal, they turned their attention to the special session of the legislature, just as repealists had done, for relief of their grievances.

As already noted, Governor Murray had not alluded to beer or repeal in his message to the special session of the legislature. Revenue measures had been the executive's sole concern. But, under pressure, he had expanded his call to allow for consideration of repeal of the Twenty-first Amendment. The beer bloc now faced a similar challenge. Some revenue-conscious legislators who opposed the Governor's income and sales tax program, believed beer taxes could serve as a reliable substitute. Moreover, many lawmakers regarded any possible levy on beer as much less controversial than the taxes proposed by the Governor. It it was to be successful, the beer bloc must obtain the support of these legislators. Before "Alfalfa Bill" presented his message to the legislature, beer leaders asked him to request state payment of the election. Murray remained noncommittal; but his refusal to mention the matter implied his temporary rejection of their demand.

But if the Governor by silence had thwarted the will of the beer advocates, they were now in position to thwart his will. Above all, as suggested previously, Murray wanted emergency clauses attached to the tax measures passed by the regular session which would make them operative immedi-

---

[53] Up to the last of April, wets had assumed that the cost of the election would be reduced by the elimination of counters. The state election board, however, vetoed this move.

[54] Norman *Transcript*, June 8, 1933.

ately. Should the proponents of brew withhold their backing of his program, then they would force him to open the legislature to a consideration of money for the July beer election. Determined to test the Governor's steel allegiance to his own desires, and content upon the achievement of their personal legislative aims, 3.2 supporters successfully introduced a resolution entreating the Governor to permit discussion of the beer issue. To place the burden of a public question upon the shoulders of private interests, the resolution stated, was unfair.[55] By an impressive vote of 72 to 29, the house approved the resolution, and the senate passed it 26 to 12.[56]

Grim reality now greeted the politician who prided himself a master politico. As Murray saw his tax program, especially the sales tax, amended to the likings of a legislature sensitive to a populace which did not relish having extra pennies taken from its pocket in an age of depression, beer strategy slowly began to reap results. The usually strong "Alfalfa Bill" showed signs of weakening by the first of June when he proclaimed that "I have no desire to defeat a vote by the people on [the] question."[57] But if any person, he said, "thinks that he will use the word 'beer' as an excuse to serve [his own selfish interests] by opposing the tax program[,] he is mistaken."[58]

On June 5, Murray informed his legislative lieutenants of a forthcoming message on funds for the referendum. He would do nothing, however, until the legislature passed the income tax emergency clause.[59] By subtle pressures, political debt collection, and outright browbeating, the emergency clause, as indicated, went through by exactly a two-thirds

---

[55] For the text of the resolution, see House *Journal*, 1933, II, 4203–4205.

[56] *Ibid.*, 4223; and Senate *Journal*, Extraordinary Session, 1933, 67.

[57] Murray had also suggested that the legislature consider a bill eliminating counters.

[58] Norman *Transcript*, June 1, 1933.

[59] Mertz, "Year of Repeal, 1933," 100.

majority. Many observers reasoned that the beer bloc had
been responsible for its success and they eagerly pointed to
the votes cast by Leon Phillips, M. L. Misenheimer, and Sam
Sullivan. The truth is "that no single reason can be assigned
for the appearance of two-thirds majority where none had
been before," but undoubtedly beer men played a vital role,
and without the loosening of their lines, the emergency clause
could never have been passed.[60]

Murray lived up to his promise. In a special message he
suggested payment for the beer election from general revenue
funds "if the legislature in its judgment thinks best."[61] He
further urged the lawmakers to appropriate money in advance
to pay election officials rather than anticipate paying them
from beer taxes. The Governor also felt that the beer question
should be voted upon at a time when no candidates were
running for office. Thus, he officially set July 11, 1933, as the
date for the election.[62] Generally, public opinion sustained
Murray's action, for there was a growing realization that all
citizens had a stake in every statewide political issue and
contest.[63]

The legislature moved quickly to appropriate money to
defray election costs. In June the house approved $140,000
for the beer referendum and for a vote on the reduction of
ad valorem taxes. The senate, however, chopped $8,000 off
this amount; a conference committee finally set aside $66,000
for the beer election alone.[64] The clash in the legislature between drys and wets over an appropriation produced only a
mild skirmish compared to the devastating wars of days past.
While a few never-say-die prohibitionists offered stubborn
resistance in the lower chamber, they could muster only 12

[60] *Ibid.*, 104.
[61] House *Journal*, 1933, II, 4316.
[62] *Ibid.*, 4315.
[63] Mertz, "Year of Repeal, 1933," 106.
[64] *Ibid.*

"SUDS," THAT'S ALL: REPEAL AND BEER

votes for their faltering cause, and only 7 in the senate. The fact that many drys ceased opposition reflected not only the prevailing public will, but also the optimistic attitude they shared of a triumph at the ballot box.[65]

During the month and one-half prior to the election, the Beer for Oklahoma League feverishly pressed its economic arguments, while drys violently refuted what they described as exaggerated claims. The Tulsa *World* put the case very pointedly for the advocates of 3.2 when it predicted benefits for farmer, landowner, and wage earner alike.[66] Could the other thirty-three states which had already approved the "moderate drink," asked the wets, be entirely wrong in their economic assumptions? To put such a question to drys was to answer it in the affirmative. Their reply had a historical orientation now familiar to most Sooners: beer (or liquor) needlessly diverted money from legitimate purchases—milk, meat, and clothing for the wife and family. Moreover, they asserted, much of the beer money would not stay in Oklahoma, but would find its way into the brewery coffers in Milwaukee and St. Louis.

The Woodward *News Bulletin* in a reasonably detached and highly perceptive comment gave an astute observation of the possibilities of beer which came closer to the truth than much of the verbiage poured forth by the antagonists in the battle of 1933:

> Our guess is that, regardless of how the election comes out, both sides will be disappointed. The return of beer isn't going to make a great deal of difference to the future of the state. Its return will not alone bring prosperity and solve all the problems confronting a financially troubled populace. Nor will its return mean the ruin of the younger generation, the tearing down of the home and wrecking of community standards.

[65] *Ibid.*, 107.
[66] Tulsa *World*, July 11, 1933.

–125–

From reports from all other states where . . . brew has returned, after the first few days of rejoicing the return has been
a disappointment . . . .

The greatest lure to beer now is that it is forbidden and it
always has been man's nature to never be satisfied until he
has tasted that which has been denied him.[67]

To strengthen what seemed a failing campaign, the Anti-
Saloon League secured the services of one of the country's
most renowned prohibitionists, Bishop James Cannon. History, however, later revealed this as an act of dubious wisdom,
for controversy had been no stranger to the Bishop's life.[68]
Within his own denomination he had come under fire for allegedly misappropriating funds in the 1928 presidential election; and to the consternation of some of his Methodist
brethren, he had also played (gambled) in the stock market. While the clergyman had been exonerated of any wrong
doing, to be sure, the suspicion aroused by his activities sent
puritanical tremors through Bible-belt Oklahoma. Little
wonder wets entertained few fears; in fact, their reaction
bordered on the periphery of jubilation.[69] If Cannon's visit
was "properly" handled, and if the full story of the Bishop's
nonreligious doings was transmitted to the public, wets reasoned that his sojourn would surely redound to their advantage.[70]

The "exposure" of Cannon went according to schedule. Before his arrival in the state the pro-beer Oklahoma *News*
opened with a series of searching articles on the preacher's
past. For four days in June,[71] the paper carried front page
stories, the last of which dealt with his indictment by a fed-

67 Quoted in *Harlow's Weekly*, June 23, 1933.
68 Virginius Dabney's *Dry Messiah: The Life of Bishop Cannon* remains
the best biography of the Methodist clergyman.
69 Mertz, "Year of Repeal, 1933," 128.
70 Tulsa *World*, June 10, 1933; *Daily Oklahoman*, June 16, 1933.
71 June 15, 16, 17, and 18, 1933.

eral jury and appeared upon Cannon's arrival in Oklahoma. Bitterly assailing the minister, the Tulsa *World* viewed his presence in the state as nothing less than a godsend.[72] "If Christ came to earth today," wrote one Tulsan, "his first act would be to whip Cannon out of the college of bishops," just as he had driven money-changers from the temple.[73]

One of the most devastating results of Cannon's visit was dissension within the dry ranks in many areas of the state. An incident at Norman reflected this division. W. L. Losinger of the Anti-Saloon League wanted the Bishop to speak in the city and he secured permission for the use of McFarlin Methodist Church from its pastor, the Reverend A. Norman Evans. The local Ministerial Alliance failed to become enthusiastic over his coming and refused the Bishop an official invitation. The Reverend Emerson Houser, more forthright than many of his brethren of the cloth, came directly to the point without equivocation when he said that Cannon's leadership "has been discredited and so far as I know, none of the ministers are [sic] in favor of his appearance here."[74] The Reverend Mr. Evans, caught in a dilemma, could not diplomatically extricate himself from this embarrassing circumstance and finally had to retain his original position. After all, Cannon was a Methodist. On July 5, the Bishop spoke at Norman to a crowd of 500 people and harangued the wets in his usual style; but his coming did little to solidify the prohibitionist forces in that central Oklahoma town.[75]

Pretend as they may that Cannon's trip out "West" would win them votes, wets had no way of confirming their convictions. Besides, he did symbolize power, and for some odd rea-

[72] Tulsa *World*, June 28, 1933.
[73] *Ibid.* For a cross section of press opinion, see *Harlow's Weekly*, June 17, 1933.
[74] Norman *Transcript*, June 16 and 21, 1933, and *Daily Oklahoman*, June 17, 1933.
[75] Norman *Transcript*, June 16, 1933.

son, power oftentimes obscures suspicions of doubtful morality. Beer forces had announced early in July that they would
not dispatch special speakers to recoup any losses suffered in
the wake of the Cannon storm through Oklahoma. It would be
a "useless and wasteful expense of time and money," said one
official of the Beer League, "to send anyone over the state,
as all reports [suggest] he has helped more than hurt the
cause of legalizing beer."[76] But the beer people had a change
of mind. Reversing former plans, their leaders announced
that R. M. McCool, State Democratic Committee chairman,
would tour Southeastern Oklahoma.[77] The *Daily Oklahoman,*
noticing this redirection of wet strategy, applauded the move
—McCool would surely ruin things for them; he would help
drys regain the losses suffered from the Cannon visit. "At last
a 'break' has come to bless the embattled forces of prohibition," said the once ardently wet but now decidedly dry paper,
because "Chairman McCool of a thousand unwon victories
is to go forth like death on the pale horse and deliver big
speeches in behalf of beer." If he kept up his "moist out-
bursts" long enough, the majority for beer, the *Oklahoman*
speculated, "will be nothing like so overwhelming as Bob
Graham . . . and the other Einsteins of the wet army have
predicted."[78]

Every available sign pointed toward a beer triumph,[79] despite the admirable crusade by drys to stem the 3.2 tide. Garland thought beer would pile up a 200,000-vote majority. The
Reverend Mr. Penn of the Prohibition Thousand regarded his
opponent's forecast as a product of emotional intoxication

[76] *Daily Oklahoman,* July 2, 1933.
[77] *Ibid.,* July 3, 1933.
[78] *Ibid.,* July 5, 1933.
[79] In anticipation of victory, prospective wholesale dealers formed a per-
manent organization, the Beer Distributors Association of Oklahoma. See
ibid., July 1, 1933.

which had momentarily obscured his good sense.[80] While he conceded a close election, righteousness, as in the past, would prevail. If the wets won by 200,000 votes, said another dry leader, it would be because 300,000 of his followers stayed at home,[81] or because the decent people of Oklahoma had been thoroughly confused by the injection of the economic issue into the campaign by mercenary wets. The *Baptist Messenger*, detecting evidence of public lethargy, tried to inspire members of the faith to go to the polls, and not heed the old argument of revenue. "Judas," said the *Messenger*, "sold our Lord for revenue but that one deed was the shame of the ages." The wicked brothers of Joseph did the same—but that did not justify their act.[82] In the considered opinion of one devout prohibitionist, if the state chose to adopt the infamous beer bill, then the church had decided to "believe in lies."[83]

The church may not have believed in lies, but Oklahomans did believe in beer. The 3.2 referendum carried by an impressive vote of 224,598 to 129,582.[84] Even the weather on the day of the election conspired against the drys. Temperatures throughout the state ranged above the century mark, with Oklahoma City recording a blistering 107 degrees, the highest in forty-three years for that particular day. Thus, predictions of an extremely heavy vote proved too optimistic. Failure of voters to turn out in great numbers was taken as an indication of lack of interest by some observers; but wets contended that many drys stayed at home rather than vote against a popular bill. Prohibitionists blamed the band wagon movement for keeping their usually faithful at home. The stunned Reverend A. M. Jayne of Prohibition Thousand, admitting a "knockout," lamented in a democratic spirit that "if the

[80] *Ibid.*, July 2, 1933.
[81] Norman *Transcript*, July 3, 1933.
[82] *Baptist Messenger*, July 6, 1933.
[83] *Daily Oklahoman*, July 10, 1933.
[84] *Directory and Manual of . . . Oklahoma, 1961*, 1962.

majority of the people want suds the rest of us will have to sit back until they are weaned away from the appetite."[85]

Beer commanded a wide following throughout the state. A total of only twenty counties of the seventy-seven returned dry (anti-beer) majorities: Alfalfa, Beaver, Cotton, Custer, Dewey, Grant, Greer, Harmon, Harper, Jackson, Jefferson, Kiowa, Major, Payne, Roger Mills, Texas, Tillman, Washita, Woods, and Woodward.[86] By and large, western Oklahoma with its relative absence of large towns presented an arid front except in a precious few spots where beer won by small majorities. Significantly, the beer forces had centered their greatest attention in those areas of heaviest population. All of the eastern and central counties, excluding Payne, a WCTU stronghold, went for 3.2. The crushing blow, however, came from the large cities. In Oklahoma City the referendum carried by at least 4 to 1 in each ward, and in Tulsa only one precinct in the entire county voted dry; Muskogee piled up an even more impressive victory.[87] It was highly possible, one student of the election has concluded, that "most of the voting in [many areas] was done by convinced wets while indifferent drys stayed at home."[88] Unquestionably, although many urbanites were recently arrived rustics, the impersonalization of the city and lessening influence of the churches had their effects. Whatever, Oklahoma was now the thirty-seventh state to sanction beer since its relegalization by Congress.

The election did not terminate the fiery controversy over "suds." Governor Murray held that beer was not legal until he officially issued the results of the vote. But Attorney Gen-

[85] *Daily Oklahoman*, July 12, 1933; also *Baptist Messenger*, July 20, 1933.

[86] One of the best accounts of the election is found in the Tulsa *Tribune*, July 12, 1949.

[87] For brief surveys of the election, see Tulsa *World*, July 13, 1933; Tulsa *Tribune*, July 12, 1933; and *Daily Oklahoman*, July 12 and 13, 1933.

[88] Mertz, "Year of Repeal, 1933," 143.

eral J. Berry King, a Murray antagonist, maintained that the bill became effective the moment the people approved it. Always jealous of his prerogatives, and determined that "Oklahoma will not have beer until I say so," the Governor went to bed the night of July 11 convinced that if the state had waited twenty-six years for brew, it could wait until Bill Murray decided to act.[89] Thousands of carloads of 3.2 stood on Oklahoma tracks consigned to other states, but awaited immediate diversion. To prevent any premature actions, the Governor declared martial law and then called out the National Guard in Oklahoma City to patrol all railway yards. Taking his own time, the executive procrastinated during the morning of July 12, but finally he called R. C. Garland to his office and gave him the honor of verifying the election with the state election board.[90] Later in the day, "Alfalfa Bill" lifted military law; and thirsty citizens who had gathered at the yards in Oklahoma City began to drink the brew frantically as workers unloaded it. More than two and one-half decades of drought produced a momentary lack of restraint which some wets considered entirely excusable, but drys a sinful shame.

The legislature had yet to pass an enforcement and administrative measure. The beer bill itself provided that manufacturers pay a state tax of $2.50 a barrel and a license fee of $1,000; wholesalers and retailers were to pay $250 and $100 respectively. The enforcement bill established a number of regulatory features. Brewers were permitted to sell only to wholesalers who had to purchase a license for each of their distribution points. The legislature gave the Oklahoma Tax Commission authority to collect all taxes, and to require the keeping of records by manufacturers, distributors, and re-

89 *Daily Oklahoman*, July 12, 1933.
90 Mertz, "Year of Repeal, 1933," 140.

tailers. For violation of federal and state liquor laws or the beer act, licenses could be revoked.[91]

When the legislature adjourned July 15, 1933, wets had every reason to rejoice in their hard-won victories. For the first time since statehood, they had been able to modify the state constitution indirectly by permitting the sale of "non-intoxicating" 3.2 beer. Likewise, a bill establishing a convention to ratify the Twenty-first Amendment had been approved, but before the Sooner State could act, the Eighteenth Amendment had gone into eclipse. Had Oklahoma expressed its will on the amendment, there is much to suggest its conformity to the rest of the nation. Yet, one thing remained certain; the prohibition bastion in Oklahoma still displayed strength, and even if the people of the state had accepted a half-way measure in the beer bill, it was not because they looked forward to repeal and hard liquor. It would take many more years before wets pushed Sooners off the dry beach into the fast flowing liquor stream which by then carried forty-eight states along in its swift current.

[91] Both the Enforcement Act and the Beer Act may be found in *Session Laws*, 1933, 338–44 and 478–90 respectively.

VIII

LIBERALITY STIFLED: ERA OF REFERENDA

THE VICTORY of Oklahoma wets in 1933 in legalizing beer encouraged a false sense of power which deluded them into thinking that the state would willingly sip from the fountain of hard liquor. The sixteen years following 1933 saw the apostles of drink press valiantly, yet vainly, for the resurrection of John Barleycorn. While prohibitionists triumphed at the polls in the three repeal elections held in the state during the period 1936–49, keen observers noted the small but gradual decline in the percentage of their votes. This development could be attributed to such factors as steadily increasing urbanism, the influence of the national tendency toward legalized liquor, and also a more permissive attitude among Sooners which esteemed a person's right to imbibe or not to imbibe.

By mid-century, however, the wet forces had been unable to work their will completely upon a rural Protestant populace inseparably welded to years of tradition. Moreover, by dominance of the legislature, drys easily rebuffed wets in their attempts at legalization of alcohol. Prohibitionists' control over the state's governors also reinforced their strength.

Indeed, it is highly significant that from 1907 to 1958, only one chief executive, E. W. Marland, boldly advocated outright repeal. Ill-advised, Marland thoroughly misread public sentiment in 1936—and dearly he paid. Dry forces brought to bear upon his political ambitions the full weight of their righteous wrath; never, they said, would the "traitor" to the "cause" again hold office. Marland's very unusual, and suicidal, stand clearly attests that the overwhelming majority of Oklahoma politicians, whether at the state or local level, regarded repeal as "too hot to handle."

The first few years following 1933 saw a number of abortive repeal efforts. Not until 1936 was the Oklahoma Temperance League able to bring the issue before the people. Representing principally hotel and restaurant interests, and encouraged by Governor Marland, the league employed a former judge, George S. Henshaw, to devise a control bill. Besides his service on the bench, Henshaw had been corporation commissioner and an assistant attorney general. As a distinguished member of the Oklahoma Constitutional Convention, he had, oddly enough, voted to include the prohibition provision in the state constitution. But by 1936 deplorable conditions in Oklahoma had thoroughly convinced him that the most sensible way to regulate the traffic in intoxicants was to place them under state control.[1]

The proposal drafted by the Judge mirrored Governor Marland's ideas as well as his own. Under the projected plan the Governor would appoint three "temperance commissioners" who would have authority to set up a liquor monopoly and establish state wholesale liquor warehouses; but private business would handle retail sales. The commissioners would also fix the margin of profit; in short, the retail price of whisky would be, to a large degree, a state determination.

[1] An informative sketch of Judge Henshaw appears in the Tulsa *Tribune*, November 1, 1936.

It was left to the legislature to designate administrative officials, to establish a schedule of taxation, and to set license fees. The Henshaw bill spelled out the distribution of tax revenues, allocating most of them to the general fund and to old-age pensions. The proposed law permitted hotels and restaurants to sell intoxicants by the drink when served with meals, but otherwise the bill limited the distribution of liquors to sealed packages. Finally, the measure allowed for the creation of a "temperance court of appeals" composed of nine district judges selected by the chief justice of the Oklahoma Supreme Court.[2]

By April, 1936, the Temperance League had successfully circulated initiative petitions. With roughly 155,000 signatures, more than 60,000 in excess of the required number, repealists hoped to bring the issue forward at the second state primary, July 28.[3] Drys, to the surprise of no one, said they would seek to delay official certification of the petitions and, hence, the election. Such a challenge, of course, implied the laborious task of examining each signature and the taking of testimony, and a possible appeal to the state supreme court. Should the wets survive this ordeal, the fate of the referendum would then reside with the Governor; and Governor Marland, after his election, had closely allied himself with the repealists, although in April, 1936, he had not yet publicly declared for the Henshaw measure. If the petitions received certification, Marland had declared he would give the people a chance to vote on the continuance of prohibition "the first opportunity after the July 7th primary."[4] Since the Governor had pledged not to let repeal mar the issues of the

2 The best digest of the proposed constitutional amendment is in *Harlow's Weekly*, January 11, 1936; but see also the "Prohibition Leaflets" in the Redmond C. Cole Collection, University of Oklahoma Library.

3 *Harlow's Weekly*, May 2, 1936.

4 *Ibid.*

general election in November, the first opportunity was the July 28 primary, exactly what wets wanted.

Prohibitionists had begun to close ranks in 1935 in anticipation of an onslaught upon their dry Sooner edifice. In that year, Mrs. Elizabeth House, president of the WCTU, called together sixty-three religious and civic leaders who assembled at the Blue Room of the State Capitol and formed the United Oklahoma Dry Association, an agency designed to direct and co-ordinate the efforts of dry groups.[5] Mrs. House still vividly recalls that "Marland really was not behind us."[6] For the next sixteen years the United Oklahoma Drys became the major guiding force in the Oklahoma prohibition movement. After the 1936 election it experienced a decline in enthusiasm and the group almost faded, but in 1940 it was reconstituted to ward off another attack from wets. Nine years later it was reorganized as the United Dry Association.[7] Close analysis reveals that United Dry leadership came chiefly from the clergy. In sixty of the seventy-seven counties in 1956, for example, ministers served as chairman; and of the remaining seventeen positions, ten were vacant, while the other seven were held by persons outside the clergy.[8]

Drys viciously assailed the Henshaw plan from every possible angle. But the one single issue which they advanced most vigorously was the possibility of corruption in state government through manipulation of the liquor-control machinery. For the state to place complete authority in the hands of an appointive commission would open the doors to "the biggest

[5] Personal interview with Mrs. Elizabeth House, Stillwater, May 20, 1966.

[6] *Ibid.* For comment on the drys and Marland, see John Joseph Mathews, *Life and Death of an Oilman*, 232.

[7] Tulsa *World*, April 12, 1940, and *Oklahoma Dry*, April, 1947. To lessen confusion, both groups will be referred to as the United Drys.

[8] *Oklahoma Dry*, January–February, 1956. Issues of this publication may be found in the files of the Sooner Alcohol and Narcotic Education Association at Bethany, Oklahoma.

political graft the state has ever known."[9] Inevitably, it was contended, money from distillers would flow readily into the state to ensure the election of a governor partial to their interests.[10] The Lawton *Constitution* and the Bartlesville *Examiner* accepted this speculative view, adding that the Henshaw proposal clothed the commission "with the power of a Czar."[11] With such sweeping authority, commented the Oklahoma City *Times*, "it is ridiculous to presume that the commission would fail to recognize and use its political power."[12]

Prohibitionists also deplored the wets' idea of attaching repeal to the old-age pension program. Receipts from liquor, said they, would provide only a small portion of the amount needed for the old-timers, and those who believed differently were sadly mistaken. The Reverend Claude Hill of the United Drys characterized the repealists' attempt to capitalize upon the misery of the aged by allocating liquor revenue to the pension system nothing short of sinful deception. Such unholy tactics, chimed the *Baptist Messenger*, could be expected from wets, for they were, by far, the most "unashamed set of liars" ever seen.[13] Senior citizens should not become overjoyed. "In the first place," observed the Reverend Mr. Hill, "there would not be any [money] left after the salaries and expenses of the political machine were paid." And even if there were, "God help us if we can only take care of our old people by taking . . . bread and milk from the mouths of children."[14] What the petition should have provided for, said the drys,

9 See the statement of the Reverend Claude Hill, eastern director of the United Drys, in *Harlow's Weekly*, May 30, 1936.

10 *Ibid.*; and Tulsa *Tribune*, November 1, 1936.

11 See the statements of the *Constitution* and the *Examiner* in *Harlow's Weekly*, February 15 and May 30, 1936.

12 *Ibid.*, May 30, 1936.

13 *Baptist Messenger*, September 24, 1936.

14 *Harlow's Weekly*, May 30, 1936.

was the care of families impoverished because of drinking husbands.

Other objections drys had voiced continuously since statehood. Repeal occasioned increased deaths on the highways, corrupted youth,[15] fostered more bootlegging, damaged the economy, and encouraged unrestrained lawlessness. If Oklahoma did not want a return to the saloon and brass-rail days which had been the shame of Oklahoma Territory, then the Henshaw dragon had to be slain. The Sapulpa *Herald* conveyed the spirit of traditionalism which had helped to keep the state in the dry column when it extolled the virtues of prohibition, and cautioned that "now is not the time to begin experimenting."[16] To the most hardened drys, liquor was a veritable menace, and a decided boom to anarchy.

The Henshaw plan dissatisfied a substantial group of wets, who joined drys in urging its defeat. Judge Robert L. Williams, who had grown critical of the state's prohibition policy, had long urged a good liquor bill, but he turned his back on this particular proposal. Williams felt that the Henshaw plan would result in irreparable injury to the state, would virtually "destroy [Oklahoma] as a part of the Republic," and would lead inevitably to the creation of a corrupt political machine.[17] Criticism such as this from one who had previously endorsed legalization of intoxicants created a serious impediment to wet ambitions. Likewise, the critical attitude of many out-of-state liquor interests, to whom repealists looked for financial support, proved equally as discouraging. Fear existed among some of them that the liquor commission would exclude their brands from the Oklahoma market; so why aid an undertaking which offered nothing definite or, in the case of liquor wholesalers, actually denied them profits?[18]

[15] Presbyterian *Minutes*, 1936, 13.

[16] *Harlow's Weekly*, February 15, 1936.

[17] See Williams' statement reprinted in part in *Baptist Messenger*, July 16, 1936.

The most ardent defender of the Henshaw plan besides its author and the Temperance League was Governor Marland, whose political fortunes became inextricably interwoven with its fate. Before he took office, drys had regarded Marland with suspicion after he had offended one of their workers who tried to force him to sign a pledge. After he entered the senatorial race in 1936 (the second year of his incumbency as governor), most people assumed that he dared not risk his political fortunes on as potentially destructive an issue as repeal. They miscalculated. No one can be certain when Marland planned his coup against the dry regime, although early in his administration there had been rumors of his contact with wets, notably Henshaw. Convinced by his own logic that the people wanted to journey another step farther than they had in 1933, and that the state would adopt a "new deal" for an antiquated social policy, he gambled with his political ambitions when a noncommittal stand would have been expedient, if not prudent. The Frederick *Leader*, among other papers, admired Marland's courage and willingness to sacrifice himself to principle, but questioned his political sagacity in embracing the repeal program.[19]

Boldly breaking with time-honored precedents set by his predecessors, Governor Marland made his position unmistakably clear. The prohibition section of the constitution had outlived its usefulness—it must be scrapped. "Personally," he said,

> I am in favor of repeal. This is not a question of a wet or a dry state. Oklahoma is already wet, as wet, if not wetter, than the states where prohibition has been repealed. The ques-

[18] J. W. Williamson, executive secretary of the United Drys, charged near the end of the initiative campaign that wets were raising money by promising a monopoly of the liquor business in several counties to certain persons. The statement, however, was never confirmed. See the Tulsa *Tribune*, October 4, 1936.

[19] *Harlow's Weekly*, February 15, 1936.

tion is, who shall get the profits from the handling and sale of liquor—the state or the bootlegger? Prohibition was a beautiful dream—one of those noble experiments that wouldn't work. Whether the repeal measure will carry or not I do not care to hazard a guess. Many of the finest men and women in the state are for prohibition. Many of the voters who favor repeal will not bother to vote on the subject of repeal because . . . liquor is plentiful in Oklahoma and cheaper . . . than in other states, because it does not pay a state tax. The state is being deprived . . . of millions of dollars that it should have instead of the bootleggers.[20]

Some commentators saw the Governor's advocacy of the Henshaw bill as a serious blunder in his bid for a Senate seat. All of the major contenders for the Democratic nomination, namely Josh Lee and Gomer Smith, bore the dry label, as did the incumbent, Senator Thomas Gore.[21] Each of them was expected to join the United Drys in its resolute endeavor to turn back repeal, and thus capitalize upon Marland's commitment to the wets. The candidate with the most to gain, however, from the Governor's forthright avowal was Josh Lee, devoted churchman and ardent dry.

Marland sought to minimize the dangers to his candidacy by his refusal to campaign actively for the Henshaw bill prior to the July 7 primary. In an apparent effort to erect additional safeguards, it will be recalled, he had postponed the repeal election until the second primary. The Governor noted that he did not desire the election to become confusing since other referenda were up for a vote.[22] The critical *Daily Oklahoman*,

20 *Ibid.*, May 30, 1936. For clarity, paragraphing has been omitted.

21 Mrs. House admitted that the WCTU occasionally had to "prod" politicians. She recalled that once Gore "thought of refusing" an invitation to one of the women's banquets. She advised Gore to "show up." He replied "buy two tickets for Gore." House interview, May 30, 1966.

22 *Harlow's Weekly*, April 11, 1936. The most important referenda scheduled for the July 7 primary related to general welfare and perpetuation of

in observing Marland's reason for the postponement, surmised that he "had rather go into the senate campaign at this stage of the race without liquor as an issue and the drys actively fighting him." The editor of the paper believed that Marland cleverly contrived his move to deal a blow to the dry Josh Lee.[23] But was it politically wise for the Governor to exclude the issue from the first primary, and then announce its prospective presentation at the second? What if he and the prohibitionist Lee met in the runoff with repeal on the ballot?

Results of the first primary left Marland with some hope, but with even greater problems. The final tally showed that Lee had out-distanced the Governor by a vote of 168,030 to 121,433. Smith came in third with 119,585 votes, while the incumbent Gore received only 91,581 votes.[24] Now Marland faced the dilemma he had taken little care to avoid—a runoff with Lee and repeal on the same ballot.

Again the Governor acted decisively. Quickly reversing himself, he announced that the initiated proposal would not be placed on the ballot, and that it was unlikely if a vote would ever be held during his incumbency.[25] Both wets and drys criticized Marland's action, accusing him of trying to advance his own political stock in violation of sacred promise. In defense the embattled senatorial candidate retorted that dissatisfaction with the Henshaw plan in both groups motivated his decision. The Ponca City *News* accepted the Governor's response as a tacit admission that the repeal proposal had encountered general opposition and had become a piercing thorn in his political side. But the *News* asserted that "postponing the election is not going to soften [things]," for

the Conservation Commission. See *Directory and Manual of Oklahoma, 1961*, 194–95.

23 *Daily Oklahoman*, April 10, 1936.

24 *Directory and Manual of Oklahoma, 1961*, 64.

25 *Harlow's Weekly*, July 4–11, 1936.

the Governor. Repeal belonged to Marland: "He had it written, accepted it, presented it to the public and has supported it."[26]

If the propriety of removing repeal from the ballot stimulated debate, so did the constitutional issues it raised. The state constitution did not clearly specify the procedure for presentation of initiated petitions, but a 1916 statute decreed that they should be submitted to the people for approval or rejection at the next regular election. But it also stipulated that the governor had the power, at his discretion, to call a special election to vote upon such questions, or to designate the mandatory primary election as a special election for that purpose.[27] The language of the law gave the governor much latitude. Those who would force Marland to bring repeal to a vote in accordance with the constitution overlooked the option he could exercise.

Ultimately, the state supreme court resolved the controversy. Drys sought to force the Governor and the state election board to place the issue on the July 28 ballot. Even a few wets wanted to get it over. Naturally the supporters of Josh Lee still considered a vote to their advantage, despite Marland's half-hearted attempts to divorce himself momentarily from the liquor-control plan. The supreme court, however, in a 5 to 4 decision ruled in the Governor's favor—that the primary was not a general election and that it could not order him to submit the question.[28] Marland's success, nevertheless, did not long endure. In the runoff primary, Lee trounced the "wet New Dealer" 301,259 to 186,899.[29] From the beginning his chances of defeating Lee appeared slim, but there is much to suggest that the campaign in behalf of repeal,

[26] *Ibid.*, July 18, 1936.

[27] *Session Laws*, 1916, 89.

[28] *State ex rel, Williamson et al.* vs. *Carter, Secretary of State, et al.*, 177 Okla. 384.

[29] *Directory and Manual of Oklahoma, 1961*, 64.

and the effort to keep it off the ballot, increased the vote against him.[30]

The shattering disaster at the polls did not end the Governor's problems. From the outset he opposed a vote on repeal at the general election, lest the liquor issue obscure more important economic problems and also adversely affect the Democratic party. Many Oklahomans remembered too well Roosevelt's "dripping wet" position in 1932, and no assurance existed that their political vengeance would not arrive belatedly. The only alternative to the general election in November was a costly special election, which repealists preferred and drys detested. In determining a date Governor Marland solicited the co-operation of the state press in ascertaining the will of the people.

The chief executive's request left him open for criticism. The Poteau *News Democrat*, like many other state papers, refused to run a poll of its readers on the advisability of a special election and emphatically proclaimed that it would not help the Governor "pull a [single] chestnut from the [fiery] furnace." The Hollis *Daily News* informed him that the people of Harmon County "didn't give a continental whether you call a special election on the liquor question." The Ponca City *News* dismissed the whole thing as a "mess," and the Guthrie *Leader* charged that Marland sought to make "goats" of the newspapers. The more considerate Frederick *Leader* tried to lessen the Governor's fear that repeal would hurt FDR at the general election. The issue in the national campaign, said the *Leader*, involved economic matters which concerned the daily lives of every person, and voters would not vent their feelings upon the Democratic nominee over a

[30] Scales, "Political History of Oklahoma," 382–83. Lee went on to defeat the Republican candidate, Herbert Hyde, a political dry, by more than 260,000 votes. Both ignored the debates on the Henshaw bill after declaring against it. The best discussion of the campaign is found in Monroe L. Billington, *Thomas P. Gore: The Blind Senator from Oklahoma*.

repeal bill already totally discredited.[31] Marland never made public the results from those papers which did co-operate in the poll, but his choice of the November election suggested the outcome.[32]

Statehouse politics gathered few new friends for the wet cause. The Tulsa *World* believed that Marland had hurt prohibition repeal by his own action and thus enabled the prohibitionists' leaders to force the petition upon the ballot at a time when they had the silent vote as an ally.[33] Try as he might in the month preceding the election to alter Sooner attitudes toward the Henshaw bill by exhorting that prohibition did not prohibit, and by a crackdown on bootlegging, Marland and other wets made little headway.[34] At one point he threatened to request of the legislature an act declaring it a crime to *purchase* liquor if repeal failed. Few took him seriously; and those who did knew that such a bill would never get past the hopper of the legislature, even if there were a brave soul foolish enough to introduce it. Moreover, legislators did not eagerly welcome the opportunity to write their own colleagues' jail sentences.

Wets did add one major ally to their ranks a few weeks before the election—the retail beer dealers.[35] Threats to 3.2 beer by the WCTU and the Anti-Saloon League prompted the alliance more than did any high regard for the Henshaw bill. In June, 1936, the spirited WCTU held its national con-

[31] Excerpts from various papers found in *Harlow's Weekly*, September 19, 1936.

[32] Many wets believed that Marland abandoned them by delaying a vote and by his refusal to call a special election.

[33] *Harlow's Weekly*, October 17, 1936.

[34] One dry seriously suggested that the Governor call in the National Guard if state authorities could not stop the sale of liquor; but the United Drys believed they could accomplish the job if authorized. See the Tulsa *Tribune*, October 15, 1936; and for a related comment, Mathews, *Death of an Oilman*, 253.

[35] Tulsa *Tribune*, October 13, 1936.

vention in Tulsa and went on record as favoring action against "nonintoxicating" brew once the women defeated the Henshaw bill.[36] The rising demand for stronger beer, according to some 3.2 spokesmen, also entered in as another factor encouraging support of hard liquor. The inability to supply a more potent beverage under the present law, they explained, had led to increased violations, as evidenced by the 2,700 persons in Oklahoma who possessed federal liquor stamps.[37]

At the November election the people turned down the Henshaw bill 391,983 to 267,285.[38] By and large, wets depended upon the centers of population, but they only received sizable backing in the state's three largest cities, Oklahoma City, Tulsa, and Muskogee. The few eastern counties in the state which piled up majorities for repeal were more than counterbalanced by those of the traditionally arid west.[39] The meaning of the election was clear: the people of Oklahoma simply could not accept the badly drawn Henshaw measure, and, more importantly, the state was not ready for any kind of liquor-control plan. The provisions of the initiated petition did not alone spell its doom, they only increased the margin of defeat.

Nearly four years elapsed before the battered wets fully recuperated from the beating of the Marland era. Recovery was greatly hastened by the elevation of Leon "Red" Phillips to the statehouse. Phillips coyly clouded his true identity, at times appearing both wet and dry. During the fight over the Twenty-first Amendment, he had stood directly in the dry's path. The Anti-Saloon League had also accused him of stalling the Murray program in the Fourteenth Legislature until the

[36] House interview, May 20, 1966. The seven hundred women who attended the convention set aside a special time to pray both silently and audibly for the defeat of repeal.

[37] Tulsa *Tribune*, October 15, 1936.

[38] *Directory and Manual of Oklahoma, 1961*, 195.

[39] See *Daily Oklahoman* and Tulsa *World*, November 4, 1936.

beer bloc had its way.[40] But when "Red" Phillips ran for governor, his stance was that of any other politician who recognized the power of the church vote.

Phillips carried out such an impressive enforcement crusade during his first year in office, it even struck fear in the hearts of some hard-drinking drys. Not since the days when Lee Cruce personally took to raiding "honky-tonks" had the governor's office warred so violently against those predisposed to violate the law. So effective was Phillips in his drive that one dry official remarked that he "has accomplished more for us than any other governor."[41] In the summer of 1940, United States District Attorney Charles E. Dierker said that Oklahoma was drier than at any other time in the state's history.[42] Indeed, the Governor attacked the trade in intoxicants with such vigor that it appeared he was determined to impress indelibly upon the church people the reality of his ultra-dryness—that he was drier than any other Sooner, including Senator Josh Lee who would be up for re-election the year Phillips left the governor's office.[43]

A fundamental part of the executive's program consisted of a law enlisting federal assistance in the rigid enforcement of state prohibition. His first message to the legislature called for the enactment of a so-called permit statute in compliance with a congressional act passed in 1936 which aimed at excluding, with the aid of the central government, the importa-

[40] See the critical statement of W. J. Losinger of the Anti-Saloon League made after Phillips' election, in the Tulsa *World*, March 22, 1940.

[41] Undated clipping in prohibition scrapbook, Leon Phillips Collection, University of Oklahoma Library (hereafter cited as Phillips Collection prohibition scrapbook).

[42] *Ibid.*

[43] Lee had been swept into office by a flood of church votes. Phillips realized that if he were to run against Lee, he must gain their support, especially those of Lee's own Baptist denomination. Thus the Methodist governor set out through enforcement to win systematically the largest group of the Oklahoma church bloc.

tion of whisky from wet to dry territory.[44] The Oklahoma legislature approved the law with little debate. It gave the tax commission authority to issue permits for alcohol for scientific and medicinal purposes, and wines for religious services.[45] Subsequent to its passage, the bill became the object of a test case in which its unconstitutionality was alleged; the Oklahoma Supreme Court, however, upheld the act.[46]

Seemingly, Phillips had abandoned his wet friends. Some of the more astute and perceptive, nevertheless, realized that such a dramatic clean-up could play into their hands. Encouraged by what struck them as a grand opportunity, wets began to speak seriously of another repeal election. *If* they could acquire sufficient signatures, and *if* Phillips would, unlike any other governor, call a special election when the silent vote offered no disadvantage, *then* success would appear within their grasp. A little enforcement terror drummed up by the Governor would even help to push the state nearer the liquor oasis. Drys, however, placed complete faith in the Governor's sound judgment. W. R. Wallace, president of the Baptist Laymen's Association, reflected this confidence when he suggested that "wets will be fooled if they think Governor Phillips will aid them in their efforts to get a [special] vote on repeal."[47]

Wet intention to circulate a petition pushed Phillips to a definite stand. In late 1939 he rejected the idea of a special election, but he consented to have the issue decided at the same time other measures came forward for a vote.[48] If the

[44] A very extended discussion of the permit system is found in the Governor's message in Senate *Journal*, 1939, 156–61.

[45] *Session Laws*, 1939, 16–19.

[46] Enlisting federal aid in enforcement did not arrest liquor running into Oklahoma. As the editor of one journal stressed, "nothing short of a federal law making possession of tax-paid liquor in a prohibition state *prima facie* evidence of introduction of such liquor, will be of aid in Oklahoma." *Harlow's Weekly*, April 1, 1939.

[47] Undated clipping, Phillips Collection prohibition scrapbook.

[48] *Ibid.*; and Tulsa *World*, August 2, 1939.

initiated proposal, however, contained a provision earmarking revenue for schools or old-age benefits, Phillips vowed not to submit it. "I don't think repeal is the solution to the state's ... problems," said the leader of financially hard-pressed Oklahoma; the tax angle was "not the proper way to approach the liquor question."[49] To wets who had assured themselves of Phillips' active support of their plan because of its revenue features, his announcement came as an excruciating jolt.

On the other hand, drys were not happy with the Governor's statement. They preferred no election at all, and his willingness to submit the anticipated referendum at the primary justifiably revived old fears.[50] What irritated the prohibitionists was that Phillips allegedly broke a pre-election promise to place any liquor question on the *general election* ballot. Whether he made such a pledge or not is difficult to determine. The real difference between the Governor and his dry friends, who had so recently showered him with ego-satisfying praise, was one which revolved upon the conception of the executive's official duty—of whether the governor should respect a legally perfected petition or arbitrarily deny citizens the right to have it decided at the most convenient time. Drys maintained that whatever the executive did, his action should demonstrate an interest in the welfare of the state, which meant, of course, placing repeal up for a vote when wets would be at a disadvantage.

Phillips did gain some support for his stand. The dry Frederick *Leader* hailed the Governor's decision as fair and democratic. Phillips' personal convictions, said the *Leader*, did not prevent him from honoring the intent of the initiative and referendum sections of the constitution. An election at any time, the paper assured its readers, would "set the [liq-

[49] Tulsa *World*, August 2, 1939.

[50] See, for example, the statement by W. J. Losinger in Tulsa *Tribune*, November 15, 1939.

uor] advocates back on their haunches for another decade."
The Altus *Times Democrat* reviewed the Governor's accomplishments and joined in his defense; the castigation of Phillips was uncalled for and unfair. To refuse wets a chance at
the ballot box would be autocratic, exclaimed the Anadarko
News.[51] Drys, however, consumed with the desire to sustain
a policy they considered morally defensible and socially cred-
itable, failed to reckon with what their own reaction would
have been had they exchanged places with their hated opponents.

In January, 1940, Phillips deferred the election until November. Wets grieved, drys rejoiced. The Governor gave as
his reason the fact that the repeal group then circulating petitions, the Oklahoma Commission for Liquor Control, would
not have a proposal ready for the July primary. Further, he
denied that he had ever intimated any intention of placing
the issue on the ballot but, apparently, Phillips suffered from
momentary amnesia, for indeed he had once suggested that to
reporters.[52]

Unless wets mustered enough names for a valid petition,
previous squabbling over the election would remain purely
academic. In late 1939 the commission had selected C. A.
Cardwell of Oklahoma City to conduct its campaign. Cardwell
banked heavily upon the downward trend in revenues which
threatened to plunge the state into deeper economic hardship.
The amendment pushed by the commission allocated 90 per
cent of all liquor taxes to the general fund; the other 10 per
cent the commission set aside for enforcement. It permitted
the package sale of liquor as well as its distribution by the
drink in hotels, restaurants, and cafes. Counties could exercise
the choice of local option.[53] In May, 1940, Cardwell filed the

51 See summary of press opinion in *Harlow's Weekly*, November 18, 1939.
52 Undated clipping, Phillips Collection prohibition scrapbook.
53 Tulsa *Tribune*, December 5, 1939, and Tulsa *World*, January 28, 1940.

commission's amendment with the secretary of state. Although drys challenged the sufficiency of the petition, the secretary upheld its validity.

At the general election the state again rejected liquor for the fourth time; the control measure failed by a vote of 374,911 to 290,752.[54] Wets, however, witnessed a modest gain over their showing in 1936. Victory for the drys had resulted in no small part from the co-operative attitude of Governor Phillips. For the remainder of his term, he continued to give prohibitionists his unstinting support and to reject the wets' thesis that liquor revenues would signal an end to many of the state's economic difficulties. His view was best expressed in his special message to the legislature in March, 1941, when he told that body that repeal was "neither good business nor good government." Adopting an argument typical of any good dry, he told the Eighteenth Legislature it would be impossible to calculate "the broken lives . . . incident to legalizing intoxicating liquors in Oklahoma."[55]

Only four years had transpired between the "Battle of '36" and that of 1940, but it took nearly a decade for wets to again summon renewed strength to engage the drys. Their revived hope came in part from the success of repeal in Kansas, which in 1948 cast aside that state's noble experiment. Continued failure to obtain submission through a legislative referendum also inspired them in 1949 to resort to the commonly employed initiative process.

Characteristically, the repeal drive in 1949 gave rise to a new wet organization, the Oklahoma Economic Institute.

[54] *Directory and Manual of Oklahoma, 1961*, 198. Dissension plagued the wet camp prior to the election. C. A. Cardwell charged that the commission owed him more than $2,000. M. J. Rhinehart, president of the organization, alleged that he had been paid. Cardwell resigned, predicting defeat for the proposal. See Tulsa *World*, October 27, 1940.

[55] See Governor Phillips' statement to the legislature in House *Journal*, 1941, I, 1266–67.

Chartered in December, 1948, and composed principally of businessmen, it had as its leader, A. G. Kulp, an Oklahoma City attorney. Kulp clearly spelled out the institute's policy: there would be no attempt to argue the evil or good of alcoholic beverage. "We certainly don't advocate their use," said the repealist, but "we simply cannot afford to continue a practice that is financing the underworld and depriving the state of revenue from taxation."[56] That wets chose not to attack the dry position militantly represented a clever approach, for they had finally come to realize that to do so cast them in the uncomfortable role of opposers of morality.

The institute could not completely omit, however, a refutation of many customary dry contentions. Where drys argued, for example, that drinking was an unfortunate lapse in morality, leaders of the institute described it as a disease incurable by prohibition.[57] When prohibitionists portrayed John Barleycorn as a callous and reckless destroyer of home and family, the repealists marshaled statistics showing that the divorce rate in Oklahoma exceeded the national average. Consumption of spirits under control would decrease, despite dry opinion to the contrary. Few things, they concluded, were worse than the present corruption and hypocrisy produced by prohibition.

The institute needed 100,000 names to place the issue on the ballot. The organization secured those in March, 1949, and submitted the petition to the secretary of state. David Shapard, attorney for the United Drys, asked for a ninety-day period to examine the signatures, a request immediately denied by the secretary. Unlike the previous amendments, the one drawn by the institute reposed almost complete authority

[56] *Daily Oklahoman*, December 25, 1948.

[57] "Don't Hide the Facts," a pamphlet prepared by the Oklahoma Economic Institute, in Leonard I. Pearlin, "An Application of Correlation Methods to the Results of the 1949 Prohibition Referendum," 21 (hereafter cited as Pearlin, "Results of the Prohibition Referendum").

in the legislature to "enact laws for the strict regulation, control, licensing, and taxation of the manufacture, sale and distribution of intoxicants . . . ." Significantly, it forever forbade the "open saloon" (bars) and empowered the legislature to define the term.[58]

Although the repeal amendment was unquestionably the best ever devised by any of the many wet groups, the United Drys found much to criticize. Shapard charged that it left no opportunity for the legislature to prohibit liquor anywhere in the state, thus excluding the possibility of local option. But Kulp answered that other states with similar laws, namely Kansas and Texas, permitted counties to vote out liquor. Drys also leveled fire at the section of the amendment which granted the legislature the right to define the term "open saloon."

Governor Roy Turner, who succeeded Robert S. Kerr, announced that he would put repeal on the same ballot with a bond issue at a *special election*. Irate drys accused the Governor of betraying their trust, just as they had Phillips before the 1940 election. According to the Reverend R. E. Holloman of the United Drys, Turner had told his people that "I will have nothing to do with repeal. It is no part of my program . . . ."[59] Turner explained his action by stressing that he called the election because the petition had been ruled valid and because he wanted to end the turmoil over the situation.

For the first time at a special election, the people of Oklahoma voted on repeal in September, 1949. Their response was the same as it had been in 1936 and 1940. For the third time in less than two decades, wets failed to convince Sooners of the necessity for change. Prohibition remained a part of the constitution, 323,270 to 267,870.[60] Wets had assumed that a

[58] *Daily Oklahoman*, September 24, 1949.

[59] *Baptist Messenger*, June 23, 1949. Wets had pushed for a referendum in the legislature but had failed.

large turnout would strengthen their chances. But in a very careful mathematical analysis of the 1949 vote, Leonard I. Pearlin has concluded that "the wets profited from the apathy of . . . non-voters. That is, it appears that if a larger proportion of voters had gone to the polls, the margin of defeat of the wets would have been greater."[61]

Of the state's seventy-seven counties, eleven approved the amendment. All but three of those (Muskogee, Comanche, and Coal) border on either Oklahoma or Tulsa counties, the heaviest populated and the most urbanized. Those counties adjacent to states surrounding Oklahoma were the ones with the highest percentage of the dry vote, clearly a suggestion that persons close to legalized liquor felt no compulsion to vote for repeal. Conversely, Oklahomans who relied upon bootleggers or to whom liquor was not readily accessible inclined more toward the wet position.[62]

After the defeat of the 1949 referendum, wets pondered whether or not the state would ever abolish its hypocritical policy. Most discerning observers realized that the only possibility for change lay in a more liberal church attitude, expanding industrial and commercial activity, the continued growth of urban centers, and the emergence of courageous and dynamic political leadership. Only then would the old order pass, yielding place to the new.

[60] *Directory and Manual of Oklahoma, 1961*, 202. Observers had expected the legislative referendum authorizing the state to issue $36,000,000 in bonds to attract a huge vote.
[61] Pearlin, "Results of the Prohibition Referendum," 27.
[62] *Ibid.*, 36–73.

IX

AWAY WITH "SUDS": DRYS ATTACK BEER

PROHIBITIONISTS' successes in the years following 1933 sustained their faith in the worth of their cause and compelled them to strike out against the "drink of moderation." To drys, beer was alcohol, and the statute which legalized it as a nonintoxicating beverage, they said, perverted, if not contradicted, the antiliquor portion of the state constitution. Oklahoma needed a return to constitutionality by ridding it of sin-inspiring 3.2. After the approval of the beer bill in 1933, the Anti-Saloon League tried to accomplish this task, but faltered in the wake of the "beer mania" induced by the New Deal cry for revenue. By 1957 drys thought the time had come to oust beer from much, if not all, of the state. Advocates of beer, on the other hand, believed drys perceived nothing more than an old anti-3.2 illusion from pre-beer days.

Wets now took solace in the fact that beer constituted an item of considerable importance to the economy. Indeed the status of beer as a revenue-producing agent would become one of the most debated issues in the 1957 campaign for local option. Prior to the legalization of the beverage, it will be recalled, predictions of possible income from the sale of beer ranged all the way from nothing to $10,000,000 a year, depending on whether wets or drys did the predicting. Beer had fared well economically since 1933, but revenue never reached the inflated figures forecast by its proponents. The year following the adoption of 3.2, total tax collections came to slightly more than $700,000, and not until three years hence did they top $1,000,000.[1] Between 1938 and 1941, however, beer income dropped below this amount. Although it is difficult to assign reasons for this phenomenon, one may surmise that general economic conditions coupled with a slight decline in the state's population played at least a small role in this reduction.[2] By 1945 beer collections had reached the $2,000,-000 mark, an estimate which had been vigorously paraded before the people by some wets. Six years later the state for the first time received an income from beer beyond $6,-000,000; subsequently, it never fell below this figure. In the year immediately preceding the prohibitionists' crusade to return Oklahoma to sobriety, taxes from beer stood at $6,330,-541, which totaled 2.89 per cent of all tax receipts.[3] Although beer revenue did not match that of some commodities—cigarettes, for example—it proved an arduous job for drys to dispel the notion that money from 3.2 was not an important item in the state budget.

Throughout the early 1940's drys pressured the legislature to outlaw beer or to limit its distribution to only package sales. None of the measures presented in the legislature drew serious

[1] See summary table No. 1, "Tax Collections from Principal Sources from 1916 to 1956," in Oklahoma Tax Commission, *Twelfth Biennial Report*, 1956, 14.

[2] In 1930, Oklahoma had a population of 2,396,040 compared to 2,336,434 ten years later, which represented a 2.5 per cent decrease. The next decade saw a greater dip, with a decrease of 4.4 per cent. See Bureau of the Census, *Census of Population: 1950*, Vol. II, *Characteristics of the Population*, pt. 36, *Oklahoma*, 36–39.

[3] Oklahoma Tax Commission, *Twelfth Biennial Report*, 1956, 14.

attention, and consequently failed.[4] In 1949 the United Drys
adopted as its major program the achievement of local option,
and the organization informed beer interests of its intention
to wage a determined campaign until that had been achieved.[5]
A few years later a leading Oklahoma clergyman, the Reverend Roy E. Holloman, again emphasized the immediate ur-
gency of restricting 3.2 when he noted that "beer consumption
has increased at an alarming rate" and that more beer establishments dotted the Oklahoma terrain than schools or
churches. According to the minister's own statistics, in 1951
there were 4,219 beer taverns in Oklahoma compared to 3,200
churches and 2,543 schools.[6] David Shapard, echoing the same
sentiments, put it bluntly—"beer must go."[7]

In the 1950's ever vigilant drys continued to insist upon
restrictive action in every session of the legislature. The clos-
est they came to success was in 1955 when the house approved
a referendum which prohibited the sale of 3.2, but the senate
never voted on the measure.[8] Importantly, one of the anti-
beer bills introduced in the senate in this period came from
Senator Raymond Gary of Madill, who in 1955 won the governorship and threw the full force of his office behind the United
Dry program.[9]

Their legislative ambitions smashed, drys turned to an old
method previously employed by wets in the prohibition movement—the initiative. In June, 1955, Dr. Stanley Niles, executive secretary of the United Drys, announced the circulation
of a petition calling for a vote on a constitutional amendment
for local option at a special election. Prohibitionists, he said,

[4] The best summary of legislation during this period is Dwayne W. Sterling,
"The Repeal of Prohibition in Oklahoma," 5.

[5] *Daily Oklahoman*, November 17, 1949.

[6] *Baptist Messenger*, April 19, 1951.

[7] *Ibid.*

[8] House *Journal*, 1955, 874.

[9] Sterling, "Repeal of Prohibition," 5–6.

would also seek to outlaw advertising in dry counties if the amendment passed and to require a bond for trucks which moved through dry areas. Governor Gary gave the petition his strong endorsement. An ardent dry, Gary noted that the initiative was necessary since the legislature would not approve a local-option bill.[10]

With visions of victory, drys opened their campaign in October, 1955. Niles predicted his group would have 200,000 names affixed to its petition, although only 90,000 were needed. The Board of Directors of the Baptist General Convention pledged its membership alone to 100,000.[11] Significantly, one of the most prominent members of that faith, namely the Governor, adopted the United Dry program as his program, and as a gesture of his allegiance, he officially proclaimed October, "Temperance Month."[12] Presbyterians, who regarded the drinking of all alcoholic beverages as "a character-destroying personal indulgence, and as a betrayal of social responsibility," urged ministers to preach the evils of intemperance. But the church subtly displayed a growing liberality within its ranks in discreetly admonishing "that all members of our churches should *if their conscience allows them to do so, sign the petition.*"[13] The ladies of the WCTU, however, interested themselves in signatures despite conscience, and they set up booths at the Oklahoma City and Tulsa state fairs. Out-of-state assistance also came from the

10 *Daily Oklahoman,* June 12, 1955.

11 At first glance this figure may look large. Assuming, however, that only one-third of the Baptists signed the petition, the number could have been obtained, for in 1956 the church had 399,255 parishioners. Methodists had the next largest group, with 206,523, followed by the Disciples of Christ and the Presbyterians (USA), with 99,032 and 36,321 respectively. Membership in non-fundamentalist churches came to slightly more than 100,000 out of a total of 1,000,000 persons who had their names on the church rolls. Statistics from *Baptist Messenger,* March 7 and March 21, 1957.

12 *Daily Oklahoman,* October 10, 1955.

13 Presbyterian *Minutes,* 1955, 17. Italics are those of the author.

National Temperance League, which sent speakers to Oklahoma.[14] Prohibitionists had launched a co-ordinated offensive calculated to blast the state back to "normalcy."

As expected, drys encountered little trouble in getting the requisite number of signatures. That they were only able to acquire 137,500, not the predicted 200,000, represented an omen yet unclear. The beer industry, organized under the name of Oklahoma United and led by M. F. Dykema, immediately protested the petition in behalf of a Lawton distributor.[15] Accordingly, the secretary of state, Andy Anderson, set February 9, 1956, for hearing objections to the measure.

Oklahoma United deemed the short period allotted by Anderson inadequate to check all the names on the local-option petition and thus asked for a continuance of the hearing.[16] Cognizant of the tremendous job which faced the beer industry, the secretary gave the organization an additional thirty days beyond the time originally scheduled. During the intervening period before the second hearing, Oklahoma United set up IBM machines in the secretary's office and continued its scrutiny of the petition.[17] On March 10, 1956, the date of the second hearing, wets pleaded for another delay on the ground that they had been able to invalidate 28,000 names and that this percentage of the total warranted a postponement. The secretary, however, was no longer amenable to another extension. He reasoned that no matter what his final decision, the loser would appeal to the state supreme court; thus, he gave the petition his approval on March 19, 1955.[18] With his

[14] *Baptist Messenger*, September 27 and October 13, 1955; and Sterling, "Repeal of Prohibition," 13–14.

[15] *Daily Oklahoman*, February 7, 1956.

[16] *Ibid.*, February 9, 1956.

[17] The petition also provided Oklahoma United with a valuable mailing list. Sterling, "Repeal of Prohibition," 17.

[18] *Daily Oklahoman*, March 20, 1955.

declaration began the long court battle which prevented a vote on local option for many months.

Oklahoma United appealed Anderson's decision to the Oklahoma Supreme Court in behalf of Jackson R. Webb, a beer distributor. Rowe Cook, Webb's attorney, contended in his brief that "the unreasonable and arbitrary" time limits set by the secretary had caused all work by the appellant "to be done piecemeal." Cook's most powerful argument, and one which created much difficulty for the justices, was that the drys' petition actually proposed a constitutional amendment in the form of a legislative act; therefore, it was "a complete legal nullity."[19] Cook, nevertheless, asked the tribunal to appoint a referee to check the petition *if* it ruled the proposal constitutional.[20]

From the beginning, the beer forces valued the importance of time, and they bargained for every precious minute through the legal process. By September, 1956, they had begun to fear the consequences of their stalling tactics. In a surprise move, which caught drys and practically everyone off balance, Cook requested the dismissal of his client's case. Prohibitionists envisioned a clever motive behind this legalistic maneuvering. And indeed the wets had soberly and very methodically charted their course: if the court threw out the case, the referendum would come up at the general election in November, 1956, where local option would have to acquire *a majority of all votes cast.*[21]

Wet strategy encountered two major obstacles. One of these represented the political craftsmanship of Governor Gary, who emphatically said he would not present the issue at the general election regardless of judicial action. Gary knew his prerogatives as governor, for the supreme court had already

19 *Ibid.*, March 29, 1955.

20 *Ibid.* and Sterling, "Repeal of Prohibition," 18.

21 *Daily Oklahoman*, September 26, 1956.

declared in the summer of 1956 that an executive could, if he desired, submit the issue at his discretion.[22] The second difficulty proceeded from an unexpected quarter. Wets could rationalize Gary's position or, at worst, dismiss it with a curse and a sigh of dismay. But it was not so easy for them to decipher the motives of one William Beardsley. Disclaiming any connection with drys or wets, Beardsley asked the court to grant him sixty days to check the sufficiency and legality of the local-option measure. Although the court denied the request, it delayed the election for at least another month, making a November vote practically impossible.

The supreme court rendered a decision on United's original motion in July, 1957. By that time wets had already conceded the validity of the proposal. In essence the court said that while the proposed amendment greatly resembled a legislative act which had once been proposed in the Oklahoma legislature, this similarity was by no means fatal to its submission.[23] The persistent Rowe Cook filed for a rehearing, which promptly drew a denial. The way now appeared clear for the election. Obviously the beer interests, had they reckoned it to their advantage, could have further delayed a vote through continued legal action, but they would have run the risk of alienating many neutral citizens. As some of the leading figures in the beer camp testified years after the campaign, the long delay had given them time to organize, raise funds, and test the patience of the drys.[24]

Governor Gary called the special election for December 3, 1957. His choice was not arbitrary, and it came only after a significant compromise agreement between drys and wets.[25] Dykema, president of Oklahoma United, wanted to avoid a

[22] The case has been examined *ibid.*, April 11, 1956.

[23] Sterling, "Repeal of Prohibition," 20.

[24] See interviews with various beer leaders *ibid.*, 22–23.

[25] The Governor's special proclamation found in the files of the Oklahoma Malt Beverage Association.

contest during the latter part of November when people were away for Thanksgiving or uninterested. Therefore, he asked Gary to postpone the election until a later date;[26] in return, he agreed to drop further litigation. The Governor put the suggestion of the December vote to George Miller, United Dry attorney, who had drafted the petition and defended it in the courts. Following consultation with Stanley Niles and others, Miller consented to the date advanced by Gary.[27] That the drys received the worst end of the compromise seems an inescapable conclusion. Had prohibitionists refused consent to the beer interests' proposal, thus forcing them to sustain their court fight, they could have capitalized upon adverse public sentiment which probably would have mounted against them. Most Oklahomans, as witnessed in the liquor referenda in the 1940's, believed that any issue with substantial backing demanded a hearing at the polls.

If the preceding two years following the filing of the United Dry petition had given birth to the unexpected, the few weeks prior to the election brought additional surprise. The politically conscious and verbally flamboyant George Miskovsky, state senator from Oklahoma County, apparently believing he possessed constitutional insights others lacked, detected grave defects in the local-option measure. On November 2, 1957, the eager Miskovsky filed a protest with the court, listing a number of things wrong with the dry measure. His most important objection was that it *did not amend* the prohibition provision of the state constitution. He proposed, therefore, to change the title so as to inform voters of the specific portion of the constitution being amended. In addition, he said the petition did not really authorize county option.[28] To question Miskovsky's good faith is to dismiss his possible honest in-

[26] *Daily Oklahoman*, October 2, 1957.
[27] *Ibid.*
[28] *Ibid.*, November 3, 1957.

tentions; to ignore his political ambitions is to misinterpret the nature of a politician.

The Miskovsky bombshell produced a curious, yet understandable, co-operative attitude between wets and drys. Both groups, now with their machinery in high gear, asked the court to dispose of the protest immediately. Miller of the United Drys tried to dispel any illusions about this mutual action, noting that "we don't want it to appear we are marching shoulder to shoulder . . . with the beer industry."[29] To clear all confusion, the Oklahoma Supreme Court finally drafted a ballot title of its own.

Impediments to the election had now been cleared away after two years of legal controversy. Wets had begun to formulate their strategy in October, 1957, at the Biltmore Hotel in Oklahoma City. Members of the executive committee of Oklahoma United adopted a three-pronged attack: they would concentrate on citizen groups, wives of beer employees, and business organizations.[30] Sound and dynamic leadership which could appeal to a large segment of the state came from George A. Fisher of Oklahoma City whom wets chose to handle their campaign. Fisher, vice-president of the American First Title and Trust Company of Oklahoma City, had also been connected with former Governor Roy Turner's campaign and had held a position in the Citizens for Eisenhower organization in 1956. A retired officer of the 45th Division and a recipient of Oklahoma's Distinguished Service Medal, Fisher brought to the hierarchy of Oklahoma United an enviable reputation. And very importantly, he was a church member who taught an adult Sunday school class at the Northwest Christian Church.[31]

[29] *Ibid.*, November 9, 1957.
[30] Sterling, "Repeal of Prohibition," 30.
[31] Biographical information on Fisher from *Daily Oklahoman*, October 7, 1957.

Drys, of course, had always prided themselves in an abundance of religious leadership. Mobilization for them, then, meant essentially three things: intensifying their church activities, disseminating educational materials, and raising money. The last of these posed a problem. At the end of 1956, the United Drys' financial report showed a deficit of $4,210.32.[32] Expenses for 1957 came to nearly $76,000, and only a little more than $35,000 of this amount was spent after October 1, 1957, the commencement of the dry campaign. Beyond any doubt, drys were never able to match the finances of the wets. One has to remember, however, that in the past it had been possible for prohibitionists to carry out a concerted attack without unusual outlays of money.[33] But in 1957 the difference in expenditures of the two antagonists figured prominently in the eventual outcome of the election. Indeed, it was a year when Christian leadership could not eclipse the power of money, wet strategy, and a community attitude which had become liberal enough to sanction the moderate "non-intoxicating beverage."[34]

As earlier suggested, if any one particular issue dominated the election debate, it was that of beer revenue and its worth to the state. Wets faced the task of persuading the public that money from 3.2 beer constituted an important and necessary item in the state's budget and that its legalized sale benefited other businesses. All during the campaign Oklahoma United repeatedly emphasized that local option would produce repercussions throughout Oklahoma and would take away a high annual payroll.[35]

[32] *Oklahoma Dry*, January–February, 1957.

[33] Sterling, "Repeal of Prohibition," 24–25.

[34] Compared to other citizens of the nation, Sooners consumed very little beer. In 1957, for example, Americans drank 15.7 gallons of beer per capita; Oklahomans consumed 8.4 gallons per capita. Wisconsin led all states with a per capita consumption of 25.5 gallons. See Ada *News*, October 19, 1957.

[35] Undated clipping, Oklahoma Malt Beverage files.

The letter section of the Oklahoma Malt Beverage Association files in Oklahoma City vividly reveals the effort expended by Fisher and his staff in presenting the revenue theme. In letters to real estate brokers and salesmen, for example, Fisher admonished them to "consider carefully the impact on [your] profession" if 3.2 met destruction. "Think of how many hundreds of business . . . vacancies there would be in Oklahoma towns." Lower purchasing power for homes, higher taxes, and mortgage delinquencies resulting from persons thrown out of jobs would all follow if the fanatical prohibitionists had their way. In correspondence to home builders, Oklahoma United noted that the building industry was already curtailed by the money situation and that it could not afford to lose any business.

Other illustrative letters reflected the determination and skill employed by the wets in projecting the tragedy to befall Oklahoma if drys prevailed at the polls in December. Unwittingly, prohibitionists could create hardships for practically every citizen. "County option on 3.2," the beer interests told state employees, "would mean that there would be fewer dollars to pay your salary with and less money for other state expenses"; and to ranchers, Fisher suggested that any loss of revenue in taxes from beer would lessen their chances of getting relief from sales taxes on seed, feed, and fertilizers. He informed woefully underpaid Oklahoma teachers that restrictions on beer would shatter their hopes of adequately financing the school system, the aged that the size of their welfare checks stood in jeopardy; and doctors that county option "is not consistent with an enlightened society."[36] Correspondence to other citizens and businesses pointed up with equal clarity the dire consequences of local option to their trade or profession.

Drys accused wets of deception, exaggeration, mercenary

[36] All letters cited above are in letter section, *ibid.*

objectives, and outright lies. The *Baptist Messenger*, commenting on the anticipated unemployment of 11,000 workers in the beer industry, thought it strange "to see [the wet crowd] shedding crocodile tears for [its] company employees." The wages they received were the lowest in the nation, wrote its editor; if workers had to find other employment in a more decent occupation, better for them. "County option," he continued, "may kick them into a [higher] income bracket." Wets were trying to deceive good, honest, God-fearing people.[37] Stanley Niles, laboriously trying to combat the emphasis upon dollars and cents, relied upon the drys' strongest deterrent to iniquity—morality: "How many men, women, and children," he asked, "are we willing to slaughter to keep Progress Brewing Company [the state's lone brewery in 1957] open, 5,000 tavern owners in business and a few tributary industries happy?"[38] Fisher and the beer interests had mastered the art of extravagant claims in asserting a state loss of nearly $11,000,000 from beer income; tax receipts really amounted to $6,000,000[39]—an insignificant sum.

Governor Gary did not fail his dry followers who had invested their faith in his wisdom. In fact Niles indicated after the election that "without Raymond's help I never would have gone into the thing [local-option fight]."[40] The Governor's alliance with the United Drys transcended purely political consideration, for he had long held that the state should *regulate* (prohibit) liquor (including beer) through its police power. He once admitted, however, that "there is no law on earth which can prevent a person from destroying homes," but he believed government had "an obligation to do everything possible to keep our citizens from developing a strong desire for

[37] *Baptist Messenger*, November 14, 1957.

[38] Stanley Niles, comp., *The Casebook for County Option for Ministers, County Officers and Other Workers*, 8.

[39] For the argument, see the *Baptist Messenger*, November 14, 1957.

[40] Sterling, "Repeal of Prohibition," 30–31.

intoxicants." Man alone could not discipline his appetites. "It's my impression," Gary once speculated, "few people can honestly be described as moderate drinkers. The fellow who so classifies himself may be moderate most of the time, but there will be occasions when he slips over into the excessive class."[41]

Gary's economic arguments against beer were just as direct as his moral pronouncements. In a radio address delivered the day prior to the election, he forcefully offered his rebuttal to wet contentions. State government did not need beer taxes: "I am telling you now, as Governor of Oklahoma," he told listening Sooners, "that we can support this government . . . without any tax on beer or whiskey." According to Gary, at the end of his first year in office there had been a surplus in the general fund of $7,000,000, and $18,000,000 the second. He blamed wets for utilizing scare tactics. The local-option vote, said he, had no direct bearing upon old-age pensions, homestead exemptions, teachers' salaries, highways, or anything else. The campaign for beer, "as is typical of that industry," was deliberately trying to mislead the people of Oklahoma.

Any contribution beer had made to state government, Gary viewed as totally negative. Three-point-two had forced his administration to spend additional funds on large relief rolls; it had brought increased crime, more automobile accidents, and, correspondingly, a greater burden upon the taxpayer. And, in the true tradition of Oklahoma prohibitionists, the Baptist Governor urged all those concerned with the state's welfare to "rise up and march to the polls by the thousands . . . carrying the Christian Flag, and uphold the cause of righteousness." His battle was that of the Lord's: "I am happy to stand on the side of 3,500 churches in opposition to

[41] *Oklahoma Dry*, July, 1957, and Purcell *Register*, July 25, 1957.

a commodity that is causing [destruction to homes] and . . . young people to wind up in a life of crime."[42]

Beer leaders had no personal quarrel with the Governor, or any other dry, but they did question the validity of his factual statements. Fisher took the executive to task over his "poor arithmetic." At one point Gary had denied that beer contributed nearly $37,000,000 a year to the state in wages and taxes. Fisher said that the beer industry had a payroll of $26,000,-000 annually, and it paid excise taxes totaling more than $6,000,000, which constituted the fifth largest to that fund. Furthermore, beer paid state, county, corporation, ad valorem, and other kinds of taxes which exceeded $5,000,000. If Gary did not need the money, why had it been necessary for his administration to raise gasoline taxes to pay for bridges and highway construction? To pretend that the state did not need the money was so much "hogwash," said Oklahoma United's campaign director. Gary and the drys were endeavoring to "woof" the public.[43]

For wets to condemn the Governor's addition was not sufficient; exposing the shortcomings of his administration had some advantage. They alluded to the illegal use of state funds by one of Gary's right-hand men, and to the fact that a state park lodge employee turned up with a federal liquor stamp. And why, they wanted to know, had the Governor permitted liquor in his presence at a party held in Oklahoma City when Vice-President Richard Nixon visited the state? Why did he not call the "law" or exercise it himself?[44] Just

[42] *Daily Oklahoman*, December 2, 1957.

[43] *Ibid.*

[44] In October, 1957, a number of journalists from across the country assembled for a national conference at Oklahoma City. They staged a party at a local hotel with Governor Gary and Vice-President Richard Nixon as guests. To the Governor's embarrassment the writers freely partook of liquor in his presence. The editor of the *Oklahoma Dry* bitterly castigated the sponsors of the affair, but refused to indict Gary for not upholding the law. *Oklahoma Dry*, September–October, 1957.

or unjust, convincing or unconvincing, this criticism was biting, and to Governor Gary, no doubt, hurting.

The repeal of the constitutional provision against liquor could not help edging its way into the 1957 beer controversy. Drys charged that a hard-liquor group, the Christian League for Liquor Control, served as a front for the beer industry. Dykema refuted this allegation and challenged Stanley Niles of the United Drys to submit evidence supporting his statement. Niles, however, never rendered incontestable facts in defense of his claim and could only reply that it was his judgment, and that of the man on the street. He reasoned that the timing of the formation of the league demonstrated "that the brewing industry...had something to do with it." Spokesmen for the league heatedly assailed drys for their unfounded charges and noted that their members were busy raising money to repeal prohibition and to support wet candidates in the next gubernatorial election.[45]

Judging from some reports, there had been an increase in bootlegging in the state, and beer leaders took note of this fact in arguing for the continued licensed sale of 3.2. They pleaded to the public not to drive the beverage into the back alleys as was the case with hard liquor. In 1956 the federal government had issued more than 500 retail liquor licenses to retail dealers, and some 700 the following year. At $50 a license, this meant that bootleggers who chose not to gamble with the federal government paid out $25,000 and $35,000 for the two years respectively.[46] If securing a license constituted prima-facie evidence of an intent to use it for its prescribed purpose, and it probably did, then one could assume that a goodly portion of the purchasers did just that. A youthful and very perceptive student at the University of Oklahoma agreed

[45] *Daily Oklahoman*, October 5, 1957; see also *Baptist Messenger*, October 10, 1957.

[46] Tulsa *World*, November 2, 1957.

that liquor dispensers had no trouble marketing their products. "Anyone with the money can buy *moisture* here regardless of age," said the youth. Oklahoma was not dry—it was "soggy." Except for the mass corruption of law-enforcement officers and contempt for the judiciary, Oklahoma's set-up, wrote the young Sooner, "is ideal."[47]

If the persistent theme of prohibition hypocrisy reverberated throughout the state in an election which involved a non-intoxicating beverage, so did the question of the theory and practice of local option and majority rule. If drys had really trusted the people, and if they had believed in democratic government, they would not have forced Gary to call a special election, said wets.[48] The dry Laverne *Leader Tribune*, however, scolded the opponents of option as anti-democratic in that they would deny citizens of a county the right to majority rule.[49] The Shawnee *News-Star*, on the other hand, believed that local option "merely added confusion [to] a troublesome issue." The people should know better than to approve a proposal which would foster more bootlegging, and which provided for an election in the counties every two years.[50] There always had been an "option" said the Hinton *Record*—of buying beer from local distributors or of not buying it.[51] Jack Heatwole of Tulsa wrote in a letter to the *Tribune* that, theoretically, local option sounded wonderful, but as for him, if Tulsa County went dry, he would simply get on his telephone or speed off to the nearest wet county to purchase his refreshments.[52] The Ponca City *News* asked why drive beer underground, thus bringing back the roaring days of the gay twen-

---

[47] *Oklahoma Daily*, November 2, 1957.

[48] Leaflet in the Oklahoma Malt Beverage files.

[49] Laverne *Leader Tribune*, October 31, 1957.

[50] Shawnee *News-Star*, October 17, 1957.

[51] Hinton *Record*, October 17, 1957.

[52] See Heatwole's letter in the Tulsa *Tribune*, October 31, 1957.

ties "when young people were called flaming youth and didn't live long enough to finish sowing their wild oats."[53]

For many years drys had been the happy beneficiaries of the unwavering support of the influential *Daily Oklahoman*, owned by E. K. Gaylord. Despite his opposition to repeal, Gaylord penned one of the most critical indictments of the theory of local option. It was not the same thing as in years past, said Gaylord. Local option once conformed squarely with Jeffersonian principles, but the automobile and technology had transformed society. "No one would have denied the rightness of local option on any matter whatsoever when this country was young, but nowadays," admitted the *Oklahoman*, "[it] runs counter to prevalent American policy."[54] In short, local option was a relic of the distant long ago.

For many years drys had been the happy beneficiaries of theories of governmental philosophy. To most the issue was simple—to have beer or not to have beer in counties of the state; that was the real question. In November unfavorable signs which caused trembling among the drys flashed across the Oklahoma horizon. Between October 28 and November 2, 1957, Central Surveys Incorporated of Shenandoah, Iowa, conducted a state poll to determine attitudes on the forthcoming election. All together, Central chose for its study 600 voters who represented a political cross section in thirty precincts. Of the persons questioned, 36 per cent favored local option, 54 per cent opposed it, and 10 per cent had no opinion.[55] Varied comments by participants in the poll ranged from utterly humorous to the profoundly serious. "People will drink this damn beer anyway," said one candid citizen;

[53] Ponca City *News*, November 1, 1957.

[54] *Daily Oklahoman*, October 3, 1957.

[55] See *Probable Attitudes in Oklahoma Concerning Local Option in the Sale of Liquor, A Re-examination of Interviews in a Survey Conducted . . . on a Proposal for County Option in the Sale of Beer*, found in James Nance Collection, University of Oklahoma Library.

AWAY WITH "SUDS": DRYS ATTACK BEER

and another claimed complete "sovereignty" for people of his county—they were going to do what they wanted to, which meant consuming beer even if they voted dry. Others turned to the matter of revenue despite drys' allegation of insignificance: "We can use that money," and "If we had more beer ... there would be more tax money for schools," remarked two Sooners obsessed with the pecuniary benefits of beer. Drys generally replied in moralistic terms with such statements as "Beer is a ruination to the young race."[56]

At the special election the drys were drowned in an ocean of pro-beer ballots. Local option went down by a vote of 275,528 to 214,012.[57] A total of forty-three counties voted dry in 1957. Of all Oklahoma counties, Cimarron, with a small rural population, had the greatest percentage for local option, while Muskogee stacked up the largest vote against the amendment. The heavily populated counties of Oklahoma and Tulsa voted 63.92 per cent and 71.09 per cent respectively against the amendment.[58]

To explain the United Dry defeat is not an easy task. When Governor Gary said that the issue failed because many church people did not vote Yes, he came close to the truth. But his assertion that many people voted against the amendment because of miscomprehension was of doubtful validity.[59] Both wet and dry papers simplified the issue so that only near illiterates could fail to understand what stood at stake. The Governor's sentiments, however, were echoed by the WCTU[60] and by Baptists who lamented after the election that "we live

[56] *Ibid.*, 9–12, for above quotations.

[57] *Directory and Manual of Oklahoma, 1961*, 207.

[58] Norman *Transcript*, December 4, 1957; *Daily Oklahoman*, December 4 and 10, 1957; and scattered undated clippings in the Special Collection on Prohibition, Tulsa Public Library.

[59] Clinton *Daily News*, December 11, 1957.

[60] *Daily Oklahoman*, December 8, 1957.

in a pagan society."[61] Had drys been honest with themselves, they would have admitted that the fear of the loss of revenue, the well-organized campaign of George Fisher, the subtle force of urbanization, and the twenty-four-year tradition of beer had worked their will. Moreover, drys helped to wreck their own ambitions by unrestrained and undocumented statements, their unwise expenditure of money in areas already on their side, and their failure to bombard the business interests constantly with their educational materials.

The 1957 beer election signaled the beginning of the end for Oklahoma's noble experiment. Indeed, the drys' first major offensive since statehood had carried within its own powerful thrust deadly seeds of massive destruction. The *Daily Oklahoman* correctly prophesied after the election that the defeat of the constitutional amendment would bring repeal to the forefront. Drys, who relied upon the church and tradition, refused to believe that Sooners were ready to rewrite history.[62] What their leaders overlooked was that sentiment for liquor was slowly encroaching upon established habits. Much of the prohibitionists' strength had come from rural areas where fundamentalist churches exercised a stronger hold on their parishioners than churches in the cities and towns did on theirs. Strikingly, by 1950, Oklahoma was more than 50 per cent urban.[63] It is a fact of much importance that of the counties with cities of populations above 10,000 (a total of twenty-five), *all but four voted against the local option amendment*. Another omen, not yet clear, had been cast across the Oklahoma landscape.

[61] *Baptist Messenger*, December 12, 1957.

[62] Comments in *Daily Oklahoman*, December 4, 1957.

[63] The 1950 *Census* listed Oklahoma as 51 per cent urban and 49 per cent rural.

X

BARLEYCORN'S RESURRECTION: THE END OF AN ERA

THE PREDICTION that the annihilation of the drys in the 1957 beer referendum would push the liquor issue into the governor's race the following year proved accurate. In the past most state politicians, especially gubernatorial candidates, studiously avoided repeal, deeming it too delicate an issue to touch.[1] But if political triumph had once depended upon the avoidance of the explosive question, a few hopeful aspirants reasoned that success in 1958 hinged, in part, upon a declaration to let Sooners decide the fate of the fifty-two-year-old prohibition movement. Certainly the one person who party held the key to the repeal kingdom was the state's governor, for in the final analysis, he would have the responsibility of pressing a referendum through the legislature or of placing repeal before the people at a favorable time. Clearly then, a wet executive could render great service to the cause of legalized liquor. This fact was plainly underscored in Sep-

---

[1] See the very fine study by Robert S. Walker and Samuel C. Patterson, *Oklahoma Goes Wet*, 3. The author owes much to Dwayne Sterling and to Professors Walker and Patterson upon whom he has relied heavily in writing this particular chapter.

tember, 1957, when the Christian League for Legal Control informed its disciples that "The . . . first thing we must do is elect a governor who is friendly to our program."[2]

The first candidate to declare for repeal in the 1958 governor's campaign was state Senator George Miskovsky. In June, 1957, at Oklahoma City, Miskovsky proposed a state program based on repeal, reorganization, and reapportionment.[3] After the formation of the Christian League, he welcomed its support, and he enthusiastically applauded the group for creating a vehicle whereby the liberal Christian element of Oklahoma might face the liquor question in 1958 with "realistic idealism." The time had come, said the Senator, to "take our heads out of the sand."[4] More candidly than any other serious contender for the governorship in the state's history, Miskovsky decried the "religious fanaticism" drys employed in fighting alcohol. And he went further to denounce the "hypocrisy, corruption and dishonesty in Oklahoma government for fifty years." It was time for a change. Prohibitionists had been "milking" the honest Christian people long enough, said the Episcopalian from Oklahoma City. "They've cost the state millions," and "their failure is a state disgrace and a national joke." Miskovsky thought that if wets were offered a repeal measure as a tax program with controls written into the law, it would carry. The people back in 1949 had been asked to vote for a bad bill—a "pig in a poke," as he phrased it.

Miskovsky's blazing of the repeal path made it more difficult for other candidates to evade the prohibition issue. His outspoken pronouncements again turned the people's attention to the question, gave dejected wets renewed enthusiasm,

[2] *Daily Oklahoman*, September 28, 1957.

[3] Walker and Patterson, *Oklahoma Goes Wet*, 3.

[4] See Miskovsky's statement in full in *Daily Oklahoman*, September 29, 1957.

and made it something less than blasphemy for a candidate to take a stand publicly on a liquor-control policy.[5] Other major Democratic candidates who finally favored repeal or a vote of the people were state Judge Andrew Wilcoxen, state Senator James A. Rinehart, and Tulsa attorney J. Howard Edmondson. The leading Republican candidate, Phil Ferguson, personally desired outright repeal.[6] Indeed a few Republicans found an interesting reason to support submission; it was because in Democratic Oklahoma "bootleggers consistently [aided] Democratic candidates from sheriff to governor with the tacit understanding that they will ignore or soft pedal Oklahoma's prohibitory laws."[7] Despite this allegation, prohibition in 1958 never became a partisan political matter.

Prohibitionists did not go unrepresented in the campaign. The leading dry contender was Democrat W. P. "Bill" Atkinson. A personal abstainer, this Midwest City millionaire was regarded by political observers as the man to beat in the early stages of the campaign.[8] The only other serious Democratic contestant for the dry vote was William Doenges. A wide and very costly split developed in the dry camp when the Methodists insisted upon United Dry endorsement of Doenges' candidacy. Baptists, however, wanted the group to remain formally uncommitted. But the fact that Doenges had advanced part of his personal holdings as collateral for a United Dry loan made some Methodist brethren more determined to back him, and no doubt he had expected an endorsement. Atkinson, on the other hand, had also contributed to the drys. The failure to concentrate all of their power behind one man did considerable damage to the United Drys'

5 Walker and Patterson, *Oklahoma Goes Wet*, 4.
6 *Daily Oklahoman*, September 11, 1957.
7 *Ibid.*, February 24, 1958.
8 Walker and Patterson, *Oklahoma Goes Wet*, 4.

efforts. As a dry official said after the election, either Atkinson or Doenges could have won had Methodists and Baptists buried their obstinacy.[9]

The bitterly fought Democratic primary campaign dashed to the ground the hopes of those who wanted the wet-dry issue kept in the background. As minor candidates fell by the wayside, Atkinson, Edmondson, and Miskovsky emerged as the strongest contenders for their party's nomination. Atkinson, with plentiful resources and a powerful organization, reasoned that he could easily overcome the Oklahoma City senator and send Edmondson, the boy politician from Tulsa, back to school for more training.[10] But the young reformer from the Oil City taught them both a hard and unwanted lesson. Before the primary, Edmondson had projected a program which pleased wets but invited the ire of drys. "I believe people are fed up with prohibition as now written and enforced," said the attractive and dynamic young lawyer. The state had to tighten enforcement by the use of the proper agencies when local officers failed to exercise their responsibilities. If elected, Edmondson promised a special election on repeal.[11] The political program offered by the youthful Tulsan drew many Oklahomans to his side in the primary, and he completely confounded the experts, beating out Atkinson by a narrow 742 votes; Miskovsky, Doenges, and William Coe followed in that order. Had Doenges not entered the race, it is almost certain his dry votes would have gone to Atkinson.

Neither Edmondson nor Atkinson gained a majority of the ballots cast, thus making a runoff necessary to determine an opponent for the Republican Phil Ferguson, who handily won his party's nomination. Both Democratic candidates moved hurriedly to consolidate their strength. Atkinson augmented

9 Sterling, "Repeal of Prohibition," 39.
10 Ibid., 40–41.
11 Daily Oklahoman, May 22, 1958.

his camp with support from Coe, Rinehart, and Governor Gary. Edmondson won the allegiance of Miskovsky and Doenges, who defected from the dry camp. Noticeably, the aggressive campaign carried out against the "boy" from Tulsa, as some in Atkinson's ranks characterized Edmondson, earned him more friends than his opponents had anticipated.[12]

The approaching runoff saw Edmondson continue to espouse his views on submission, while Atkinson gradually liberalized his former stand on repeal. Apparently, the Midwest City politician now realized that he needed part of the wet vote if he was to defeat Edmondson. Therefore, a week after the first primary, he indicated a willingness to submit repeal at a special election if a person or group offered an initiative petition. Drys exploded with verbal fury;[13] but Atkinson was their last hope, and the United Drys continued to back him. Despite his shift in position, however, Atkinson could not match the political strength generated by Edmondson, who defeated his rich opponent by one of the most impressive runoff primary majorities in state history.

Except those who believed in miracles in Oklahoma politics, few doubted the Democrats' chances of trouncing the Republicans at the polls. Neither of the candidates greatly differed on the liquor question. Edmondson, however, conscious of the lack of a unified opinion among wets over a control measure, refused to get involved in any squabbles.[14] Likewise, he prudently did not declare for or against repeal, and only pledged himself to submission within ninety days after inauguration. Ferguson, on the other hand, announced unequivocally that in his administration "prohibition will be repealed."[15]

12 For a discussion of the political alliances after the primary, see Walker and Patterson, *Oklahoma Goes Wet*, 6.

13 Sterling, "Repeal of Prohibition," 41.

14 *Daily Oklahoman*, August 31, 1958.

15 Walker and Patterson, *Oklahoma Goes Wet*, 7.

In an effort to capitalize on the stand of the two candidates, a political unknown named D. A. Bryce entered the race as an Independent. Confronted with two bad choices between the major parties, and with a fifty-year tradition hanging precariously in the political balance, the United Drys gave the unheralded and obscure Bryce its support. Edmondson, nevertheless, prevailed over his opponents by the greatest margin in state history.[16] The sleeping John Barleycorn had received the first signs of revival.

With victory achieved, the governor-elect appointed a committee headed by W. Lee Johnson of Pawnee to study a repeal proposal. The committee consisted of members who represented a wide range of opinions from varied professions. In appointing the study group Edmondson emphasized that he would recommend submission to the legislature, but he did not rule out the possibility of an initiative petition.[17] Prior to the establishment of the committee, two major repeal groups organized to circulate a repeal measure in the event Edmondson could not ram repeal through the legislature. The first of these, the Citizens Committee to Repeal Bootleg Control, consisted mostly of Miskovsky's supporters. The Citizens Committee was the Senator's own creation "and he was the dynamic force that made it an influence in Oklahoma Repeal politics."[18] In November, 1958, members of the committee met at the Municipal Auditorium in Oklahoma City to commence their drive for 83,000 signatures. Their plan called for privately owned package stores, county option, and a system whereby one-third of liquor revenue went to wet cities and towns, and two-thirds to the state; it also prohibited sale by the drink. Miskovsky's actions irritated Edmondson, who

---

[16] The vote read 399,504 to 107,495; Bryce received 31,840, a record high for an Independent. See *Directory and Manual of Oklahoma, 1961*, 27, 232.

[17] *Daily Oklahoman*, November 7, 1958.

[18] Walker and Patterson, *Oklahoma Goes Wet*, 10.

argued that he should have waited until the study committee made its report. But the Senator wanted to become "Mr. Repealist." He proceeded to criticize the Edmondson group for its unusual size, and he warned in one of his comments that "it will be surprising if they can agree on the Ten Commandments before they are through."[19] He proudly pointed to the virtues of his "conservative" plan which would foster temperance and moderation.

The second repeal group, the Oklahoma League for Legal Control, was as intent as the Citizens Committee in wiping prohibition from the constitution. A Tulsa organization headed by Neil Bogan, the league, like the Citizens Committee, circulated a petition for a vote which implied, of course, differences of opinion among wets. Essentially, Bogan's organization preferred *local* (city) option and sale by the drink in certain establishments. The league was very critical of the Miskovsky proposal, especially *county option*; its members argued that city option would protect small communities within counties.[20] The league fell far short of its goal, and most of the signatures it obtained came from within the city of Tulsa.

The study group worked rapidly and in late December, 1958, made its report to the governor-elect. Edmondson did not attend any of its meetings, but one member of his staff, Whit Pate, sat in on the proceedings.[21] The committee endeavored to devise a plan which would attract a broad following and at the same time benefit the state. It called for:

[19] *Daily Oklahoman*, November 17, 1958.

[20] *Daily Oklahoman*, December 23, 1958, and Walker and Patterson, *Oklahoma Goes Wet*, 12.

[21] The study committee divided itself into four separate groups, each of which handled a specific area of the repeal question: (1) revenue, (2) local option, (3) package stores, and (4) state versus private sales. Mrs. June Benson, Gene Grubitz, Loren Williams, and N. G. Henthorne respectively headed these subcommittees.

(1) privately owned package stores in towns of 2,000 population or more, county seat towns, and state lodges, (2) revenue to be divided on the basis of one-third to cities and towns, and two-thirds to the general fund, (3) a 2 per cent sales tax on all alcoholic beverages in addition to other taxes, (4) no county option at the beginning of repeal, but for an election in two years to determine a county's preference. One of the committee members remarked that this proposal would "please the old folks, the rural element, the moderate drys and the wets. You might say it's a plan under which everybody can have their cake and eat it too."[22]

Local option posed one of the greatest barriers to wet unity. The study committee had recommended a delayed vote after the repeal election. Miskovsky and others always felt that the people would reject any proposal without this feature.[23] Edmondson agreed that a simultaneous vote on repeal and local option had some merit, but he argued that it would deny Sooners the chance to see how an effective control system operated. The influential Gaylord of the *Oklahoman* sided with Miskovsky, and in an editorial, "Like Rock and Rye," he assailed the governor-elect for bowing to the suggestions of the study committee in what struck some people as an "awkward and crablike approach to the option question." Oklahoma's record, said Gaylord, showed that option and repeal were as mixed "as the gin and Vermouth in a dry martini." The dry editor knew his politics—and his drinks. And with years of prohibition history stuffed away in his mind, he cautioned that any attempt to push repeal down rural throats "parched by preference is bound to stick . . . in the craws of representatives from dry counties."[24]

[22] *Daily Oklahoman*, December 21, 1958.

[23] Revenue heavily influenced their opinion. In his testimony before the repeal committee, Miskovsky estimated that if the state held a local-option election, only twenty-five counties would vote wet. See his comment *ibid.*, November 23, 1958.

Edmondson could not ignore the influence of George Miskovsky in his search for a workable plan that would hurdle the legislature. In January, 1959, he and the Senator met and discussed their differences; the following month, Miskovsky announced an alignment of forces with the Governor. In explanation of his about-face, he only "modestly" suggested that "wise men change their minds"; he agreed with Edmondson "100 per cent," and he would join supporters of his program "shoulder to shoulder."[25] Moreover, Miskovsky dropped his petition and prepared another one in line with Edmondson's ideas. The compromise between the Governor and the Senator cemented a formidable coalition and served notice on the drys that a battle lay ahead in the legislature. Truly, ill winds blew in the drys' direction.

In late December, 1958, floor leaders of both houses had met with Edmondson to map out a repeal resolution for presentation at the opening session of the legislature. They agreed to give repeal priority because of its controversial nature, and because revenue hinged on it.[26] Edmondson again underscored the vital connection between repeal and revenue in his address to the joint session of the legislature when he told that body that the administration needed to know whether to include taxes from liquor sales in the budget. Prior to his message, he had bluntly informed legislators that he would use the full power of his office to prompt submission.[27]

Edmondson's election and subsequent actions produced near frantic reactions among prohibitionists. The United Drys tried to gain the unity they had lost during the gubernatorial campaign by elevating Dr. Sam Scantland to executive director, replacing Stanley Niles who had been a source of fric-

---

[24] *Ibid.*, January 7, 1959.
[25] Walker and Patterson, *Oklahoma Goes Wet*, 13.
[26] *Daily Oklahoman*, December 30, 1958.
[27] *Daily Oklahoman*, January 8, 1959.

tion. A Baptist, Scantland headed that denomination's missions program and was well known in religious circles. Unfortunately, he suffered from political neophytism,[28] and the pressures he later encountered found him unconditioned for the task at hand. Nevertheless, the clergyman entered his new position with optimism, and with all the religious fervor at his command, he blasted those who wished to "baptize Oklahoma with liquor."[29] And he pledged Sooner ministers to stand as Henry Petain at Verdun and say, "They shall not pass!" Prayer would constitute part of their heavy artillery.[30]

What prayer needed to accomplish most within dry ranks was solidarity among the churches. Non-fundamentalist sects, of course, had always been a negligible part of the prohibitionists' establishment, and some groups such as the Catholics, Jews, and Episcopalians had quietly, if not openly, assumed a hostile attitude toward the drys. Unity then meant cohesion of the Protestant churches. Methodists, in particular, presented a problem. Many resented the dominance of Baptists in the United Dry organizational structure; others viewed their Baptist brethren as too extreme in temperament. To cement the association, its executive committee elevated Dr. Joseph Shackford (a Methodist), to the presidency, succeeding the Reverend Max Stanfield.[31] The effort to lessen discord bore some results, but full unity never materialized. At no other time had the church people experienced a split of such proportions—and at a moment when the legislature readied itself for one of the most critical fights in its history.

Four basic repeal proposals came before the Twenty-seventh Legislature. The ideas of Bogan's Repeal League were embodied in House Joint Resolution No. 508; those of

[28] Sterling, "Repeal of Prohibition," 56.
[29] Oklahoma City *Times*, November 7, 1958.
[30] Elk City *News*, November 9, 1958.
[31] Walker and Patterson, *Oklahoma Goes Wet*, 14.

the Citizens Committee became House Joint Resolution No. 502; and a plan for state-owned stores showed up in House Joint Resolution No. 505. Edmondson's study committee report was found in House Joint Resolution No. 501 and Senate Joint Resolution No. 1.[32] Legislative leaders and the Governor agreed that joint hearings should be held on the bills, but that each committee concerned with the repeal proposals should retain the right to act independently. Accordingly, committee chairmen set hearings, to consist of two four-hour sessions, for January 20 and 21, 1959.

Wets of varying shades presented their case on the first day. Senator Miskovsky (who in January had not yet compromised with Edmondson on local option) appeared to urge approval of his group's plan, and to attack the suggestion of Senator Jim Nance, chairman of the Committee on Revenue and Taxation, that the legislature place a $5.00 tax a barrel on liquor. Senator Louis Ritzhaupt and Neil Bogan pushed the Repeal League's proposal, while Senator Tom Payne and Representative Robert Lollar argued in favor of the Edmondson proposal. Those who desired state-owned liquor stores had their views voiced by Dr. H. V. Thornton, professor of government at the University of Oklahoma. Ministers of non-fundamentalist churches also pleaded the wets' case.[33]

The fervor of dry testimony more than matched that of the wets. Moralism and de-emphasis on revenue prevailed in 1959 as it had for the past half century. In 1966, Mrs. Elizabeth House still recalled the intensity with which she told the committee to "keep Sin out of Oklahoma."[34] One United Dry spokesman admitted the imperfect nature of prohibition, but said legalized liquor would bring more bootlegging and mount-

---

[32] See the excellent discussion in Sterling, "Repeal of Prohibition," 62.

[33] For full coverage, see Tulsa *World*, January 21, 1959, and *Daily Oklahoman*, January 21, 1959.

[34] House interview, May 20, 1966.

ing social destruction. The president of Phillips University at Enid, Dr. Eugene Briggs, strove to discredit repealists' claims of huge revenue; and Dr. Shackford said that all states which had adopted legalized liquor in some form could be wrong; Oklahoma should not rush to conform.[35]

With the hearings completed, the senate settled down to what developed into an unforgettable session. Fortunately, the compromise between Governor Edmondson and Miskovsky, described earlier, had been reached by February. It provided for two separate ballots at the same election, one for repeal, the other for option.[36] When the Miskovsky-Edmondson compromise bill came to the floor of the senate, several legislators made vigorous attempts to alter the plan. The senate passed a number of amendments pertaining to prices on wholesale liquors, their sale in towns of certain sizes and to minors and the insane, advertising, and the revocation of licenses. Perhaps the most important amendment required legislative approval of members of an Alcoholic Control Board which the act would establish. Finally, as a penalty for past actions, persons who had held federal liquor stamps or who had been convicted of a felony were forbidden to purchase a state permit.[37]

The administration encountered a momentous challenge in pushing the referendum through the senate. For the first time in history, however, the upper chamber passed a repeal measure, 29 to 15 on February 11, 1959; and it provided for a special election April 7 by a vote of 31 to 13.[38] A total of thirty votes was needed to call such an election, and victory came only after a bitter five-hour debate. The most crucial votes were those of Senators Ryan Kerr of Altus and Byron Davis

[35] Muskogee *Times Democrat*, January 21, 1959.
[36] Walker and Patterson, *Oklahoma Goes Wet*, 16.
[37] For the struggle in both houses of the legislature to alter the plan, see Sterling, "Repeal of Prohibition," 69–74.
[38] Senate *Journal*, 1959, 233.

of Gotebo, both of whom voted against the amendment itself, but changed their minds on its submission to the people at a special contest. The dry Joe B. Cobb scolded the administration for steam-rolling the bill through the senate in one day, and he desired that his colleagues in the house administer it the *coup de grâce*. The cryptic Senator Ray Fine characterized the bill as the image of the devil himself.[39] Obviously the resolution could never have passed unless some former drys had changed their minds. The truth is, writes a student of the subject, "the Senate Drys who voted to support the repeal referendum did so on the grounds that it was preferable, if there was to be a state-wide vote on repeal, for the proposal to be drafted by the legislature, rather than by private citizens' groups operating through the initiative procedure."[40]

Edmondson's task now shifted to the house. Dry strategy to offset the senate action soon displayed itself: drys would amend the bill to death by attaching a provision for state-owned stores. And that, they were certain, Oklahomans would not accept. Thus, United Dry leaders put forth every effort urging citizens to write their representatives encouraging them to torpedo the inclination toward iniquity.[41]

While the house debated the repeal bill, an important development occurred which undoubtedly affected that body's decision. In February the Reverend Mr. Scantland alleged that some legislators may have been bribed and indicated the possible need for an investigation. Both wet and dry lawmakers, the honor of their august assemblage at stake, were furious. Speaker of the house Clint Livingston verbally blistered the preacher, admonishing that Scantland should "keep his big fat mouth shut." The Baptist clergyman, now on

---

[39] For comments by various senators, see the *Daily Oklahoman*, February 12, 1959.

[40] Walker and Patterson, *Oklahoma Goes Wet*, 17.

[41] *Daily Oklahoman*, February 13, 1959.

the defensive, asserted that he had voiced a rumor to which he wanted to "strike a match." He did—and it burned Scantland and the drys. When asked whether he had actually seen money change hands, Scantland suggested evasively that George Miskovsky probably would have some idea. Miskovsky uneuphemistically called the minister a "categorical liar" and accused Scantland of going "arm and arm with the underworld because he is adopting their tactics."[42] The Senator urged an apology from the minister and encouraged him to tell the people of Oklahoma that he got carried away and really did not know what he was saying. At the invitation of the house, Scantland appeared before a committee and offered a humble apology, but the damage he had done was irreparable.

The debate in the house on repeal began with the galleries packed with interested parties. The administration had a formidable job—to push the bill through *without any changes.* Just as important, Edmondson needed sixty votes to pass the measure and eighty to get a special election. For a house which had never come any closer to passing a liquor referendum than many sincere drys to a fifth of Old Crow or Jim Beam, those were a lot of votes. The Governor and his leaders pressured house members while both wets and drys collared nervous legislators in the lobbies to give them the message from the "folks back home." The tenseness of the moment was reflected on the floor of the house; at one point tempers became so taut that the speaker had to remind his colleagues that "we're all blood brothers," and besides "we're on TV."[43]

For six and one-half hours lawmakers heatedly considered Barleycorn's legal resurrection from a long slumber. Old arguments couched in new language popped forth. To drys

[42] *Ibid.*, February 17, 1959.

[43] "Vote Becomes Price of Oklahoma Drinking," *Life*, Vol. XLVI (March, 1959), 22.

the house should not legalize the "master tranquilizer"; the tranquilizer, said wets, was as close as the nearest bootlegger or moonshiner.[44] Intent upon frustrating the Governor's plans, prohibitionists in the house offered a number of unsuccessful amendments in an effort to force the bill into conference. Shortly after 8 P. M. on February 18, the house voted; the repeal resolution carried *without a single change* by a vote of 65 to 33, and the provision for a special election, 81 to 37.[45] To the advantage of wets, a total of eighteen legislators changed their votes to call the April 7 special vote.

Governor Edmondson committed himself to strict enforcement of the prohibition law as long as it remained a part of the state constitution. He pledged to give Sooners a clear choice—legal liquor or none. Although the crackdown on bootleggers and moonshiners did not attract national attention until after he took office, and until he appointed Joe Cannon commissioner of public safety, it had really begun before then on the local level in some areas.[46] Cannon acted with directness. The thirty-four-year-old commissioner informed clubs and hotels that the liquor traffic must stop; and he told the sheriffs of Oklahoma's seventy-seven counties to clean up their domain, or he would take action. The "crew cut commando," as some labeled him, also announced that the highway patrol would assist in the enforcement program. This decision brought a tirade of criticism from some citizens

[44] For fiscal 1958–59 the Internal Revenue Service issued 585 retail liquor stamps and one wholesale license. Statistics are from the records of the Internal Revenue Service, 1958–59, Oklahoma City.

[45] House *Journal*, 1959, 231–32.

[46] Officials in Oklahoma City and Tulsa, for example, began to carry out concerted raids as early as November, 1958. By January, 1959, things had become "so hot" that some legislators seriously pondered whether or not the governor's ball in January, 1959, would be wet or dry. One senator quipped that "it probably will be a buttermilk ball, and you can bring your own cow." See Oklahoma City *Times*, January 8, 1959, and also "Corking Up the Jug," *Newsweek*, Vol. LIII (March 2, 1959), 25.

and lawmakers, especially the chairman of the senate Committee on Public Safety, Everett Collins. Cannon and the Governor insisted, however, that the patrol could successfully pursue bootleggers while handling highway problems.

Edmondson's decision to dry up Oklahoma was not an impulsive gesture. His response represented a deliberate plan. He had heard of the enforcement program in Kansas and how it had hastened repeal a decade earlier; he "just didn't believe Oklahomans wanted enforced prohibition."[47] In November, 1958, a newspaper in the Governor's home town had discussed the Kansas experiment and the effective policy of state officials who ordered illegal joints to close up or get raided. Panic followed, liquor became scarce, and soon the price of a good fifth had skyrocketed to $20—almost a "prohibitive" price. "Solid citizens" became "boiling mad" and repeal followed. The Tulsa *Tribune* warned the United Drys that instead of cheering the Governor's program, they should be shaking in their shoes, for Oklahomans simply would not tolerate expensive liquor.[48] And it could have added, strict enforcement.

At first the Cannon raids evoked only mild disgust among bootleggers and hard-drinking Sooners who accepted the "youngster's immature action" as one of Edmondson's infant jokes. After all, it was a new administration, and the people needed something for public consumption. But Cannon and Edmondson were deadly serious, and they had decided that whatever the public needed, it was *not* illegal liquor. The constitution must be defended. Cannon threw up road blocks, searched here and there, and at times gave the impression of universality. Bootleggers, turning to technology to outwit him, installed radios in their vehicles to keep track of the

---

[47] See Sterling's interview with Edmondson in his "Repeal of Prohibition," 76.

[48] Tulsa *Tribune*, November 19, 1958.

"commando," but only reaped frustration resulting from a specially devised patrol code.[49] Cannon, of course, never assumed that he could dry up the whole of Oklahoma, but he did set out to significantly reduce the supply of liquor, and to frighten tavern owners and bootleggers into obedience. And he did. For the first time in many a year, said one paper in northeast Oklahoma, "Spavinaw [Mayes County] is dry."[50] A lot of other Spavinaws dotted the Oklahoma landscape by April, 1959.

Drys hated to admit it, but the enforcement they had demanded for years worked against them. The Cannon crusade not only limited the flow of intoxicants but gave the impression that ardent spirits abounded in plenitude. Prohibitionists, of course, pretentiously praised the young Edmondson, but everyone detected the forced laudations. The raids disturbed the business community in the state, particularly hotels which had to cancel parties suddenly because a man hired to do his job did just that—and without favor. Consequently, it was not difficult to comprehend why, during the debate over repeal in the legislature, legislators' mail became increasingly wet. Cannon was partly the answer. Relentlessly he continued to press his campaign until the people of Oklahoma went to the polls and gave the lie to Will Rogers' old assertion about Sooners voting dry as long as they could stagger to the polls.[51]

Although wets had been divided before the legislative battle, by February, 1959, they were in better condition than at any other time in the state's history. They co-ordinated their campaign under the United Oklahomans for Repeal, directed by H. W. McNeil, an Oklahoma City oilman.[52] McNeil ac-

49 "Corking Up the Jug," *Newsweek*, Vol. LIII (March 2, 1959), 25.

50 Tulsa *Tribune*, March 5, 1959.

51 The best discussion of the Cannon raids is in Sterling, "Repeal of Prohibition," 79–81.

52 *Daily Oklahoman*, February 27, 1959.

cepted his position only upon agreement that he would have full control of the entire operation. Since his executive committee consisted of strong personalities such as Miskovsky and Bogan, old soldiers with scars from the repeal battle which only victory could heal, prudence no doubt dictated McNeil's demand for a free hand. The group acquired indirect support from the governor when McNeil persuaded Edmondson to appoint Whit Pate an ex officio member of the organization, thus implying the Governor's sanction of the campaign, if not repeal; officially Edmondson maintained a neutral position.[53]

McNeil organized his attack with consummate skill and enviable energy. He established a central office at Oklahoma City composed of two troubleshooters, a specialist in preparing newspaper releases and advertisements, two secretaries, and two publicity men. He then created county organizations which kept in contact with headquarters through district agents. All these local groups resembled each other; each had a chairman, a vice chairman, a secretary-treasurer, and usually a steering committee.[54] McNeil's leadership, however, allowed for reasonable flexibility although general policy was established by headquarters.

The United Oklahomans acquired support from other groups not directly a part of their superstructure. Before approval of the referendum, the beer interests had stated their intention of avoiding the repeal battle as long as it did not disturb 3.2 beer. In fact, there had been much talk of disbanding the old Oklahoma United which in 1957 had turned back local option on 3.2 beer.[55] But if the prohibitionists triumphed over the repealists, would they not assault the

[53] Walker and Patterson, *Oklahoma Goes Wet,* 22.
[54] Sterling, "Repeal of Prohibition," 83.
[55] *Daily Oklahoman,* September 18, 1958.

moderate drink again? Answering in the affirmative, Oklahoma United joined the ranks of the "true wets," bringing with them the majority of the workers in beer and related businesses.[56] Also, Miskovsky's personal political organization, which never became a part of the United Oklahomans for Repeal, lent its powerful assistance.[57]

Drys, on the other hand, had never approached a campaign laden with as many multitudinous problems. Its leadership exhibited drive and enthusiasm, to be sure, but lacked vital political experience so necessary to steer the "forces of righteousness" over those of "demon rum." Neither Scantland nor Shackford could fill the bill; one was a novice, the other a newcomer to the state, unschooled in Sooner attitudes. The coolness of some denominations, as already suggested, did little to inspire leaders who, more than ever before, badly needed it. Genuine brotherly co-operation escaped the drys. After the election Scantland specifically complained of deficient Methodist support. Within some other groups—Presbyterians, for example—ministers such as the dry Ralston Smith of Oklahoma City and the pro-repeal Kenneth Feaver of Norman battled to win acceptance of their views.

Beyond the split in the church, the greatest problem drys confronted stemmed from money to finance their defense of prohibition. Naturally it is difficult to estimate dry expenditures since prohibitionists relied heavily upon local congregations which often did not channel their contributions through United Dry headquarters. From January to April, 1959, the drys spent nearly $79,000, while the WCTU ex-

[56] Little fear existed among beer men over huge losses of revenue if repeal passed. Personal interview with Louis Gatti, executive secretary, Oklahoma Malt Beverage Association, Oklahoma City, August 20, 1966.

[57] McNeil and Miskovsky could never agree on strategy. The former claimed that the senator broke his promise to allow him to run the campaign.

pended another $30,000 in its own campaign. The best estimate of their opponents' expenses is $300,000.[58] That the antiliquor forces augmented their campaign chest by funds from self-interested bootleggers has for years been a commonplace, yet unsupported, assertion. Prohibitionists would have been unwise, indeed insane, to have admitted the acceptance of this money. One writer, however, has reasoned that "the truth of the matter seems to have been that bootleg money did flow into the dry treasuries, but by indirect and circuitous routes."[59] When an Oklahoma bootlegger appeared on national television in March, 1959, and expressed the desire for a dry victory, some Sooner suspicions became immediately transformed into incontestable fact. Any dogmatic generalization about bootleg support, however, runs the risk of inexcusable error; but it is true that Oklahoma prohibition, like its politics, often made strange bedfellows.[60]

Wets and drys took out their old campaign records for a dramatic replay. Prohibitionists preached prayer and moralism—wets, revenue and freedom of choice.[61] McNeil, however, conducted his campaign with much more finesse than wet leaders in the past. He stressed the strong controls written in the amendment, and he avoided the confusion of the moral issue. He did not waste time on devout drys, nor on staunch wets, but applied unrelenting pressure to those who wavered back and forth.[62] McNeil received support in this effort from

[58] Compare Sterling, "Repeal of Prohibition," 89, and Walker and Patterson, Oklahoma Goes Wet, 25.

[59] Walker and Patterson, Oklahoma Goes Wet, 28.

[60] Many speculated that the recognizable increase in the cost of liquor went to support the dry campaign. The rise of whisky prices, however, could have resulted from the disparity between supply and demand.

[61] See "Look Out Oklahoma," a pamphlet prepared by the United Dry Association in the files of the Sooner Alcohol and Narcotic Education Association, Bethany; and Walker and Patterson, Oklahoma Goes Wet, 27.

[62] Sterling, "Repeal of Prohibition," 85. McNeil held that there was a swing group of perhaps 120,000 voters, composed mostly of women.

the Oklahoma City Volunteer Churchmen for Repeal which argued that if the possibility of the wrong choice was taken away from man, the virtue of temperance could never develop. Notably, the churchmen did not question the drys' sincerity.[63]

As in the past, revenue occupied a prominent place in the wet-dry debate. In 1958–59, Oklahoma politicians had talked of the possibility of increased taxation. Levies on liquor, McNeil told taxpayers, could provide a reliable substitute for other kinds of taxes; it was, of course, an old argument. With additional money, city governments could raise employees' salaries and provide a number of new and better services. Seemingly, this approach in 1959 had its telling effects. Professional groups such as the grossly underpaid teachers, for example, saw in repeal the hope for higher salaries, although their state association remained neutral on repeal.[64]

Newspapers have always been both molders and reflectors of public attitudes. How much influence they have been able to wield at a given time on a particular issue is debatable. Professors Robert W. Walker and Samuel C. Patterson in their study of Oklahoma newspapers during the 1959 prohibition election found that editors pursued a policy consonant with their perception of community attitudes. The Sooner State in 1959 had 122 daily and weekly papers. The Walker-Patterson study revealed that the overwhelming majority of these (87 per cent) either favored repeal or took no clear-cut position, while only a very few (13 per cent) came out full blast against it. More than half (54 per cent) of those who favored the amendment edited dailies, while nearly two-thirds (60 per cent) of those who took no stand edited weeklies. Sig-

[63] The position of the churchmen is stated in "Support Repeal," a pamphlet prepared by the Volunteer Churchmen for Repeal, in the author's possession.
[64] Walker and Patterson, *Oklahoma Goes Wet*, 31.

nificantly, almost three-fourths (73 per cent) of the editors who opposed the liquor bill published weeklies.[65] Undeniably then, the Oklahoma press, like the national press in the 1920's, had much to do with prohibition's fate.

If drys experienced pessimism as April 7 neared, there was ample reason. Every sign pointed to calamity. During the latter part of March, polls showed them running far behind the pace-setting repealists. One study revealed that of 495 persons who had voted for local option on beer in 1957, 290 said they would vote for repeal, 169 remained steadfastly dry, and 36 had not yet made up their minds. On the other hand, a total of 606 citizens out of 869 who voted wet in 1957 said they would repeat their act in April; and only 47 of this total were undecided.[66]

In the minds of many drys April 7, 1959, is a day which will forever ingloriously adorn the pages of Oklahoma history. The people went to the polls and took the humor out of Will Rogers' joke. They approved repeal 396,845 to 314,380. Local option failed 469,503 to 221,404.[67] An entire era in Oklahoma's social and political life had been ushered out, and a new business ushered in.

Devout and professional drys found it hard to keep faith. They looked, however, to the immediate return to the calm and peaceful days when righteousness ruled supreme. Liquor was legal, thundered the *Baptist Messenger*, but "Sin is Sin," and a bottle of state-sanctioned whisky would produce the same results as a bottle of bootleg "hooch."[68] The WCTU echoed similar sentiments.[69] More crime, more tragedy, more

[65] Robert S. Walker and Samuel C. Patterson, "The Political Attitudes of Oklahoma Newspapers: The Prohibition Issue," *Southwestern Social Science Quarterly*, Vol. XLII (December, 1961), 278–79.

[66] For the result of the poll, see the *Daily Oklahoman*, March 29, 1959.

[67] *Directory and Manual of Oklahoma, 1961*, 208.

[68] April 16, 1959.

[69] *Daily Oklahoman*, April 9, 1959.

poverty, more deaths, moaned one dry. But a ray of hope beamed through the dark clouds of evil: "Three to five years from now, with the bitter results of free-flowing whiskey evident on every hand and the utter impossibility of legal control demonstrated," citizens would return to the straight path.[70] At this writing, the prediction has not come true, and there are few visible signs that Oklahomans will return to the social experiment begun in 1907 and which for more than half a century commanded obedience to its mandates.

[70] *Baptist Messenger*, April 16, 1959.

BIBLIOGRAPHY

MANUSCRIPTS

Internal Revenue Service, Oklahoma City.
National Archives, Washington, D.C.
    General Records of the Department of Justice, Record Group 60.
    National Commission on Law Observance and Enforcement Research Records, Record Group 10.
Office of the Secretary of State, Oklahoma City.
Oklahoma Historical Society, Oklahoma City.
    Frederick S. Barde Collection
    Special Collection on Prohibition
    Woman's Christian Temperance Union Collection
Oklahoma Malt Beverage Association, Oklahoma City.
Sooner Alcohol and Narcotic Education Association, Bethany, Okla.
Special Collection on Prohibition, Tulsa Public Library.
University of Oklahoma Library, Norman.
    Redmond C. Cole Collection
    Charles N. Haskell Collection
    Historic Oklahoma Collection
    Henry S. Johnston Collection
    William H. Murray Collection
    James Nance Collection

BIBLIOGRAPHY

Leon Phillips Collection
William and Zoe Agnes Tilghman Collection
Charles West Collection

PUBLIC DOCUMENTS

Federal

Bureau of the Census. *Census of Population: 1950.* Vol. II, *Characteristics of the Population.* Pt. 36, *Oklahoma.*
————. *Special Reports: Religious Bodies, 1906. Summary and General Tables,* Part I.
————. *Thirteenth Census of the United States, 1910. Abstract, with Supplement for Oklahoma.*
Congressional Record. 62d Cong., 3d sess., 1913. Vol. XLIX, pt. 5, 4291–92.
Congressional Record. 65th Cong., 1st sess., 1917. Vol. LV, pt. 3, 2171.
House of Representatives. *Hearings on Prohibition in the Proposed State of Oklahoma before the Committee on Territories.* 59th Cong., 1st sess.
National Commission on Law Observance and Enforcement. *Enforcement of the Prohibition Laws. Official Record of the National Commission on Law Observance and Enforcement . . . .* 6 vols. Washington, Government Printing Office, 1931.
Statutes at Large. Vols. XXXIV, XXXVII, and XLI.
Treasury Department. Bureau of Industrial Alcohol. *Statistics Concerning Intoxicating Liquors.* Washington, Government Printing Office, 1921–33.

State

Address of Governor C. N. Haskell . . . Before the Oklahoma Prohibitionists, April 15, 1908. Guthrie, Leader Printing Co., 1908.
Biennial Report of Benjamin F. Harrison, Secretary of State of . . . Oklahoma for the Two Years Term Ending November 30, 1912. Oklahoma City, Peerless Press, 1912.

Carter, Dorset, comp. *Indian Territory Statutes (1899).* St. Paul, West Publishing Co., 1899.

Constitution of Oklahoma.

Directory and Manual of ... Oklahoma, 1961.

First Message of the Governor to the Second State Legislature, January 5, 1909. Guthrie, Leader Printing Co., 1909.

Inaugural Address of Governor C. N. Haskell, November 16, 1907. Guthrie, Leader Printing Co., 1907.

Message of Governor Robert L. Williams to the Sixth Legislature of the State of Oklahoma, January 4, 1917. Oklahoma City, n.p., 1917.

Meyer, Leo, comp. *Oklahoma State Manual, 1909.* Guthrie, Leader Printing Co., 1909.

Oklahoma House of Representatives. *Journal.* Biennial, 1907–59.

Oklahoma Senate. *Journal.* Biennial, 1907–59.

Oklahoma Tax Commission. *Twelfth Biennial Report.* 1956.

Proceedings of the Constitutional Convention of the Proposed State of Oklahoma. Muskogee, Muskogee Printing Co., 1907.

Regular Biennial Message of Governor Lee Cruce to the Legislature of 1913. Vinita, Leader Printing Co., 1913.

Session Laws of Oklahoma. Biennial, 1907–59.

Seventh Special Message of the Governor to the First Legislature, December 12, 1907. Guthrie, Leader Printing Co., 1907.

Snyder, Henry G., comp. *The Compiled Laws of Oklahoma.* Kansas City, Pipes-Reed Co., 1909.

Statutes of Oklahoma, 1890.

Williams, Robert L., comp. *Constitution and Enabling Act of Oklahoma, Annotated, with Reference to the Constitution, Statutes, and Decisions of Other States and the U.S.* Kansas City, Vernon Law Book Co., 1912.

Wilson, W. F., comp. *Wilson's Revised and Annotated Statutes of Oklahoma, 1903.* 2 vols. Guthrie, State Capital Co., 1903.

NEWSPAPERS

Altus *Times.*

Alva *Weekly Courier.*

BIBLIOGRAPHY

American Issue.
Baptist Informer.
Baptist Messenger.
Beaver County *Democrat.*
Beaver County *Herald.*
Beaver *Journal.*
Blackwell *Times-Record.*
Cherokee *Advocate.*
Cherokee *Messenger.*
Chickasha *Daily Express.*
Cleveland County *Leader.*
Clinton *Daily News.*
Daily Oklahoman.
Daily Oklahoma State Capitol.
El Reno *News.*
Elk City *News.*
Eufaula *Indian Journal.*
Eufaula *Republican.*
Frederick *Enterprise.*
Guthrie *Daily Leader.*
Guymon *Herald.*
Harlow's Weekly.
Hinton *Record.*
Kingfisher *Free Press.*
Laverne *Leader Tribune.*
Lexington *Leader.*
Mangum *Star.*
Muskogee *Daily Phoenix.*
Muskogee *Times Democrat.*
New York *Times.*
Norman *Transcript.*
Oklahoma City *Times.*
Oklahoma City *Times Journal.*
Oklahoma Dry.
Oklahoma *Messenger.*
Oklahoma *News.*
Pauls Valley *Enterprise.*

Ponca City *News*.
Purcell *Register*.
Sayre *Headlight*.
Shawnee *Daily Herald*.
Shawnee *News-Star*.
Stillwater *Gazette*.
Tulsa *Daily Democrat*.
Tulsa *Times*.
Tulsa *Tribune*.
Tulsa *World*.
Union *Signal*.
Vinita *Weekly Chieftain*.
Watonga *Republican*.
Wilburton *News*.
Woodward *News Bulletin*.

MINUTES AND PROCEEDINGS

Anti-Saloon League. *Proceedings* of the National Convention, 1915–33.
Oklahoma Baptist General Convention. *Minutes*, 1908–58.
Oklahoma Methodist Episcopal Church (South). *Minutes*, 1905–58.
Oklahoma Woman's Christian Temperance Union. *Minutes*, 1907.
Southern Baptist Convention. *Annual*, 1920–36.
Synod of the Oklahoma Presbyterian Church (USA). *Minutes*, 1899–1958.

COURT CASES

Crossland et al vs. *State*, 74 Okla. 58.
DeHasque vs. *Atchison, Topeka, and Santa Fe Railroad Co.*, 68 Okla. 182.
Robert Lozier vs. *Alexander Drug Company*, 23 Okla. 1.
State ex rel, Williamson et al. vs. *Carter, Secretary of State, et al.*, 177 Okla. 384.
Swan vs. *Wilderson*, 62 Pac. 422.

BIBLIOGRAPHY

Watkins vs. *Grieser*, 66 Pac. 332.

INTERVIEWS

Louis Gatti, Oklahoma City, August 20, 1966.
Mrs. Nellie Holmes, Tulsa, March 16, 1963.
Mrs. Elizabeth House, Stillwater, Okla., May 20, 1966.
J. F. Shallenberger, Tulsa, May 27, 1966.

THESES AND DISSERTATIONS

Heckman, Dayton E. "Prohibition Passes: The Story of the Association Against the Prohibition Amendment." Ph.D. dissertation, Ohio State University, 1939.
Mertz, Paul. "Oklahoma and the Year of Repeal, 1933." Master's thesis, University of Oklahoma, 1958.
Neal, Nevin E. "A Biography of Joseph T. Robinson." Ph.D. dissertation, University of Oklahoma, 1958.
Pearlin, Leonard I. "An Application of Correlation Methods to the Results of the 1949 Prohibition Referendum." Master's thesis, University of Oklahoma, 1950.
Scales, James R. "Political History of Oklahoma, 1907–1944." Ph.D. dissertation, University of Oklahoma, 1949.
Sterling, Dwayne W. "The Repeal of Prohibition in Oklahoma." Master's thesis, University of Oklahoma, 1965.
Zwick, Gwen W. "Prohibition in the Cherokee Nation, 1820–1907." Master's thesis, University of Oklahoma, 1940.

BOOKS[1]

Alexander, Charles. *The Ku Klux Klan in the Southwest.* Lexington, University of Kentucky Press, 1965.

[1] The volume of material on the national prohibition movement, especially for the Twenties, is staggering. Only those books and articles cited in the notes have been listed. Significantly, state studies of prohibition have not been cited although some of them proved very useful, most notably Gilbert Ostrander's work on California and Norman Clark's on the state of Washington.

Asbury, Herbert. *Carry Nation: The Woman with the Hatchet.* New York, Alfred A. Knopf, 1929.

———. *The Great Illusion: An Informal History of Prohibition.* Garden City, N.Y., Doubleday and Co., 1950.

Bandy, William. *Commentary on Intoxicating Liquor Laws in Oklahoma.* St. Paul, West Publishing Co., 1953.

Billington, Monroe L. *Thomas P. Gore: The Blind Senator from Oklahoma.* Lawrence, University of Kansas Press, 1967.

Catlin, George E. *Liquor Control.* New York, Henry Holt and Co., 1931.

Cherrington, Ernest H., ed. *The Anti-Saloon League Year-Book,* 1909–1919, 1931. Westerville, Ohio, American Issue Publishing Co., 1909–19.

———. *The Evolution of Prohibition in the United States: A Chronological History* . . . . Westerville, Ohio, American Issue Publishing Co., 1920.

———. *Standard Encyclopedia of the Alcohol Problem.* 6 vols. Westerville, Ohio, American Issue Publishing Co., 1925.

Colvin, D. L. *Prohibition in the United States: A History of Prohibition Party, and of the Prohibition Movement.* New York, George N. Doran Co., 1926.

The Cyclopedia of Temperance and Prohibition. New York, Funk and Wagnalls, 1891.

Dabney, Virginius. *Dry Messiah: The Life of Bishop Cannon.* New York, Alfred A. Knopf, 1949.

Dale, Edward E., and Jesse L. Rader, comps. *Readings in Oklahoma History.* New York, Row, Peterson and Co., 1930.

———, and James D. Morrison. *Pioneer Judge: The Life of Robert L. Williams.* Cedar Rapids, Iowa, Torch Press, 1958.

Democratic National Committee. *Campaign Addresses . . . of Governor Alfred E. Smith* . . . . Washington, The Committee, 1929.

Dobyns, Fletcher. *The Amazing Story of Repeal: An Exposé of the Power of Propaganda.* New York, Willett, Clark and Co., 1940.

Dunford, Edward B. *The History of the Temperance Movement.* Washington, Tem Press, 1943.

Earhart, Mary. *Frances Willard: From Prayers to Politics.* Chicago, University of Chicago Press, 1944.

Ellis, A. H. *History of the Constitutional Convention of the State of Oklahoma*. Muskogee, privately published, 1923.

Eubanks, John E. *Ben Tillman's Baby: The Dispensary in South Carolina, 1892–1915*. Augusta, privately published, 1950.

Foreman, Grant. *A History of Oklahoma*. Norman, University of Oklahoma Press, 1942.

——. *The Five Civilized Tribes*. Norman, University of Oklahoma Press, 1934.

Fowler, Oscar. *The Haskell Regime: The Intimate Life of Charles Nathaniel Haskell*. Oklahoma City, Boles Printing Co., Inc., 1933.

Gibson, A. M. *Oklahoma: A History of Five Centuries*. Norman, Harlow Publishing Corp., 1965.

Gordon, Anna. *Frances Willard*. Revised and abridged. Chicago, Woman's Christian Temperance Union Publishing Association, 1921.

Gordon, Seth, and W. B. Richards, comps. *Oklahoma Redbook, 1912*. 2 vols. Tulsa, Tulsa *Daily Democrat*, 1912.

Haynes, Roy A. *Prohibition Inside Out*. New York, Doubleday, 1923.

Hillerman, Abbie B. *History of the Woman's Christian Temperance Union of the Indian Territory, Oklahoma Territory, and the State of Oklahoma*. Sapulpa, Jennings Printing and Stationery Co., 1925.

Hines, Gordon. *Alfalfa Bill: An Intimate Biography*. Oklahoma City, Oklahoma Press, 1932.

Hoover, Herbert. *The Memoirs of Herbert Hoover*. 3 vols. New York, Macmillan Co., 1951–52.

Johnson, William E. *The Federal Government and the Liquor Traffic*. Westerville, Ohio, American Issue Publishing Co., 1911.

——. *Ten Years of Prohibition in Oklahoma*. Westerville, Ohio, American Issue Publishing Co., 1917.

Krout, John A. *The Origins of Prohibition*. New York, Alfred A. Knopf, 1915.

McRill, Albert L. *And Satan Came Also: An Intimate Story of a City's Social and Political History*. Oklahoma City, Britton Publishing Co., 1955.

Mathews, John Joseph. *Life and Death of an Oilman*. Norman, University of Oklahoma Press, 1951.

Mertz, Charles. *The Dry Decade*. Garden City, N.Y., Doubleday, Doran and Co., 1930.

Miller, Floyd. *Bill Tilghman: Marshal of the Last Frontier*. Garden City, N.Y., Doubleday, 1968.

Miller, Robert M. *American Protestantism and Social Issues*. Chapel Hill, University of North Carolina, 1958.

Murray, William H. *Memoirs of Governor Murray and True History of Oklahoma*. 3 vols. Boston, Meador Publishing Co., 1945.

Niles, Stanley, comp. *The Casebook for County Option for Ministers, County Officers and Other Workers*. [Oklahoma City, United Dry Association], 1956.

Odegard, Peter H. *Pressure Politics: The Story of the Anti-Saloon League*. New York, Columbia University Press, 1928.

The Oklahoma Annual Almanac and Industrial Record, 1908. Oklahoma City, Oklahoma Publishing Co., 1908.

Rosenman, Samuel, ed. *The Public Papers and Addresses of Franklin D. Roosevelt*. 13 vols. New York, Random House, 1938–50.

Schmeckebier, Laurence F. *The Bureau of Prohibition*. Washington, Brookings Institute, 1929.

Sinclair, Andrew. *Era of Excess: A Social History of the Prohibition Movement*. New York, Harper and Row, 1962.

Sinclair, H. M. *Making Oklahoma Safe for the Democratic Party or How the Williams Machine Stole the Election of 1916*. Oklahoma City, privately published, 1917.

Stewart, Dora A. *The Government and Development of Oklahoma Territory*. Oklahoma City, Harlow Publishing Co., 1933.

Tilghman, Zoe A. *Marshal of the Last Frontier: Life and Services of William Matthew (Bill) Tilghman, for 50 Years One of the Greatest Peace Officers of the West*. Glendale, Calif., A. H. Clark, 1949.

Timberlake, James H. *Prohibition and the Progressive Movement, 1900–1920*. Cambridge, Harvard University Press, 1963.

Walker, Robert S., and Samuel C. Patterson, *Oklahoma Goes Wet: The Repeal of Prohibition*. Eagleton Institute Studies in Practical Politics, No. 24. New Brunswick, N.J., Rutgers University Press, 1960.

Wardell, Morris L. *Political History of the Cherokee Nation, 1838–1907*. Norman, University of Oklahoma Press, 1938.

The Yearbook of the United States Brewers' Association, 1909–19. New York, United States Brewers' Association, 1909–19.

ARTICLES

"Beer Wet Oklahoma Votes for Hard Liquor," *Report on Man's Use of Alcohol*, Vol. XVII (May–June, 1959), 3–4.

"Billups Booze Bill," *Outlook*, Vol. LXXXIX (June, 1908), 311.

Brown, L. Ames. "Nation-wide Prohibition," *Atlantic Monthly*, Vol. CXV (June, 1915), 735–47.

Brown, William. "State Cooperation in Enforcement," *Annals* of the American Academy of Political and Social Science, Vol. CLXIII (September, 1932), 30–38.

"Corking Up the Jug," *Newsweek*, Vol. LIII (March 2, 1959), 25–26.

Foreman, Grant. "A Century of Prohibition," *Chronicles of Oklahoma*, Vol. XII (June, 1934), 133–41.

Foxcroft, Frank. "Prohibition in the South," *Atlantic Monthly*, Vol. CI (May, 1908), 627–34.

Furbay, H. G. "The Anti-Saloon League," *North American Review*, Vol. CLXXVII (September, 1903), 434.

Goddard, Mary. "Well Went Dry Just 50 Years Ago," *Daily Oklahoman*, November 13, 1957. Magazine section.

"How Wet Is Wet?" *Newsweek*, Vol. LII (September 8, 1958), 31–32.

Hudson, Peter J. "Temperance Meetings Among the Choctaws," *Chronicles of Oklahoma*, Vol. XII (June, 1934), 130–32.

Jeffery, Earl C. "News About Whiskey-wet Oklahoma," *Report on Man's Use of Alcohol*, Vol. XVIII (March–April, 1960), 4–5.

Moley, Raymond. "The Drys Last Hurrah," *Newsweek*, Vol. LIII (March 9, 1959), 116.

Nesbitt, Paul, ed. "Governor Haskell Tells of Two Conventions," *Chronicles of Oklahoma*, Vol. XIV (June, 1936), 189–217.

"Number of Dry States Doubled," *Literary Digest*, Vol. L (March, 1915), 536.

"Oklahoma Votes on Whiskey," *Report on Man's Use of Alcohol*, Vol. XVII (March–April, 1959), 1–11.

"Prohibition Party," *Independent*, Vol. LXVII (April, 1909), 929–30.

"Prohibition Winning the West," *Literary Digest*, Vol. XLIX (November, 1914), 997–98.

Reinmiller, G. A. "Oklahoma City's First Civic Clean-up," *Sturms*, Vol. IX (January, 1910), 27–32.

———. "West vs Reardon," *Sturms*, Vol. IX (February, 1910), 35–36.

Simpson, R. W. "Near Prohibition in the South," *Harper's Weekly*, Vol. LIII (July, 1909), 15.

"The Saloon in the South," *Outlook*, Vol. LXXXVIII (March, 1908), 581–82.

"To Dam the Interstate Flow of Drink," *Literary Digest*, Vol. XLIV (January, 1912), 106–107.

"Vote Becomes Price of Oklahoma Drinking," *Life*, Vol. XLVI (March, 1959), 20–24.

Walker, Robert, and Samuel C. Patterson. "The Political Attitudes of Oklahoma Newspapers: The Prohibition Issue," *Southwestern Social Science Quarterly*, Vol. XLII (December, 1961), 271–79.

Whitener, Daniel J. "The Dispensary Movement in North Carolina," *South Carolina Quarterly*, Vol. XXVI (January, 1937), 33–58.

"Will the Webb Law Work?" *Literary Digest*, Vol. XLVI (April, 1913), 816–17.

INDEX

Booze: *see* liquor
Briggs, Dr. Eugene: 184
Broadus, Bower: 115
Brown, James L.: 8
Bryce, D. A.: 178
Bureau of Prohibition: 83, 89, 98
Business Men's Protective League: 59

Cain, F. F.: 53
Caldwell, Fred S.: 37, 38, 52, 53
Campbell, Joe: 121
Canadian County Medical Association: 32
Cannon, Bishop James: 126–28
Cannon, Joe: 187, 188, 189
Cardwell, C. A.: 149, 150n.
Caudill, W. J.: 56, 57
Central Hundred: 58–59
Central Surveys Inc.: 170
Cherrington, Ernest H.: 48
Christian League for Legal Control: 168, 174
Church: membership in Okla., 12n., 157
Citizen's Committee to Repeal Bootleg Control: 178
Citizens League: 15, 18, 20, 30
Clark, W. T.: 118
Clean-up campaign: 58, 59, 71
Cobb, Joe B.: 185
Coe, William: 109, 177
Collins, Everett: 188
Committee of One Hundred: 70, 120
Conger, George: 52
Cook, Rowe: 159, 160
Coolidge, Calvin: 103
Copeland, George: 110
Cox, Tipton: 10
Creekmore, William: 43, 71
Cromwell, Okla.: 97, 98
Cross, William: 46
Cruce, Lee: 49, 50, 51, 52, 56, 57, 61, 63, 103, 146
Crusaders: 120
Cunningham, H. S.: 26n.
Curd, P. S.: 26n.

Daily Oklahoman: opposition to

legalized liquor, 11; predicts dry victory (1907), 22
Davidson, T. H.: 63
Davis, Byron: 184–85
Davis, Clarence: 45, 63
Davison, Phillip: report of, 89ff.
DeHasque, Father Urbane: 67
Democratic party: 35, 49, 61, 99, 102, 107, 108, 175, 177
Dierker, Charles E.: 146
Dinwiddie, Rev. E. C.: 18, 21–22
Disciples of Christ: 12
Dispensary system: 16, 26ff., 30n.
Distilleries: *see* stills
Dixon, T. Woody: 113
Doenges, William: 175–76, 177
Drys: *see* Prohibitionists
Duke, A. F.: 115
Durant, Okla.: 84
Dykema, M. F.: 158, 160, 168

Edmondson, J. Howard: 175, 176–77, 181, 184, 187, 190
Eighteenth Amendment: 72, 76, 77, 78, 79, 80, 94, 95, 105, 132
Episcopal church: 69
Episcopalians: 182
Evans, Rev. A. Norman: 127

Feaver, Rev. Kenneth: 191
Ferguson "Bone Dry Bill": 66, 67, 69, 70, 72
Ferguson, Phil: 175, 177
Ferguson, Walter: 65, 70
Field, John: 161
Fine, Ray: 185
First Baptist Church (Oklahoma City): 8, 68
First Methodist Church (Oklahoma City): 7
Fisher, George A.: 162, 164, 172
Five Civilized Tribes: 12n.; *see also* Indians
Frantz, Frank: 21, 23
Freeling, S. P.: 64, 67, 70–71, 97

Garland, R. C.: 114, 117, 121, 131
Gary, Raymond: 156, 160, 165–66, 167, 171, 177

INDEX

Gaylord, E. K.: 170
German American Association: 15, 19–20, 27, 30
Gore, Thomas P.: 140 & n., 141
Gordon, Anna: 6
Goulding, J. P.: 18, 26 & n., 45
Graham, Bob: 114, 116, 117, 121
Grant, Whit: 58
Grubitz, Gene: 179
Gulick's Review: 44
Guthrie, Okla.: 11, 12, 14, 17

Hammet, Cora: 47
Harrison, Benjamin: 4
Haskell, Charles N.: 22–23, 25, 50, 51; at Constitutional Convention, 18; helps draft prohibition law, 27; opposes abolition of dispensary system, 35; and enforcement, 37ff.; and interstate shipment of liquor, 41, 42–43; stand on the initiative process, 46
Hatchet: 15
Heatwole, Jack: 169
Henshaw, George: 134; legislation introduced by, 135ff.
Henthorne, Norris: 120, 179
Hill, Claude: 137
Hillerman, Miss Abbie: 17, 62
Holloman, Roy E.: 152, 156
Holloway, William J.: 90
Holmes, Mrs. Nellie: 11 n., 31 n.
Hoover, Herbert: 89, 99, 102, 104, 108
Hotel Men's Association: 120
House, Mrs. Elizabeth: 116, 136, 183
Houser, Rev. Emerson: 127
Huckins Hotel (Oklahoma City): 120
Hughes, W. F.: 84
Hunter, Lewis: 61
Huston, A. H.: 34
Hyde, Herbert: 143n.

Indian Territory: 3, 4, 6, 18, 19, 46, 93
Indian Territory Church Federation: 14
Indians: attempt to restrict liquor from, 12–13; Five Civilized Tribes, 12n.
Inter-Church Federation: 13
Intoxicants: *see* liquor

Jayne, A. M.: 119, 129
Jews: 182
Johnson, G. O.: 26 & n.
Johnson, W. Lee: 178
Johnston, Henry S.: 102
Joplin, Mo.: liquor distributing center for Okla., 43–44

Kay County Civic League: 31
Kennamer, Franklin E.: 94
Kerr, Robert: 152
Kerr, Ryan: 184
King, J. Berry: 131
Ku Klux Klan: 101–102 & n.
Kulp, A. G.: 151

Lake Mohonk Conference: 13
Laughbaum, H. T.: 21, 64, 65, 67
Ledbetter, W. A.: 19
Lee, Josh: 140, 142, 143n., 146
Levy, I. B.: 18
Lillard, Ross: 116
Liquor: 17, 70, 77, 79, 134; laws of Oklahoma Territory, 4–5; for medicinal purposes, 16; law enforcement, 38ff., 52, 54–55, 56, 81, 82, 85, 86, 88, 89ff., 188–89; stamps, 41, 54, 145, 167, 168, 184, 187; shipped to Okla., 41–42; package stores, 178, 180; raids, 187
Liquor Men's Association: 15
Literary Digest: 107
Livingston, Clint: 185
Local option: 18, 61–62, 152ff., 164, 165, 178, 180, 194
Lollar, Robert: 183
Losinger, W. J.: 146n.
Lozier, Robert: 33, 35
Lynn, Wiley: 95, 96, 97

McCool, R. M.: 128
McCullough, William: 70
McFarlin Methodist Church (Norman): 127

INDEX

Payne, Tom: 183
Penn, Lemuel: 116, 128
Phillips, Leon: 112, 145ff., 184
Presbyterians: 12, 47, 77, 157
Progress Brewing Company: 165
Prohibition: 49, 72, 95, 98, 103, 106, 108; to be taught in Okla. schools, 62; and Progressive Movement, 75; disrespect for, 80; sentiment against national law, 106; and 1928 election, 98; and 1932 election, 108; efforts to repeal national law, 109; and 1949 repeal election, 152
Prohibition Federation: 14
Prohibition Party: 29n., 49n.
Prohibition Thousand: 110, 116, 119, 129
Prohibitionists: 21, 76, 81, 87, 133, 149, 156, 191–92; fight for restrictive liquor provision in Okla. Constitution, 12, 17, 19; and 1910 election, 47; demand stronger enforcement, 50, 57–58; and Eighteenth Amendment, 72, 79; dissatisfaction with Judge Williams, 81; stand on 3.2 beer, 110; and beer bill, 115, 117, 119; defeated at beer election, 129; and 1936 election, 142; and 1940 election, 149; and local option on beer, 159, 161; response to Governor Edmondson and repeal, 181ff.; defeat of in 1959, 194–95
Protestant churches: 12, 30, 119, 182; *see also listings for individual denominations*

Quayle, Bishop William A.: 47

Rampendahl, W. F.: 86
Ramsey, George: 120
Raskob, John J.: 101
Ravia, Okla.: 84
Repeal study group: 177
Repealists: 15, 17, 45, 48, 51, 57, 59, 67, 148, 153, 162, 165, 183
Republican party: 26, 32, 49, 61, 99, 102ff., 175, 177

Rhinehart, James A.: 175
Ritzhaupt, Louis: 183
Robert Lozier vs. *Alexander Drug Company*: 34
Robertson, J. B. A.: 72, 81, 121
Robinson, John A.: 84
Robinson, Joseph: 99
Rogers, Will: 189, 194
Roman Catholic church: 12, 67, 68–69 & n.
Roosevelt, Franklin D.: 98
Roosevelt, Theodore: 21
Rush, Benjamin: 9
Russell, Howard H.: 8

Saint Joseph's Roman Catholic Church (Norman): 67
Saloons: in Oklahoma Territory, 10ff., 15
Santa Fe Railroad: 67
Sapulpa, Okla.: 43
Scantland, Sam: 181, 185–86, 191
Seaver, W. F.: 80
Shackford, Joseph: 182, 184, 191
Shapard, David: 151–52, 156
Short, George: 81
Sirmans, W. E.: 97
Small, Samuel: 11n.
Smasher's Mail: 15
Smith, Al: 87, 98ff.
Smith, Gomer: 140
Snyder, W. K.: 63
Sons of Temperance: 32n.
Sons of Washington: 32, 45, 48
Stanford, H. E. P.: 26 & n.
Stanfield, Max: 182
State Modification and Repeal Association: 120
Stealy, C. F.: 52
Stewart, Paul: 118
Stills: 79, 84, 93 & n.
Stone, S. W.: 35
Sullivan, Sam: 124
Swan, H. E.: 116
Sweet, E. M.: 21

Taft, William H.: 42, 65
Temperance League: 135, 139
Thomas, J. Elmer: 27

-211-

Thornton, H. V.: 183
Tilghman, William (Bill): 95ff.
Tilghman, Zoe: 96ff.
Tillman, Ben: 30n.
Timmons, Henry: 117
Todd, B. W.: 115
Tribbey, Okla.: 83
Tulsa *World*: 21–22, 60, 103, 105
Turner, Roy: 152, 162
Twenty-first Amendment: 109ff., 122, 132

Unassigned Lands: 4
United Civic Association: 60
United Drys: 135, 137, 140, 152, 156, 163, 165, 171, 175, 177, 178, 181, 182, 188, 192
United Oklahoma Dry Association: *see* United Drys
United Oklahomans for Repeal: 189, 190
United States: Congress, 3, 12–15, 72, 75, 76, 87, 108, 109; Supreme Court, 64; Commissioner of Internal Revenue, 77; Congressional Committee on Territories, 83; Department of Justice, 83
University of Oklahoma: 168

Volstead Act: 76, 77, 81, 86, 99, 108

Wallace, W. R.: 147
Ware County, Ga.: 97

Waycross, Ga.: 97
Webb, Jackson R.: 159
Webb-Kenyon Act: 54, 64
West, Charles: 37–38, 43
Wets: *see* repealists
Wetzenhoffer and Turk Company: 24
Wheeler, Wayne: 75, 76, 83
Whisky: *see* liquor
Wickersham Commission: 89
Wickersham, George: 42–43
Wilcoxen, Andrew: 175
Wilebrandt, Mabel Walker: 83, 85, 86
Willard, Frances: 6, 7n.
Williams, Loren: 179
Williams, Robert: 19, 50, 61ff., 72, 80, 92, 104, 138
Williamson, J. W.: 139
Wolfe, J. E.: 31
Woman's Christian Temperance Union: (National), 6–7, 104n.; (Oklahoma), 6, 31, 47–48, 73, 104, 144–45, 157, 194; organized in, 6–7; fight for constitutional prohibition, 14; and enforcement, 36; supports clean-up campaigns, 62; and 1928 presidential election, 104; and 1957 local option election, 171–72
Woodcock, A. W. W.: 98
Woodward *News Bulletin*: 125–26

Yeager, O. J.: 26 & n.
Young, Charles Prince: 80n.

The paper on which this book was printed bears the water-
mark of the University of Oklahoma Press and has an effective life of at least three hundred years.

UNIVERSITY OF OKLAHOMA PRESS

NORMAN